Lecture Notes in Artificial I

Subseries of Lecture Notes in Comput
Edited by J. G. Carbonell and J. Siekm

Lecture Notes in Computer Science

Edited by G. Goos, J. Hartmanis and J. van Leeuwen

Springer
Berlin
Heidelberg
New York
Barcelona
Hong Kong
London
Milan
Paris
Singapore
Tokyo

Maria Teresa Pazienza (Ed.)

Information Extraction

Towards Scalable, Adaptable Systems

Series Editors

Jaime G. Carbonell, Carnegie Mellon University, Pittsburgh, PA, USA
Jörg Siekmann, University of Saarland, Saarbrücken, Germany

Volume Editor

Maria Teresa Pazienza
Department of Computer Science, Systems and Production
University of Roma, Tor Vergata
Via di Tor Vergata, I-00133 Roma, Italy
E-mail: pazienza@info.uniroma2.it

Cataloging-in-Publication data applied for

Die Deutsche Bibliothek - CIP-Einheitsaufnahme

Information extraction : towards scalable, adaptable systems / Maria Teresa Pazienza (ed.). - Berlin ; Heidelberg ; New York ; Barcelona ; Hong Kong ; London ; Milan ; Paris ; Singapore ; Toyko : Springer, 1999
(Lecture notes in computer science ; 1714 : Lecture notes in artificial intelligence)
ISBN 3-540-66625-7

CR Subject Classification (1998): I.2, H.3

ISBN 3-540-66625-7 Springer-Verlag Berlin Heidelberg New York

Typesetting: Camera-ready by author
SPIN 10705092 06/3142 – 5 4 3 2 1 0 Printed on acid-free paper

Preface

The ever-growing interest in new approaches to information management is strictly related to the explosion of collections of documents made accessible through communication networks. The enormous amount of daily available information imposes the development of IE (Information Extraction) technologies that enable one to:

- access relevant documents only and
- integrate the extracted information into the user's environment.

In fact, the classic application scenario for IE foresees, for example:

1. a company interested in getting detailed synthetic information (related to predefined categories);
2. the documents, as sources of information, located in electronically accessible sites (agencies' news, web pages, companies' textual documentation, international regulations etc.);
3. the extracted information eventually being inserted in private data bases for further processing (e.g. data mining, summary and report generation, forms filling,...).

A key problem for a wider deployment of IE systems is in their flexibility and easy adaptation to new application frameworks. Most of the commonly available IE systems are based on specific domain-dependent methodologies for knowledge extraction (they ignore how to pass to templates related to other domains or different collections of documents). The need exists for more principled techniques for managing templates in a domain-independent fashion by using the general structures of language and logic. A few attempts have been made to derive templates directly from corpora. This process is similar to deriving knowledge structures and lexicons directly from corpora. This methodological approach (*adaptability*) could push for a rapid customization to new domains of existing IE systems.

The missing availability of robust natural language processing (NLP) tools is an obstacle in developing efficient systems for information management and broadcasting.
The use of written texts as sources of knowledge lags behind other applications: it is crucial to characterize the suitable framework to support and simplify the construction phase for NL-based applications. The present software engineering methodologies are not adequate, while the automatic manipulation of unstructured natural language texts will become an important business niche.

Information Extraction technology is required to get performance levels similar to Information Retrieval (IR) systems proved to be commercially viable.

In many respects, IR and IE are very often used with a similar meaning when the interest is in *extracting*, from a very large collection of textual documents, useful information matching linguistic properties. Likewise, the Message Understanding Conferences (MUC) and the Text Retrieval Conferences (TREC) are the most qualified environments in which different IE and IR approaches, respectively, are evaluated with respect to the ability of identifying relevant information from texts. In both these competitions, innovative approaches have been implemented, evidencing the role of NLP systems. Nevertheless the definition of how accurate an approximation to explicit linguistic processing is required for good retrieval performances is still under debate.

Multilingual information extraction (IE) methodologies are more and more necessary.
Even if the most common language used in electronic texts is English, the number of languages adopted to write documents circulating and accessible through networks is increasing. Systems developed for such an application must rely on linguistic resources being available in several languages. Traditionally, these resources (mainly lexicons) have been hand-built at a high cost and present obvious problems for size extension and portability to new domains.

Most of the resources needed for IE systems are still developed by hand.
This is an highly time consuming task for very expensive human experts. A possible solution is in extracting linguistic knowledge from corpora. This requires developing systems that, in a unified approach, would be able to

1. extract such linguistic knowledge, and
2. represent it, preferably at a meta-level independently from source language and application domain.

Parallel corpora may be considered as valuable sources of this meta-knowledge, in case aligned multilingual parallel corpora are available and tools for equivalent processing have been developed.
Alignment in these texts is mandatory and it must be verified at some level (at least paragraphs and sentences). Two different frameworks exist for this task:
- use of some sort of traditional linguistic analysis of the texts, or
- a statistical approach.
The former seems to be based on the same kind of information they are trying to extract. The latter, based on simpler assumptions (e.g. a significant correlation exists in the relative length of sentences which are translations of each other), is currently used.

All these themes will be analyzed and debated at SCIE99, the SChool on Information Extraction, organized by the Artificial Intelligence Research Group of the University of Roma Tor Vergata (Italy) and supported by the European Space Agency (ESA), the Italian Association for Artificial Intelligence (AI*IA) and the National Institution for Alternative Forms of Energy (ENEA).

In recent years, SCIE99 (the second conference, SCIE97 being the first) appears to to have become an important forum in which to analyze and discuss major IE concerns,

By comparing the lectures held at the School on Information Extraction, SCIE97 (*Information Extraction: Multidisciplinary contributions to an emerging Information Technology*, Pazienza M.T.(Ed), Lecture Notes in Artificial Intelligence 1299, Springer-Verlag, Berlin Heidelberg New York, 1997) and what was debated at SCIE99 (and gathered in this book), as the current stage of the research and development in IE technology, the strong requirement for technology deployment emerges as a novelty, i.e. *the availability of robust adaptable systems to test either different methodologies or new application scenario without being forced to redefine knowledge resources and the kind of processing.* The first phase aimed at defining topics to be covered, at different extents of generality, in an IE system appears to be concluded; a new spirit calls for technological deployment for effective, adaptable IE systems!

I would like to thank individually all my colleagues from the Artificial Intelligence Research Group of the University of Roma Tor Vergata (and particularly Roberto Basili and Michele Vindigni) who supported my efforts at organizing SCIE99 and editing this book.

Roma, July 1999 Maria Teresa Pazienza

Organization

SCIE99 is organized by the University of Roma, Tor Vergata (Italy).

Program Committee

Luigia Carlucci Aiello (University of Roma "*La Sapienza*")
Elisa Bertino (University of Milano)
Domenico Sacca' (University of Calabria)
Lorenza Saitta (University of Torino)
Maria Teresa Pazienza (University of Roma, Tor Vergata)

Organizing Committee

Roberto Basili (University of Roma, Tor Vergata)
Cristina Cardani (University of Roma, Tor Vergata)
Maria Teresa Pazienza (University of Roma, Tor Vergata)
Michele Vindigni (University of Roma, Tor Vergata)
Fabio Massimo Zanzotto (University of Roma, Tor Vergata)

Supporting Institutions

The SCIE99 has been partially supported by

- AI*IA, Italian Association for Artificial Intelligence
- ENEA, National Institute for Alternative Forms of Energy
- ESA, European Space Agency
- University of Roma, Tor Vergata, Italy

Table of Contents

Can We Make Information Extraction More Adaptive?

Yorick Wilks and Roberta Catizone*

The University of Sheffield
{yorick,roberta}@dcs.shef.ac.uk

Abstract. It seems widely agreed that IE (Information Extraction) is now a tested language technology that has reached precision+recall values that put it in about the same position as Information Retrieval and Machine Translation, both of which are widely used commercially. There is also a clear range of practical applications that would be eased by the sort of template-style data that IE provides. The problem for wider deployment of the technology is adaptability: the ability to customize IE rapidly to new domains.
In this paper we discuss some methods that have been tried to ease this problem, and to create something more rapid than the bench-mark one-month figure, which was roughly what ARPA teams in IE needed to adapt an existing system by hand to a new domain of corpora and templates. An important distinction in discussing the issue is the degree to which a user can be assumed to know what is wanted, to have pre-existing templates ready to hand, as opposed to a user who has a vague idea of what is needed from a corpus.
We shall discuss attempts to derive templates directly from corpora; to derive knowledge structures and lexicons directly from corpora, including discussion of the recent LE project ECRAN which attempted to tune existing lexicons to new corpora. An important issue is how far established methods in Information Retrieval of tuning to a user's needs with feedback at an interface can be transferred to IE.

1 Introduction

Information Extraction (IE) has already reached the level of success at which Information Retrieval and Machine Translation (on differing measures, of course) have proved commercially viable. By general agreement, the main barrier to wider use and commercialization of IE is the relative inflexibility of the template concept: classic IE relies on the user having an already developed set of templates, as was the case with US Defence agencies from where the technology was largely developed (see below), and this is not generally the case. The intellectual and practical issue now is how to develop templates, their subparts (like named

* The authors are grateful to discussion and contributions from Hamish Cunningham, Robert Gaizauskas, Louise Guthrie and Evelyne Viegas, All errors are our own of course.

Pazienza (Ed.): Information Extraction, LNAI 1714, pp. 1–16, 1999.

entities or NEs), the rules for filling them, and associated knowledge structures, as rapidly as possible for new domains and genres.

This paper discusses the quasi-automatic development and detection of templates, template-fillers, lexicons and knowledge structures for new IE domains and genres, using a combination of machine learning, linguistic resource extrapolation and human machine interface elicitation and feedback techniques.

2 Background: The Information Extraction Context

Extracting and managing information has always been important for intelligence agencies, but it clear that, in the next decade, technologies for these functions will also be crucial to education, medicine, and commerce. It is estimated that 80% of our information is textual, and Information Extraction (IE) has emerged as a new technology as part of the search for better methods of finding, storing, accessing and mining such information.

IE itself is an automatic method for locating important facts in electronic documents (e.g. newspaper articles, news feeds, web pages, transcripts of broadcasts, etc.) and storing them in a data base for processing with techniques like data mining, or with off-the-shelf products like spreadsheets, summarisers and report generators. The historic application scenario for Information Extraction is a company that wants, say, the extraction of all ship sinkings, recorded in public news wires in any language world-wide, put into a single data base showing ship name, tonnage, date and place of loss etc. Lloyds of London had performed this particular task with human readers of the world's newspapers for a hundred years.

The key notion in IE is that of a "template": a linguistic pattern, usually a set of attribute value pairs, with the values being text strings, created by experts to capture the structure of the facts sought in a given domain, and which IE systems apply to text corpora with the aid of extraction rules that seek those fillers in the corpus, given a set of syntactic, semantic and pragmatic constraints.

IE as a modern language processing technology was developed largely in the US. but with strong development centres elsewhere [17], [18], [30], [34], [27] Over 25 systems world wide, have participated in the recent MUC competitions, most of which have a generic structure [34] and previously unreliable tasks of identifying, names, dates, organizations, countries, and currencies automatically – often referred to as TE, or Template Element, tasks – have become extremely accurate (over 95% accuracy for the best systems).. In interpreting MUC figures, it should also be borne in mind that the overall recall and precision of human-provided IE information as a whole is estimated to be about 20% worse [15], [13], [14] than the best human performance; it was measured by how well intelligence analysts perform the task manually when compared to a "gold star" experienced intelligence analyst.

Adaptivity in the MUC development context has meant the one-month period in which competing centres adapt their system to new training data sets provided by DARPA; this period therefore provides a benchmark for human-only adaptivity of IE systems.

This paper describes the adaptivity problem, to new domains and genres, that constitutes the central problem to the extension and acceptability of IE, and to increase the principled multi-linguality of IE systems, which we take to mean extending their ability to extract information in one language and present it to a user in another.

3 Previous Work on ML and Adaptive Methods for IE

The application of Machine Learning methods to aid the IE task goes back to work on the learning of verb preferences in the Eighties by Grishman & Sterling [31] and Lehnert [38], as well as early work at MITRE on learning to find named expressions (NEs) [5]. The most interesting developments since then have been a series of extensions to the work of Lehnert and Riloff on Autoslog [47], which was called an automatic induction of a lexicon for IE, but which is normally described as a method of learning extraction rules from <document, filled template> pairs, that is to say the rules (and associated type constraints) that assign the fillers to template slots from text. These rules are then sufficient to fill further templates from new documents.

No conventional learning algorithm was used but, since then, Soderland has extended the work by attempting to use a form of Muggleton's ILP (Inductive Logic Programming) system to that task, and Cardie [12] has sought to extend it to areas like learning the determination of coreference links. Muggleton's [52] learning system at York has provided very good evaluated figures indeed (in world wide terms) in learning part of speech tagging and is being extended to grammar learning. Muggleton also has experimented with user interaction with a system that creates semantic networks of the articles and the relevant templates, although so far its published successes have been in areas like Part-of-Speech tagging that are not inherently structural (in the way template learning arguably is).

Grishman at NYU [24] and Morgan [41] at Durham have done pioneering work using user interaction and definition to define usable templates, and Riloff [48] has attempted to use some form of the user-feedback methods of Information Retrieval, including user-marking of negative and positive <document, filled template> pairings. Collier at Sheffield [16] tried to learn the template structure itself directly (i.e. unsupervised) from a corpus, together with primitive extraction rules, rather than how to fill a given template.

4 UDIE: What Would It Be Like to Have a User-Driven IE System?

User Driven IE is a concept only at the moment: its aim is to address several areas of research such as how to use machine learning techniques to allow a system to be adapted to a new domain without expert intervention, and how the user will interact with the system. Below we discuss the structures that must be learned and proposed strategies for learning them, and the proposed interaction with users that we envision will be necessary to customize a system to a particular application.

A number of issues arise in connection with designing user-driven IE. First, the quality of the system depends partly on the quality of the training data it is provided with (cf. the above figure on the low-quality of much of the human MUC data, compared with the best human data). This makes the provision of tools to involve users in this process as part of their normal work-flow important see e.g. [23]. Secondly, the type of the learned data structures impact the maintainability of the system. Stochastic models, for example, perform well in certain cases, but cannot be hand-tailored to squeeze out a little extra performance, or to eliminate an obvious error. This is an advantage of error-driven transformation-based learning of patterns for IE with a deterministic automaton-based recognition engine, such as the work of the team at MITRE [1], following the work of Brill [8], as well as for all work done in the ILP paradigm.

4.1 Supervised Template Learning

Brill-style transformation-based learning methods are one of the few ML methods in NLP to have been applied above and beyond the part-of-speech tagging origins of virtually all ML in NLP. Brill's original application triggered only on POS tags; later [7] he added the possibility of lexical triggers. Since then the method has been extended successfully to e.g. speech act determination [50], and a template learning application was designed by Vilain [54].

A fast implementation based on the compilation of Brill-style rules to deterministic automata was developed at Mitsubishi labs [49] (see also [19]). The quality of the transformation rules learned depends on factors such as:

1. the accuracy and quantity of the training data;
2. the types of pattern available in the transformation rules;
3. the feature set available used in the pattern side of the transformation rules.

The accepted wisdom of the machine learning community is that it is very hard to predict which learning algorithm will produce optimal performance, so it is advisable to experiment with a range of algorithms running on real data. There have as yet been no systematic comparisons between these initial efforts and other conventional machine learning algorithms applied to learning extraction rules for IE data structures (e.g. example-based systems such as TiMBL [22] and ILP [42].

Such experiments should be considered as strongly interacting with the issues discussed below (section 3 on the lexicon), where we propose extensions to earlier work done by us and others [4] on unsupervised learning of the surface forms (subcategorization patterns) of a set of root template verbs: this was work that sought to cover the range of corpus forms under which a significant verb's NEs might appear in text. Such information might or might not be available in a given set of <document, template> pairs–e.g. would NOT be if the verbs appeared in sentences only in canonical forms. Investigation is still needed on the trade off between the corpus-intensive and the <document, filled template> pair methods, if templates have not been pre-provided for a very large corpus selection (for, if they had, the methodology above could subsume the subcategorization work below). It will be, in practice, a matter of training sample size and richness.

4.2 Unsupervised Template Learning

We should remember that there is also a possible unsupervised notion of template learning, developed in a Sheffield PhD thesis by Collier [16], one that can be thought of as yet another application of the old technique of Luhn [40] to locate, in a corpus, statistically significant words and use those to locate the sentences in which they occur as key sentences. This has been the basis of a range of summarisation algorithms and Collier proposed a form of it as a basis for unsupervised template induction, namely that those sentences, if they contained corpus-significant verbs, would also contain sentences corresponding to templates, whether or not yet known as such to the user. Collier cannot be considered to have proved that such learning is effective only that some prototype results can be obtained.

4.3 User Input and Feedback at the Interface

An overall aim of UDIE would be to find the right compromise for a user of IE between automatic and user-driven methods. An important aspect of UDIE that supplements the use of learning methods is a user interface quite different from developer-orientated interfaces such as GATE [21]. There will be a range of ways in which a user can indicate to the system their interests, in advance of any automated learning or user feedback, since it would be foolish to ignore the extent to which a user may have some clear notions of what is wanted from a corpus. However, and this is an important difference from classic IE descending from MUC, we will not always assume in what follows that the user does have "templates in mind", but only that there are facts of great interest to the user in a given corpus and it can be the job of this system interface to help elicit them in a formal representation.

It is crucial to recall here that one of the few productive methods for optimising traditional IR in the last decade has been the use of user- feedback methods, typically ones where a user can indicate from a retrieved document set that, say, this ten are good and this ten bad. These results are then fed back to optimise the retrieval iteratively by modifying the request. It is not easy to adapt this methodology directly to IE, even though now, with full text IR available for large indexed corpora, one can refer to sentence documents being retrieved by IR, documents of precisely the span of a classic IE template, so that one might hope for some transfer of IR optimisation methods.

However, although the user can mark sentences so retrieved as good or bad, the "filled template" part of the <document, filled template> pairings cannot be so marked by a user who, by definition, is not assumed to be familiar with template formalisms. In this section of the work we shall mention ways in which a user can indicate preferences, needs and choices at the interface that contribute to template construction whose application he can assess, though not their technical structure.

Doing this will require the possibility of a user marking, on the screen, key portions of text, ones that contain the desired facts; as well as the ability to input, in some form of an interface language (English, Italian etc.), concepts in key facts or template content including predicates and ranges of fillers). This aspect of the paper is complementary to supervised learning methods for templates, lexicons and KR structures, none of which need assume that the user does have a full and explicit concept of what is wanted from a corpus.

5 Adapting System Lexicons for a New Domain

Virtually all IE use systems use lexicons, and there is universal agreement that lexicons need to be adapted or tuned to new user domains. The disagreement is about what tuning implies and whether there is real IE benefit in terms of recall and precision. Those in the Information Retrieval tradition of information access are usually skeptical about the latter, since statistical measures tend to bring their own internal criterion of relevance and semantic adaptation. Researchers like Strzalkowski [53] and Krovetz [37] have consistently argued that lexical adaptation, taken as far as domain-based sense tagging, does improve IE. In this paper we intend to adapt and continue our work on lexical tuning to provide some evaluable measure of the effectiveness or otherwise of lexical tuning for IE. That term has meant a number of things: the notion (as far back as Wilks 1972 [56]) has meant adding a new sense to a lexicon on corpus evidence because the text could not be accommodated to an existing lexicon. In 1990 Pustejovsky used the term to mean adding a new subcategorization pattern to an existing sense entry from corpus evidence. In the IE tradition there have been a number ([46], [32]) of pioneering efforts to add new words and new subcategorization/preference patterns to a lexicon from a corpus as a prolegomenon to IE.

5.1 Background on Lexical Acquisition by Rule-Based Methods

Lexical Tuning (LT) is closely related, but fundamentally different from, a group of related theories that are associated with phrases like "lexical rules"; all of them seek to compress lexicons by means of generalizations, and we take that to include DATR [25], methods developed under AQUILEX [9], as well as Pustejovsky's Generative Lexicon [44] and Buitelaar's more recent research on under-specified lexicons [11]. All this work can be traced back to early work by Givon [29] on lexical regularities, done, interestingly to those who think corpus and MRD research began in the 1980s, in connection with the first computational work on Webster's Third Dictionary at SDC in Santa Monica under John Olney in 1966.

All this work can be brought under the heading "data compression" whether or not that motive is made explicit. Givon became interested in what is now called "systematic polysemy", and distinguished from homonymy (which is deemed unsystematic), with key examples like "grain" which is normally given an PHYOBJ sense in a dictionary, dated earlier than a mass noun sense of "grain in the mass", and this lexical extension can be found in many nouns, and indeed resurfaced in Briscoe and Copestake's famous "grinding rule" [9] that added a mass substance sense for all animals, as in "rabbit all over the road". The argument was that, if such extensions were systematic, they need not be stored individually but could be developed when needed unless explicitly overridden. The paradigm for this was the old AI paradigm of default reasoning: Clyde is an elephant and all elephants have four legs BUT Clyde has three legs. To many of us, it has been something of a mystery why this foundational cliche of AI has been greeted later within computational linguistics as remarkable and profound.

Gazdar's DATR is the most intellectually adventurous of these systems and the one that makes lexical compression the most explicit, drawing as it does on fundamental notions of science as a compression of the data of the world. The problem has been that language is one of the most recalcitrant aspects of the world and it has proved hard to find generalizations above the level of morphology—those to do with meaning have proved especially elusive. Most recently, there has been an attempt to generalise DATR to cross-language generalizations which has exacerbated the problem. One can see that, in English, Dutch and German, respectively, HOUSE, HUIS and HAUS are the "same word"-a primitive concept DATR requires. But, whereas HOUSE has a regular plural, HAUS (HAUESER) does not, so even at this low level, significant generalizations are very hard to find.

Most crucially, there can be no appeals to meaning from the concept of "same word": TOWN (Eng.) and TUIN (Dut.) are plainly the same word in some sense, at least etymologically and phonetically, and may well obey morphological generalizations although now, unlike the HOUSE cases above, they have no relation of meaning at all, as TUIN now means garden. Perhaps the greatest missed opportunity here has been any attempt to link DATR to established quantitative notions of data compression in linguistics, like Minimum Description Length which gives a precise measure of the compaction of a lexicon, even where significant generalizations may be hard to spot by eye or mind, in the time honoured manner.

The systems which seek lexical compression by means of rules, in one form or another, can be discussed by particular attention to Buitelaar, since Briscoe and Pustejovsky differ in matters of detail and rule format (in the case of Briscoe) but not in principle. Buitelaar continues Pustejovsky's campaign against unstructured list views of lexicons: viewing the senses of a word merely as a list as some dictionaries are said to do, in favour of a clustered approach, one which, in his terms, distinguishes "systematic polysemy" [11] from mere homonymy (like the ever present senses of BANK). Systematic polysemy is a notion deriving directly from Givon's examples, though it is not clear whether it would cover cases like the different kinds of emitting and receiving banks covered in a modern dictionary (e.g. sperm bank,blood bank, bottle bank etc.)

Clustering a word's senses in an optimally revealing way is some- thing no one could possibly object to, and our disquiet at his starting point is that the examples he produces, and particular his related attack on word sense disambiguation programs (including the present author's) as assuming a list-view of sense, is misguided. Moreover, as Nirenburg and Raskin [43] have pointed out in relation to Pustejovksy, those who criticise list views of sense then normally go on in their papers to describe and work with the senses of a word as a list!

Buitelaar's opening argument against standard WSD activities could seem ill conceived: his counter-example is supposed to be one where two senses of BOOK must be kept in play and so WSD should not be done. The example is "A long book heavily weighted with military technicalities, in this edition it is neither so long nor so technical as it was originally".

Leaving aside the question of whether or not this is a sentence, let us accept that Buitelaar's list (!) of possible senses (and glosses) of BOOK is a reasonable starting point (with our numbering added): (i) the information content of a book (military technicalities); (ii) its physical appearance (heavily weighted), (iii) and the events involved in its construction (long) (ibid. p. 25). The issue, he says, is to which sense of BOOK does the "it" refer, and his conclusion is that it cannot be disambiguated between the three.

This seems to us quite wrong, as a matter of the exegesis of English. "heavily weighted" is plainly metaphorical and refers to content (i) not the physical appearance (ii) of the book. We have no trouble taking LONG as referring to the content (i) since not all long books are physically large–it depends on the print etc. On our reading the "it" is univocal between the senses of BOOK in this case. However, nothing depends on an example, well or ill-chosen and it may well be that there are indeed cases where more than one sense must remain in play in a word's deployment; poetry is often cited, but there may well be others, less peripheral to the real world of the Wall Street Journal.

The main point in any answer to Buitelaar must be that, whatever is the case about the above issue, WSD programs have no trouble capturing it: many programs, and certainly that of (Stevenson and Wilks, 1997) that he cites and its later developments, work by constraining senses and are perfectly able to report results with more than one sense still attaching to a word, just as some POS taggers result in more than one tag per word in the output. Close scholars of AI will also remember that Mellish [28], Hirst [33] and Small [51] all proposed methods by which polysemy might be computationally reduced by degree and not in an all or nothing manner. Or, as one might put it, under-specification, Buitelaar's key technical term, can seem no more than an implementation detail in any effective tagger!

Let us turn to the heart of Buitelaar's position: the issue of systematicity (one with which other closely related authors' claims about lexical rules can be taken together). If he wants, as he does, to cluster a word's senses if they are close semantically (and ignoring the fact that LDOCE's homonyms, say, in general do do that!) then what has that desire got to do with his talk about systematicness within classes of words, where we can all agree that systematicness is a virtue wherever one can obtain it??

Buitelaar lists clusters of nouns (e.g. blend, competition, flux, transformation) that share the same top semantic nodes in some structure like a modified WordNet: act/evt/rel in the case of the list just given(which can be read as action OR extent or relation). Such structures, he claims, are manifestations of systematic polysemy but what is one to take that to mean, say by contrast with Levin's [39] verb classes where, she claims, the members of the class share certain syntactic and semantic properties and, on that basis, one could in principle predict additional members. That is simply not the case here: one does not have to be a firm believer in natural kinds to see that the members of this class have nothing systematic in common, but are just arbitrarily linked by the same "upper nodes". Some such classes are natural classes, as with the class he gives linked by being both animate and food, all of which, unsurprisingly, are animals and are edible, at least on some dietary principles, but there is no systemic relationship here of any kind. Or, to coin a phrase, one might say that the list above is just a list and nothing more!

In all this, we intend no criticism of his useful device, derived from Pustejovsky, for showing disjunctions and conjunctions of semantic types attached to lexical entries, as when one might mark something as act AND relation or an animal sense as animate OR food. This is close to older devices in artificial intelligence such as multiple perspectives on structures (in Bobrow and Winograd's KRL [6]), multiple formulas for related senses of a word in Wilks [55], and so on. Showing these situations as conjunctions and disjunctions of types may well be a superior notation, though it is quite proper to continue to point out that the members of conjuncts and disjuncts are, and remain, in lists!

Finally, Buitelaar's proposal to use these methods (via CoreLex) to acquire a lexicon from a corpus may also be an excellent approach. Our point here is that that method (capturing the content of e.g. adjective-noun instances in a corpus) has no particular relationship to the theoretical machinery described above, and is not different in kind from the standard NLP projects of the 70s like Autoslog [47] to take just one of many possible examples.

5.2 Another Approach to Lexical Acquisition

We now have developed a set of modular techniques in joint work between Rome University and Sheffield (under the EC-funded ECRAN project) with which to implement and evaluate lexical adaptation in a general manner, and in the context of a full pattern-matching IE system, one not yet fully evaluated in competition:

1. a general verb-pattern matcher from corpora;
2. a Galois Lattice [3] developed as a sorting frame for corpus sub-categorization frames for individual verbs to display their inclusion properties;
3. a general word sense disambiguation program that produces the best results world-wide for general text [57];
4. measures of mapping of the subcategorization patterns (with sense disambiguated noun fillers) at lattice nodes against an existing lexicon of verbs by subcategorization patterns (LDOCE).

These are now sufficient tools to experiment systematically with the augmentation of a lexicon from a corpus with (a) subcategorization and preference patterns and (b) the determination of a novel sense from lattice nodes whose pattern set falls outside some cluster measure for sense.

This aspect of the paper should be seen as interacting strongly with the section above on unsupervised learning of trial template structures from a corpus (Section 4.2 above): in that work a template is induced, seeded only by corpus-significant verbs. In this lexicon-adaptation development, the verbs are explicit seeds and what is sought is the corpus variety of subcategorization patterns within which template fillers for those verbs are to be found and partially ordered. It will be an experimental question whether the subcategorization variety located by the method of this section can be learned and generalised by any of the ML techniques of (Section 3 above).

6 Adapting Knowledge Structures for a New Domain

It is a truism, and one of IEs inheritances from classical AI, that its methods, however superficial some believe them, are dependent on extensive domain knowledge; this takes the form of, at least, hierarchical structures expressing relationships between entities in the domain world of the user. These are often shown as hierarchies in the classical manner but the relationship between child and parent nodes may be variously: part- of, membership, subset, control-over and so on. The simplest sort of example would be an upper node representing Company X, and lower children being Division-A, Division-B, Division-C, which could have relationship conventionally to be described as part-of (in that the divisions are part of the company) but which some might prefer to insist were really set membership relations over, say, employees (in that, any employee of Division-A is also an employee of Company-X—all these are matters of the interpretation of simple diagrams).

There is little dispute such structures are needed for sophisticated IE systems; the interesting questions are can they be acquired automatically for a new domain and are they distinct from lexical knowledge? As to the latter question, the types of knowledge cannot be entirely distinct. When systems like [10] attempted to locate genus hierarchies for LDOCE from parsing the definitions in the dictionary, the resulting hierarchies could be seen equally well as lexical knowledge, or as ISA-hierarchies in the world (a daisy is a plant which...etc.). Pattern matching work on corpora (Pustejovsky [45] [48] to establish and augment such relations was presented as lexicon adaptation but the results could equally well have been claimed as knowledge structure discovery. One could (over)simplify a complex philosophical area by saying that the differences–between lexical and KR interpretations of such hierarchical structure–are in part about:

- interpretation: KR hierarchies can be interpreted in a number of ways, whereas as lexical structures they are normally seen only as naive concept inclusion (e.g. the concept Plant covers the concept Daisy);
- transitivity of structure: KR hierarchies are concerned with inference and hence the transitivity of the interpretations of the ISA and part-of etc. links. This is not normally an issue in local lexical relations.
- scope/intensionality etc.: simple KR hierarchies of the sort we have suggested need to support more complex logical concepts (e.g. scope or the question of interpretation as a concept or role, as in "The President must be over 35" which is both about a current US President like Clinton and about any US President as such). Again, these are not issues in lexical relations as normally described.

Simple trial KR hierarchies for new domains could be inferred from combining for example:

1. Initial inference of the ontological population of a new domain by standard IR concepts of significant presence of a set of words compared to standard texts.
2. Attempting to locate partial KR structures for any members of that set that take part in existing EWN or other semantic hierarchies, using a word sense disambiguation program first if applicable to filter inappropriate senses from the existing hierarchy parts so selected.
3. Using some partial parser on domain corpora to locate "significant triples" over all instances of the word set selected by (i) in the manner of Grishman and Sterling [31].
4. Developing an algorithm to assign these structures (whose non-significant words will be sense-tagged and located in hierarchies, chunks of which can be imported) in combination to a minimum domain-appropriate KR structure that would then have to be edited and pruned by hand within a user-interface.

7 Adaptivity to Text Genre

Another strand of investigation we believe to be of great concern to users of IE is the adaptation, for a given domain, to a new text genre, such as moving from informal messages to formalised reports, without changing domain, and the issue of whether or not templates and their extraction rules need retraining. This was faced as a hand-crafting task in early MUCs when the genre was

US Navy messages which had a jargon and syntactic forms quite unlike conventional English. Khosravi [36] has investigated whether an IE-like approach to speech-act and message matching can transfer between dialogue and email messages and found a substantial degree of transfer, of the order of 60It has long been known that certain lexical forms are distinctive of register and genre, as in certain languages (Czech is often cited) there are still "formal dialects" for certain forms of communication. In cases like these, standard techniques (n-grams and language-recognition methods) would be sufficient to indicate genre. These could be augmented by methods such as the ECRAN-like method (see above) of adapting to new subcategorization patterns and preferences of verbs of interest in new text genres.

8 Multilingual IE

Given an IE system that performs an extraction task against texts in one language, it is natural to consider how to modify the system to perform the same task against texts in another. More generally, there may be a requirement to do the extraction task against texts in an arbitrary number of languages and to present results to a user who has no knowledge of the source language from which the information has been extracted. To minimise the language-specific alterations that need to be made in extending an IE system to a new language, it is important to separate the task-specific conceptual knowledge the system uses, which may be assumed to be language independent, from the language-dependent lexical knowledge the system requires, which unavoidably must be extended for each new language.

At Sheffield, we have adapted the architecture of the LaSIE system [26], an IE system originally designed to do monolingual extraction from English texts, to support a clean separation between conceptual and lexical information. This separation allows hard-to-acquire, domain-specific, conceptual knowledge to be represented only once, and hence to be reused in extracting information from texts in multiple languages, while standard lexical resources can be used to extend language coverage. Preliminary experiments with extending the system to French and Spanish have shown substantial results, and by a method quite different from attaching a classic (monolingual) IE system to a machine translation (MT) system

The M-LaSie (multilingual) system relies on a robust domain model that constitutes the central exchange through which all multilingual information circulates. The addition of a new language to the IE system consists mainly of mapping a new monolingual lexicon to the domain model and adding a new syntactic/semantic analysis front-end, with no interaction at all with other languages in the system.

The language independent domain model can be compared to the use of an *interlingua* representation in MT (see, *e.g.*, [35]). An IE system, however, does not require full generation capabilities from the intermediate representation, and the task will be well-specified by a limited 'domain model' rather than a full unrestricted 'world model'. This makes an *interlingua* representation feasible for IE, because it will not involve finding solutions to all the problems of such a representation, only those issues directly relevant to the current IE task.

A French-Spanish-English prototype of this architecture has been implemented and successfully tested on a limited amount of data. The architecture has been further developed in the AVENTINUS project [20].

9 Conclusion

This has been not so much a paper as a disguised research proposal and compares very unfavourably therefore with those described above who have been prepared to begin the difficult work of making IE adaptive. Another important area not touched on here (though it is to be found in Cardie [12]) is the application of ML methods to the crucial notion of co-reference (e.g. [2]), and particularly its role in relating documents together: or cross-document management, a form of data-fusion between information about individuals in different documents, who may in fact be different although they have the same names.

References

1. J. Aberdeen, J. Burger, D. Day, L. Hirschman, P. Robinson, and M. Vilain. MITRE - Description of the *Alembic* System used for MUC-6. In *Proceedings of the Sixth Message Understanding Conference (MUC-6)*, pages 141–156, 1995.
2. S. Azzam, K. Humphreys, and R. Gaizauskas. Using corefernece chains for text summarization. In *Proceedings of the ACL '99 WOrkshop on Corefernce and its Applications.* Maryland, 1999.
3. R. Basili, M. Pazienza, and P. Velardi. Aquisition of selectional patterns from sub-langauges. *Machine Translation*, 8, 1993.
4. R. Catizone M.T. Pazienza M. Stevenson M. P. Velardi M.Vindigni Y.Wilks Basili, R. An empirical approach to lexical tuning. In *Workshop on Adapting Lexical and Corpus Resources to Sublanguages and Applications , LREC, First International Conference on Language Resources and Evaluation*, Granada, Spain, 1998.
5. D. Bikel, S. Miller, R. Schwartz, and R. Weischedel. Nymble: a High-Performance Learning Name-finder. In *Proceedings of the Fifth conference on Applied Natural Language Processing*, 1997.
6. D.G. Bobrow and T. Winograd. An overview of krl, a knowledge representation language. *Cognitive Science 1*, pages 3–46, 1977.
7. E. Brill. Some Advances in Transformation-Based Part of Speech Tagging. In *Proceedings ofthe Twelfth National Conference on AI (AAAI-94)*, Seattle, Washington, 1994.
8. E. Brill. Transformation-Based Error-Driven Learning and Natural Language. *Computational Linguistics*, 21(4), December 1995.
9. E. Briscoe, A. Copestake, and V. De Pavia. Default inheritance in unification-based approaches to the lexicon. Technical report, Cambridge University Computer Laboratory, 1991.
10. R. Bruce and L. Guthrie. Genus disambiguation: A study in weighted preference. In *Proceesings of COLING-92*, pages 1187–1191, Nantes, France, 1992.

11. P. Buitelaar. A lexicon for underspecified semantic tagging. In *Proceedings of the ACL-Siglex Workshop on Tagging Text with Lexical Semantics*, Washington, D.C., 1997.
12. Claire Cardie. Empirical methods in information extraction. *AI Magazine. Special Issue on Empirical Natural Language Processing*, 18(4), 1997.
13. N. Chinchor. The statistical significance of the MUC-5 results. In *Proceedings of the Fifth Message Understanding Conference (MUC-5)*, pages 79–83. Morgan Kaufmann, 1993.
14. N. Chinchor and Sundheim B. MUC-5 Evaluation Metrics. In *Proceedings of the Fifth Message Understanding Conference (MUC-5)*, pages 69–78. Morgan Kaufmann, 1993.
15. N. Chinchor, L. Hirschman, and D.D. Lewis. Evaluating message understanding systems: An analysis of the third message understanding conference (muc-3). *Computational Linguistics*, 19(3):409–449, 1993.
16. R. Collier. *Automatic Template Creation for Information Extraction.* PhD thesis, UK, 1998.
17. J. Cowie, L. Guthrie, W. Jin, W. Odgen, J. Pustejowsky, R. Wanf, T. Wakao, S. Waterman, and Y. Wilks. CRL/Brandeis: The Diderot System. In *Proceedings of Tipster Text Program (Phase I)*. Morgan Kaufmann, 1993.
18. J. Cowie and W. Lehnert. Information extraction. *Special NLP Issue of the Communications of the ACM*, 1996.
19. H. Cunningham. JAPE – a Jolly Advanced Pattern Engine. 1997.
20. H. Cunningham, S. Azzam, and Y. Wilks. Domain Modelling for AVENTINUS (WP 4.2). LE project LE1-2238 AVENTINUS internal technical report, University of Sheffield, UK, 1996.
21. H. Cunningham, R.G. Gaizauskas, and Y. Wilks. A General Architecture for Text Engineering (GATE) – a new approach to Language Engineering R&D. Technical Report CS – 95 – 21, Department of Computer Science, University of Sheffield, 1995. Also available as `http://xxx.lanl.gov/ps/cmp-lg/9601009`.
22. W. Daelemans, J. Zavrel, K. van der Sloot, and A. van den Bosch. TiMBL: Tilburg memory based learner version 1.0. Technical report, ILK Technical Report 98-03, 1998.
23. D. Day, J. Aberdeen, L. Hirschman, R. Kozierok, P. Robinson, and M. Vilain. Mixed-Initiative Development of Language Processing Systems. In *Proceedings of the 5th Conference on Applied NLP Systems (ANLP-97)*, 1997.
24. J.Sterling.NYU E.Agichtein R.Grishman A.Borthwick.
25. R. Evans and G. Gazdar. Datr: A language for lexical knowledge representation. *Computational Linguistics 22 2*, pages 167–216, 1996.
26. R. Gaizauskas. XI: A Knowledge Representation Language Based on Cross-Classification and Inheritance. Technical Report CS-95-24, Department of Computer Science, University of Sheffield, 1995.
27. R. Gaizauskas and Y. Wilks. Information Extraction: Beyond Document Retrieval. *Journal of Documentation*, 1997. In press (Also available as Technical Report CS-97-10).
28. G. Gazdar and C. Mellish. *Natural Language Processing in Prolog.* Addison-Wesley, 1989.
29. T. Givon. Transformations of ellipsis, sense development and rules of lexical derivation. Technical Report SP-2896, Systems Development Corp., Sta Monica, CA, 1967.

30. R. Grishman. Information extraction: Techniques and challenges. In M-T. Pazienza, editor, *Proceedings of the Summer School on Information Extraction (SCIE-97)*, LNCS/LNAI. Springer-Verlag, 1997.
31. R. Grishman and J. Sterling. Generalizing automatically generated patterns. In *Proceedings of COLING-92*, 1992.
32. R. Grishman and J. Sterling. Description of the Proteus system as used for MUC-5. In *Proceedings of the Fifth Message Understanding Conference (MUC-5)*, pages 181–194. Morgan Kaufmann, 1993.
33. G. Hirst. *Semantic Interpretation and the Resolution of Ambiguity.* CUP, Cambridge, England, 1987.
34. J.R. Hobbs. The generic information extraction system. In *Proceedings of the Fifth Message Understanding Conference (MUC-5)*, pages 87–91. Morgan Kaufman, 1993.
35. W.J. Hutchins. *Machine Translation: past, present, future.* Chichester : Ellis Horwood, 1986.
36. H. Khosravi and Y. Wilks. Extracting pragmatic content from e-mail. *Journal of Natural Language Engineering*, 1997. submitted.
37. R. Krovetz and B. Croft. Lexical ambiguity and information retrieval. *ACM Transactions on Information Systems 2 10*, 1992.
38. W. Lehnert, C. Cardie, D. Fisher, J. McCarthy, and E. Riloff. University of massachusetts: Description of the CIRCUS system as used for MUC-4. In *Proceedings of the Fourth Message Understanding Conference MUC-4*, pages 282–288. Morgan Kaufmann, 1992.
39. B. Levin. *English Verb Calsses and Alternations.* Chicago, Il, 1993.
40. H. P. Luhn. A statistical approach to mechanized encoding and searching of literary information. *IBM Journal of Research and Development 1*, pages 309–317, 1957.
41. R. Morgan, R. Garigliano, P. Callaghan, S. Poria, M. Smith, A. Urbanowicz, R. Collingham, M. Costantino, and C. Cooper. Description of the LOLITA System as used for MUC-6. In *Proceedings of the Sixth Message Understanding Conference (MUC-6)*, pages 71–86, San Francisco, 1995. Morgan Kaufmann.
42. S. Muggleton. Recent advances in inductive logic programming. In *Proc. 7th Annu. ACM Workshop on Comput. Learning Theory*, pages 3–11. ACM Press, New York, NY, 1994.
43. S. Nirenburg and V. Raskin. Ten choices for lexical semantics. Technical report, Computing Research Lab, Las Cruces, NM, 1996. MCCS-96-304.
44. J. Pustejovsky. *The Generative Lexicon.* MIT, 1995.
45. J. Pustejovsky and P. Anick. Autmoatically acquiring conceptual patterns without an annotated corpus. In *Proceedings of the Third Workshop on Very Large Corpora*, 1988.
46. E. Riloff. Automatically contructing a dictionary for information extraction tasks. In *Proceedings of Eleventh National Conference on Artificial Intelligence*, 1993.
47. E. Riloff and W. Lehnert. Automated dictionary construction for information extraction from text. In *Proceedings of Ninth IEEE Conference on Artificial Intelligence for Applications*, pages 93–99, 1993.
48. E. Riloff and J. Shoen. Automatically aquiring conceptual patterns without an annotated corpus. In *Proceedings of the Third Workshop on Very Large Corpora*, 1995.
49. E. Roche and Y. Schabes. Deterministic Part-of-Speech Tagging with Finite-State Transducers. *Computational Linguistics*, 21(2):227–254, June 1995.

50. K. Samuel, S. Carberry, and K. Vijay-Shanker. Dialogue act tagging with transofrmation-based learning. In *Proceedings of the COLING-ACL 1998 Conference*, pages 1150–1156, 1998.
51. S. Small and C. Rieger. Parsing and comprehending with word experts (a theory and it's realiastion). In W. Lehnert and M. Ringle, editors, *Strategies for Natural Language Processing*. Lawrence Erlbaum Associates, Hillsdale, NJ, 1982.
52. David Page Stephen Muggleton James Cussens and Ashwin Srinivasan. Using inductive logic programming for natural language processing. In *Proceedings of in ECML.Workshop Notes on Empirical Learning of Natural Language Tasks*, pages 25–34, Prague, 1997.
53. Jin Wang T.Strzalkowski, Fang Lin and Jose Perez-Caballo. *Natural Language Information Retrieval*, chapter Evaluating Natural Language Processing Techniques in Information Retrieval, pages 113–146. Kluwer Academic Publishers, 1997.
54. Mark Vilain.
55. Y. Wilks. *Grammar, Meaning and the Machine Analysis of Meaning*. Routledge and Kegan Paul, 1972.
56. Y. Wilks, L. Guthrie, J. Guthrie, and J. Cowie. *Combining Weak Methods in Large-Scale Text Processing, in Jacobs 1992, Text-Based Intelligent Systems*. Lawrence Erlbaum, 1992.
57. Y. Wilks and M. Stevenson. Sense tagging: Semantic tagging with a lexicon. In *Proceedings of the SIGLEX Workshop "Tagging Text with Lexical Semantics: What, why and how?"*, Washington, D.C., April 1997. Available as `http://xxx.lanl.gov/ps/cmp-lg/9705016`.

Natural Language Processing and Digital Libraries

Jean-Pierre Chanod

Xerox Research Centre Europe
6, chemin de Maupertuis, 38240 Meylan, France
Jean-Pierre.Chanod@xrce.xerox.com
http://www.xrce.xerox.com

Abstract. As one envisions a document model where language, physical location and medium - electronic, paper or other - impose no barrier to effective use, natural language processing will play an increasing role, especially in the context of digital libraries.
This paper presents language components based mostly on finite-state technology that improve our capabilities for exploring, enriching and interacting in various ways with documents. This ranges from morphology to part-of-speech tagging, NP extraction and shallow parsing.
We then focus on a series of on-going projects which illustrate how this technology is already impacting the building and sharing of knowledge through digital libraries.

1 Linguistic Components

The first part of this article concentrates on linguistic tools built at XRCE, as they represent a fairly extensive suite of consistent, robust and multilingual components ranging from morphology, part-of-speech (POS) tagging, shallow parsing and sense disambiguation. They are based mostly on finite-state technology. Combinations of rule-based and statistical methods are applied whenever appropriate. They rely on fully developed language resources and are integrated into the same unified architecture for all languages, the Xerox Linguistic Development Architecture (XeLDA) developed by the Advanced Technology Systems group. These tools are used to develop descriptions of more than 15 languages and are integrated into higher level applications, such as terminology extraction, information retrieval or translation aid, which are highly relevant in the area of digital libraries.

1.1 Finite-State Calculus

Finite-state technology is the fundamental technology Xerox language R&D is based on.The basic calculus is built on a central library that implements the fundamental operations on finite-state networks. It is the result of a long-standing research effort [21], [24], [28], [30]. An interactive tutorial on finite-state calculus is also available at the XRCE finite-state home page

Pazienza (Ed.): Information Extraction, LNAI 1714, pp. 17–31, 1999.

(http://www.xrce.xerox.com/research/mltt/fst/home.html). Besides the basic operations (concatenation, union, intersection, composition, replace operator) the library provides various algorithms to improve further the compaction, speed and ease of use of the networks. The calculus also includes specific functions to describe two-level rules and to build lexical transducers. The finite-state calculus is widely used in linguistic development, to create tokenisers, morphological analysers, noun phrase extractors, shallow parsers and other language-specific components [22].

1.2 Morphology

Morphological variations can be conveniently represented by finite-state transducers which encode on the one side surface forms and on the other side normalised representations of such surface forms [23]. More specifically:

1. the allowed combinations of morphemes can be encoded as a finite-state network;
2. the rules that determine the context-dependent form of each morpheme can be implemented as finite-state transducers (cf. two-level morphology [25]);
3. the lexicon network and the rule transducers can be composed into a single automaton, a lexical transducer, that contains all the morphological information about the language including derivation, inflection, and compounding.

Lexical transducers have many advantages. They are bi-directional (the same network for both analysis and generation), fast (thousands of words per second), and compact. They also provide an adequate formalism for a multilingual approach to language processing, as major European languages and non-Indo-European languages (e.g. Finnish, Hungarian, Arabic, Basque) can be described in this framework.

1.3 Part-of-Speech Tagging

The general purpose of a part-of-speech tagger is to associate each word in a text with its morphosyntactic category (represented by a tag), as in the following example:

```
This+PRON is+VAUX_3SG a+DET sentence+NOUN_SG .+SENT
```

The process of tagging consists in three steps:

1. tokenisation: break a text into tokens
2. lexical lookup: provide all potential tags for each token

3. disambiguation: assign to each token a single tag

   Each step is performed by an application program that uses language specific data:

   - The tokenisation step [8] uses a finite-state transducer to insert token boundaries around simple words (or multi-word expressions), punctuation, numbers, etc.

   - Lexical lookup requires a morphological analyser to associate each token with one or more readings. Unknown words are handled by a guesser that provides potential part-of-speech categories based on affix patterns.

   - In XRCE language suite, disambiguation is based on probabilistic methods (Hidden Markov Model), [10], which offer various advantages such as ease of training and speed. However, some experiments [7] showed that a limited number of disambiguation rules could reach the same level of accuracy. This may become the source of interesting developments in POS tagging, as one deals with highly inflective, agglutinative and/or free-word order languages for which simple contextual analysis and restricted tagsets are not adequate [16].

1.4 Noun Phrase Extraction

Finite-state Noun Phrase extraction [6], [27],
[33], [31] consists in extracting patterns associated with candidates NPs. Such patterns can be defined by regular expressions based on sequences of tags such as: ADJ* NOUN+ (PREP NOUN)

The example above specifies that an NP can be represented by a sequence of one or more nouns [NOUN+] preceded by any number of adjectives [ADJ*] and optionally followed by a preposition and a noun [(PREP NOUN)], the optionality being indicated in the regular expression by the parentheses. Such a pattern would cover phrases like "digital libraries" "relational morphological analyser" "information retrieval system" or "network of networks". Due to overgeneration, the same pattern would also cover undesirable sequences such as "art museum on Tuesday" in "John visited the art museum on Tuesday". This highlights that simple noun phrase extraction based on pattern matching requires further processing, be it automatic (e.g. by using fine-grain syntactic or semantic subcategorisation in addition to part-of-speech information or by using corpus-based filtering methods) or manual (e.g. validation by terminologists or indexers).

1.5 Incremental Finite-State Parsing

Incremental Finite State Parsing (IFSP) is an extension of finite state technology to the level of phrases and sentences, in the more general framework of shallow parsing of unrestricted texts [19], [1]. IFSP computes syntactic structures, without fully analysing linguistic phenomena that require deep semantic or pragmatic knowledge. For instance, PP-attachment, coordinated or elliptic structures are not always fully analysed. The annotation scheme remains underspecified with respect to yet unresolved issues, especially if finer-grained linguistic information is necessary. This underspecification prevents parse failures, even on complex sentences. It also prevents some early linguistic interpretation based on to too general parameters. Syntactic information is added at the sentence level in an incremental way [2], [3], depending on the contextual information available at a given stage. The implementation relies on a sequence of networks built with the replace operator. The parsing process is incremental in the sense that the linguistic description attached to a given transducer in the sequence relies on the preceding sequence of transducers and can be revised at a later stage. The parser output can be used for further processing such as extraction of dependency relations over unrestricted corpora. In tests on French corpora (technical manuals, newspaper), precision is around 90-97% for subjects (84-88% for objects) and recall around 86-92% for subjects (80-90% for objects). The system being highly modular the strategy for dependency extraction may be adjusted to different domains of application, while the first phase of syntactic annotation is general enough to remain the same across domains.

Here is a sample sentence extracted from this current section:

Annotation:

[SC [NP _The parsing process NP]/SUBJ :v is SC] [AP incremental AP] [PP in the sense PP] [SC that [NP the linguistic description NP]/SUBJ attached [PP to a given transducer PP] [PP in the sequence PP] :v relies SC] [PP on the preceding sequence PP] [PP of transducers PP] and [SC :v can be revised SC] [PP at a later stage PP] .

Dependency extraction:

- SUBJ(description,rely)
- SUBJ(process,be)
- SUBJPASS(description,revise)
- SUBJPASS(process,revise)
- VMODOBJ(revise,at,stage)
- VMODOBJ(rely,at,stage)
- VMODOBJ(rely,on,sequence)
- VMODOBJ(be,in,sense)
- ADJ(late,stage)
- ADJ(given,transducer)
- ADJ(linguistic,description)
- NPPASDOBJ(description,attach)
- ATTR(process,incremental)
- NNPREP(sequence,at,stage)
- NNPREP(sequence,of,transducer)

- NNPREP(transducer,in,sequence)
- NNPREP(description,to,transducer)
- NUNSURE([N [PP at a later stage PP] N])
- NUNSURE([N [PP on the preceding sequence PP] [PP of transducers PP] N])
- NUNSURE([N [PP to a given transducer PP] [PP in the sequence PP] N])
- NUNSURE([N [NP _The parsing process NP] N])

1.6 Sense Disambiguation

The word sense disambiguation (WSD) system developed at XRCE is based on two existing WSD systems. The first system [32], the Semantic Dictionary Lookup, is built on top of Locolex (cf. infra). It uses information about collocates and subcategorization frames derived from the Oxford-Hachette French Dictionary [9]. The disambiguation process relies on dependency relations computed by the incremental finite-state parser.

The second system [12], GINGER II, is an unsupervised transformation-based semantic tagger first built for English. Semantic disambiguation rules are automatically extracted from dictionary examples and their sense numberings. Because senses and examples have been defined by lexicographers, they provide a reliable linguistic source for constructing a database of semantic disambiguation rules. and dictionaries appear as valuable semantically tagged corpus.

2 Some Language Applications Relevant to Digital Libraries

2.1 LOCOLEX: A Machine Aided Comprehension Dictionary

LOCOLEX [5], [13],is an on-line bilingual comprehension dictionary which aids the understanding of electronic documents written in a foreign language. It displays only the appropriate part of a dictionary entry when a user clicks on a word in a given context. The system disambiguates parts of speech and recognises multiword expressions such as compounds (e.g. *heart attack*), phrasal verbs (e.g. *to nit pick*), idiomatic expressions (e.g. *to take the bull by the horns*) and proverbs (e.g. *birds of a feather flock together*). In such cases LOCOLEX displays the translation of the whole phrase and not the translation of the word the user has clicked on. For instance, someone may use a French/English dictionary to understand the following text written in French:

Lorsqu'on évoque devant les cadres la séparation négociée, les rumeurs fantaisistes vont apparemment toujours bon train.

When the user clicks on the word *cadres*, LOCOLEX identifies its POS and base form. It then displays the corresponding entry, here the noun *cadre*, with its different sense indicators and associated translations. In this particular context, the verb reading of *cadres* is ignored by LOCOLEX. Actually, in order to make the entry easier to use, only essential elements are displayed:

cadre I: nm

1. *[constr,art] (of a picture, a window) frame
2. *(scenery) setting
3. *(milieu) surroundings
4. *(structure, context) framework
5. *(employee) executive
6. *(of a bike, motorcycle) frame

The word *train* in the same example above is part of a verbal multiword expression *aller bon train*. In our example, the expression is inflected and two adverbs have been stuck in between the head verb and its complement. Still LOCOLEX retrieves only the equivalent expression in English to be flying around and not the entire entry for *train*.

train I: nm

5 : * [rumeurs] aller bon train : to be flying round

LOCOLEX uses an SGML-tagged bilingual dictionary (the Oxford-Hachette French English Dictionary). To adapt this dictionary to LOCOLEX required the following:

- Revision of an SGML-tagged Dictionary to build a disambiguated active dictionary (DAD);
- Rewriting multi-word expressions as regular expressions using a special grammar;
- Building a finite state machine that compactly associates index numbers with dictionary entries.

The lookup process itself may be represented as follows:

- split the sentence string into words (tokenisation);
- normalise the case and spelling of each word ;
- identify all possible morpho-syntatic usages (base form and morpho-syntactic tags) for each word in the sentence;
- disambiguate the POS;
- find relevant entries (including possible homographs or compounds) in the dictionary for the lexical form(s) chosen by the POS disambiguator;
- use the result of the morphological analysis and disambiguation to eliminate irrelevant parts of the dictionary entry;
- process the regular expressions to see if they match the word's actual context in order to identify special or idiomatic usages;
- display to the user only the most appropriate translation based on the part of speech and surrounding context.

2.2 Multilingual Information Retrieval and Data Mining

Many of the linguistic tools being developed at XRCE are being used in applied research into multilingual information retrieval and more broadly in data mining [4], [14], [15], [17]. Multilingual information retrieval allows the interrogation of texts written in a target language B by users asking questions in source language A.

In order to perform this retrieval, the following linguistic processing steps are performed on the documents and the query:

- Automatically recognise language of the text.
- Perform the morphological analysis of the text using Xerox finite state analysers.
- Part of speech tag the words in the text using the preceding morphological analysis and the probability of finding part-of-speech tag paths in the text.
- Lemmatise, i.e. normalise or reduce to dictionary entry form, the words in the text using the part of speech tags.

This morphological analysis, tagging, and subsequent lemmatisation of analysed words has proved to be a useful improvement for information retrieval as any information-retrieval specific stemming. To process a given query, an intermediate form of the query must be generated which compares the normalised language of the query to the indexed text of the documents. This intermediate form can be constructed by replacing each word with target language words through an online bilingual dictionary. The intermediate query, which is in the same language as the target documents, is passed along to a traditional information retrieval system, such as SMART. This simple word-based method is the first approach we have been testing at XRCE. Initial runs indicate that incorporating multi-word expression matching can significantly improve results. The multi-word expressions most interesting for information retrieval are terminological expressions, which most often appear as noun phrases in English. Data mining refers to the extraction of structured information from unstructured text. A number of applications of linguistic processing can be applied to semantic extraction. One example of data-mining research that we are pursuing at XRCE is terminological extraction from raw text. A first pass at terminological extraction is possible once a morphological analyser and a tagger have been created for a language. One need then only define a regular pattern of tagged words that corresponds with a noun phrase in that language. At present, we are able to extract such noun phrases from English, French, German, Spanish and Italian text.

3 Some Recent Projects for Digital Libraries

The past few years have seen a remarkable expansion of digital networks and especially those using Internet. Information sources accessed via Internet are the components of a digital library (DL). They are a mixture of public and private information, free of charge or paying and include books, reports, magazines, newspapers, video and sound recordings, scientific data, etc.

The role of language processing tools is becoming prominent in a number of digital libraries projects, including:

- Callimaque : a collaborative project for virtual libraries
- LIRIX: an industrial extension of Callimaque
- TwentyOne
- PopEye and Olive

3.1 Callimaque: A Collaborative Project for Virtual Libraries

Digital libraries represent a new way of accessing information distributed all over the world, via the use of a computer connected to the Internet network. Whereas a physical library deals primarily with physical data, a digital library deals with electronic documents such as texts, pictures, sounds and video. We expect more from a digital library than only the possibility of browsing its documents. A digital library front-end should provide users with a set of tools for querying and retrieving information, as well as annotating pages of a document, defining hyper-links between pages or helping to understand multilingual documents.

Callimaque [20] is a virtual library resulting from a collaboration between XRCE and research/academic institutions of the Grenoble area (IMAG, INRIA, CICG). It reconstructs the early history of information technology in France. The project is based on a similar project, the Class project, which was started by the University of Cornell several years ago under the leadership of Stuart Lynn to preserve brittling old books. The Class project runs over conventional networks and all scanned material is in English.

The Callimaque project included the following steps:

- Scanning and indexing around 1000 technical reports and 2000 theses written at the University of Grenoble, using Xerox XDOD, a system integrated with a scanner, a PC, a high-speed printer, software for dequeueing, indexing, storing, etc. Numerised documents can be reworked page by page and even restructured at the user's convenience. 30 Gbytes of memory are needed to store the images.
- Abstracts were OCRed to allow for textual search.
- Documents are recorded on a relational database on a UNIX server.

A number of identifiers (title, author, reference number, abstract, etc.) are associated with each document to facilitate the search. With a view to making these documents widely accessible, Xerox has developed software that authorises access to this database by any client using the http protocol used by the World

Wide Web. The base is thus accessible via any PC, Macintosh, UNIX station or even from a simple ASCII terminal (The web address is http://callimaque.grenet.fr). Print on demand facilities connected to the network allow the users to make copies of the scanned material. The module for interrogation of the database is linked to a translation assistance tool developed at XRCE (see above Locolex). It will not only enable a reader unfamiliar with French to clarify certain abstracts, but also to make keyword searching more intelligent by proposing synonyms, normalising inflected forms and resolving ambiguities. Multilingual terminology will help processing non-French queries.

Language processing tools, esp. finite-state based tools, have been used during the construction of the digital library (OCR, terminology extraction). They also actively support the end-user interaction with the final system (search, translation aid):

- OCR: documents collected in the Callimaque digital libraries have been scanned, but an additional step was taken by OCR-ing the abstracts. This allows for textual search beyond basic references such as title and author names. The OCR system integrates lexical information derived from lexical transducers. This improves drastically the accuracy of the recognition, as opposed to OCR based on simple word lists. This accuracy improvement becomes even more striking when dealing with highly inflectional languages.
- bilingual terminology extraction: many of the documents integrated in the Callimaque library include bilingual abstracts, even when the body of the document is monolingual (generally written in French). Noun-phrase extraction, combined with alignment, was performed on such bilingual abstracts. This lead to the construction of a bilingual term base (French, English) which has been used as a Callimaque specific resource for indexing, cross-lingual search and translation aid.
- cross-lingual search: the bilingual term base has been encoded following the Locolex approach. This allows for matches beyond simple string matching. For instance, an English query like *"dense matrices"* match French documents containing expressions like *"matrice pleine"* *"matrice dense"* or *"matrices denses"*. This shows that matches are made regardless of morphological variations (e.g. singular or plural) or even regardless of the translation for *"dense"*. Even more, the system match *"dense matrices"* against *"matrice rectangulaire dense"*, allowing for the insertion of the adjective *rectangulaire* within the expression. This is permitted by the regular language used to described expressions encoded in Locolex.
- translation aid: a natural enhancement of the system consists in provided translation aid based on the bilingual term base. This naturally expands to any bilingual resources (e.g. a general dictionary) which can be made available to the end-user.

3.2 Lirix

Lirix is the follow-up to the Callimaque multilingual extensions. It is a multilingual information retrieval system built over Topic, the search engine from Verity, and the XeLDA linguistic platform developped at XRCE. The overall goal of the Lirix project is to design and build a general, portable, robust and innovative multilingual information system, with particular attention to CLIR (Cross Lingual Information Retrieval). The user can enter a query using his/her mother tongue, and perform retrieval accross languages (by translation/expansion of the original query). Lirix relies on general-purpose dictionaries (unlike Callimaque that is restricted to specialized term bases) and can run on any collection already indexed with Verity: no re-indexing is necessary.

CLIR (Cross Lingual Information Retrieval) systems have to cope with two difficult problems:

- They might miss relevant documents because of translation difficulties, esp. if the query translation is based on a word by word analysis. For instance, multiword expressions requires the relevant level of contextual analysis to be properly identified and then translated (e.g. *ignition key* means *clé de contact* in French, but *contact*, taken as a standalone word, cannot be translated by *ignition* and vice versa). It is also necessary to expand the query to related words that are not direct translations of the initial query (e.g. *president* in the query *presidential election*).
- The results are often very noisy because in the absence of sense disambiguation, all senses of the words found in the initial query are retained for translation (e.g. the translation of the French word *clé* could be: *key, spanner, wrench, peg, valve, clef, armlock,* etc.).

To overcome these difficulties, Lirix integrates advanced language processing capabilities:

- Multiword expressions recognition: Lirix uses the contextual dictionary lookup of XeLDA. to identify multiword expressions and provide the adequate translation (e.g. *ignition key* is translated by *clé de contact* in French). This improves accuracy and reduces noise as indicated earlier.
- Relational Morphology. This method generates all related word forms from the words in the query. This enables a fuzzy search of related words in the corpus. A query like *élection du président* will return documents containing *election of the president*, but also *presidential election.*
- Pair extraction with shallow parsing. Some words can be translated into numerous, unrelated words (cf. translations of the French word *clé* in the previous section). Searching the corpus for every possible translation will most likely retrieve a lot of non relevant documents. One way to improve this situation is through shallow parsing and extraction of syntactically related pairs. For example, if the query contains *clé de voiture (car key)* , the

system will search for the pair *car+key* in the corpus. One interesting feature of shallow parsing is that extracted pairs are derived from a wide set of dependency relations between head words, such as subject/verb, verb/object, noun/adjective, etc . As a consequence, the pairs are not limited to short distance relations as a more basic notion of co-occurrence within a window of a given size would impose. Also, the relations being syntactically motivated, they are less sensitive to noise due to word order, surface structure and proximity between otherwise unrelated elements. In the longer term, this approach could be further refined with sense disambiguation techniques as described above.

3.3 TwentyOne

Twenty-One [26], [18], [11], [34] is a EU funded project which has the target to develop a tool for efficient dissemination of multimedia information in the field of sustainable development. The project started in march 1996 and will finish in 1999. The demonstrator incorporates one of the major project results: a so-called search engine which combines full text search with several other information retrieval functions. The search engine technology has been evaluated by the user partners, and at the TREC-conferences in 1997 and 1998.

The following key features are envisaged:

- Multimedia handling: Support for the disclosure of a variety of formats : paper, wordprocessor docs, audio, video
- cross-language retrieval : Support for four languages: English, German, Dutch and French. Users can query the multilingual database in their mother tongue;

documents will be presented in translation.

Twenty-One is of potential interest for:

- people looking for information about sustainable development (end-users)
- organisations that want to disseminate their publications to interested parties in various languages (info-providers)
- digital archives (textual and/or multimedia) in need of automatic disclosure tools

3.4 PopEye: Disclosure of Video Material Using Subtitles

Reuse of library material plays an important role in keeping down the budget for audio visual production. However, cataloguing and indexing of film and video recordings is an expensive and time consuming process. It requires the expertise of specialised archivists, and has not yet been automated. There are no computer systems yet in existence that can understand and interpret moving images, or that have the unrestricted ability to recognise and comprehend speech. But there is a source of information available that can enable existing computer technology to access the content of a video: the subtitles. Subtitles are produced either to translate foreign language programmes or (for native language pro-grammes) to help people with hearing difficulties to understand the soundtrack. automated indexing Many video library systems use textual descriptions to classify a video programme; but these usually offer a description only of the entire programme, not of each separate sequence (shot) that it contains. Subtitles are time-coded; they can provide the basis for an index that points to an exact location within a video programme. Pop-Eye's indexes will connect text to image sequences, providing a completely new approach to the indexing of visual material. Natural language processing techniques are applied to the subtitles, to index them and partially translate themi nto each of the three languages supported by the Project (Dutch, English, German). Pop-Eye will extract time-coded texts from the subtitles of film or video sequences and then automatically generate multilingual indexes for the programmes. A hit in the index will reveal a still image (frame) or short clipping from the programme for the user to evaluate, not just a general indication that relevant images might be contained somewhere on a video tape. retrieval across the Internet The Pop-Eye retrieval interface is based on a standard Internet browser. Using the World Wide Web, Pop-Eye enables organisations, such as the broadcasting companies who are members of Pop-Eye (BRTN, SWF and TROS), to give users inside and outside the organisation access to their video archive. Retrieval of video sequences using Pop-Eye will be fast; this makes it cost-effective for any kind of programme production, and also opens new business opportunities: film and video archives can be made available to anyone who has access to the Internet. not just archived, but available Many systems focus on building large video archives, storing as many hours as possible of film and video on huge piles of disks. By contrast, Pop-Eye is one of the very few systems that concentrates on obtaining good recall when searching stored video material. Pop-Eye does not just add a few key words to a film or video sequence; it uses available text information (the subtitles) to guide users, in their own language, to the exact location within the video that might be of interest to them.

3.5 Olive

OLIVE [29] is developing a system which automatically produces indexes from the sound track of a programme (television or radio). This allows archives to be searched by keywords and corresponding visual or soundtrack material to be retrieved. OLIVE broadens the applicability of PopEye, which is using subtitles and video time codes to index broadcast material. The system will facilitate production of broadcast material which incorporates existing radio and video material, for example, news and documentaries. It will also be a valuable tool for programme researchers designing new programmes and other content providers, such as advertisers. Through the provision of bibliographic material, transcripts and video stills, the system will save time by allowing material to be pre-viewed before it is actually retrieved from an archive.

4 Conclusion

One of the major challenges for NLP in the process of pushing research results towards real-life applications resides not in the NLP technology itself but rather in integration, i.e. in the ability to plug NLP into contexts that are relevant for end users. Digital libraries represent one of the best cases for evaluating the impact of such integration. We are only at an early stage in this process, and future work will require continuous effort in various directions: improving the accuracy and precision of current NLP tools; expanding such tools to new languages esp. to take into consideration the growing language diversity on the internet and in electronic documents at large; pushing research in critical areas, such as semantic disambiguation, use of thesaurus, knowledge extraction, in order to build the next generation of NLP tools ; developping smarter user interfaces, taking into account the feedback collected from current DL application, integrating recent advances in distributed practices and multimodal and multimedia knowledge repositories.

References

1. Steven Abney. Parsing by chunks. In R. Berwick, S. Abney, and C. Tenny, editors, *Principled-Based Parsing.* Kluwer Academic Publishers, Dordrecht, 1991.
2. Salah At-Mokhtar and Jean-Pierre Chanod. Incremental finite-state parsing. In *Proceedings of Applied Natural Language Processing, Washington, DC*, 1997.
3. Salah At-Mokhtar and Jean-Pierre Chanod. Subject and object dependency extraction using finite-state transducers. In *ACL workshop on Automatic Information Extraction and Building of Lexical Semantic Resources for NLP Applications*, 1997.
4. Roberto Basili and Maria Teresa Pazienza. Lexical acquisition and information extraction. In *SCIE 1997*, pages 44–72, 1997.
5. D. Bauer, F. Segond, and A. Zaenen. Locolex: the translation rolls off your tongue. In *Proceedings of the ACH-ALLC conference*, pages 6–8, Santa Barbara, 1995.
6. D. Bourigault. An endogenous corpus-based method for structural noun phrase disambiguation. In *6th Conf. of EACL*, Utrecht, 1993.
7. Jean-Pierre Chanod and Pasi Tapanainen. Tagging french-comparing a statistical and a constraint-based method. In *Seventh Conference of the European Chapter of the ACL*, Dublin, 1995.
8. Jean-Pierre Chanod and Pasi Tapanainen. A non-deterministic tokeniser for finite-state parsing. In *ECAI '96 workshop on Extended finite state models of language*, Budapest, 1996.
9. M-H Corrard and V. Grundy, editors. *The Oxford Hachette French Dictonary.* Oxford University Press-Hachette, Oxford, 1994.
10. Doug Cutting, Julian Kupiec, Jan Pedersen, and Penelope Sibun. A practical part-of-speech tagger. In *Proceedings of ANLP-92*, pages 133–140, Trento, 1992.
11. Franciska de Jong. Twenty-one: a baseline for multilingual multimedia retrieval. In *Proceedings of the fourteenth Twente Workshop on Language Technology TWLT-14*, pages 189–195, University of Twente, 1998.
12. L. Dini, V. Di Tomaso, and F. Segond. Ginger ii: an example-driven word sense disambiguator. *Computer and the Humanities*, 1999. to appear.

13. F.Segond and P. Tapanainen. Using a finite-state based formalism to identify and generate multiword expressions. Technical report, Xerox Research Centre Europe, Grenoble, 1995.
14. Gregory Grefenstette, editor. *Explorations in Automatic Thesaurus Discovery.* Kluwer Academic Press, Boston, 1994.
15. Gregory Grefenstette, Ulrich Heid, and Thierry Fontenelle. The decide project: Multilingual collocation extraction. In *Seventh Euralex International Congress*, University of Gothenburg,Sweden, Aug 13-18, 1996.
16. Jan Hajic and Barbora Hladka. Czech language processing / pos tagging. In *First International Conference on Language Resources and Evaluation*, Granada, 1998.
17. Djoerd Hiemstra. A linguistically motivated probabilistic model of information retrieval. In Christos Nicolaou and Constantine Stephanidis, editors, *Proceedings of the second European Conference on Research and Advanced Technology for Digital Libraries: ECDL'98*, pages 569–584. Springer-Verlag, 1998.
18. Djoerd Hiemstra and Franciska de Jong. Cross-language retrieval in twenty-one: using one, some or all possible translations? In *Proceedings of the fourteenth Twente Workshop on Language Technology TWLT-14*, pages 19–26, University of Twente, 1998.
19. Karen Jensen, George E. Heidorn, and Stephen D. Richardson, editors. *Natural language processing: the PLNLP approach.* Kluwer Academic Publishers, Boston, 1993.
20. L. Julliard, M. Beltrametti, and F. Renzetti. Information retrieval and virtual libraries: the callimaque model. In *CAIS'95*, Edmonton, CANADA, June 1995.
21. Ronald M. Kaplan and Martin Kay. Regular models of phonological rule systems. *Computational Linguistics*, 20:3:331–378, 1994.
22. L. Karttunen, JP Chanod, G. Grefenstette, and A Schiller. Regular expressions for language engineering. *Journal of Natural Language Engineering*, 2(4):307–330, 1997.
23. Lauri Karttunen. Constructing lexical transducers. In *Proceedings of the 15th International Conference on Computational Linguistics, Coling*, Kyoto, Japan, 1994.
24. Lauri Karttunen. The replace operator. In *Proceedings of the 33rd Annual Meeting of the Association for Computational Linguistics, ACL-95*, pages 16–23, Boston, 1995.
25. Kimmo Koskenniemi. *A General Computational Model for Word-Form Recognition and Production.* PhD thesis, Department of General Linguistics University of Helsinki, 1983.
26. W. Kraaij. Multilingual functionality in the twentyone project. In *Proceedings of the AAAI spring symposium on Cross language Text and Speech retrieval*, Palo Alto, March 1997.
27. M. Lauer and M. Dras. A probabilistic model of compound nouns. In *7th Joint Australian Conference on Artificial Intelligence.*, 1994.
28. Mehryar Mohri. Finite-state transducers in language and speech processing. *Computational Linguistics*, 23:2:269–312, 1997.
29. K. Netter and F.M.G. de Jong. Olive: speech based video retrieval. In *Language Technology in Multimedia Information Retrieval. Proceedings Twente workshop on Language Technology (TWLT14)*, Enschede, 1998.
30. E. Roche and Y. Schabe, editors. *Finite-State Language Processing.* MIT Press, Cambridge, Massachusetts, 1997.
31. Anne Schiller. Multilingual finite-state noun phrase extraction. In *ECAI '96 Workshop on Extended Finite State Models of Language*, Budapest, Aug. 11-12,1996.

32. F. Segond, E. Aimelet, and L. Griot. All you can use!" or how to perform word sense disambiguation with available resources. In *Second Workshop on Lexical Semantic System*, Pisa, Italy, 1998.
33. T. Strzalkowski. Natural language information retrieval. *Information Processing and Management*, 31(3):1237–1248, 1995.
34. W.G. ter Stal, J.-H. Beijert, G. de Bruin, J. van Gent, F.M.G. de Jong, W. Kraaij, K. Netter, and G. Smart. Twenty-one: cross-language disclosure and retrieval of multimedia documents on sustainable development. *Computer Networks And Isdn Systems*, 30 (13):1237–1248, 1998.

Natural Language Processing and Information Retrieval

Ellen M. Voorhees

National Institute of Standards and Technology
Gaithersburg, MD 20899 USA
ellen.voorhees@nist.gov

Abstract. Information retrieval addresses the problem of finding those documents whose content matches a user's request from among a large collection of documents. Currently, the most successful general purpose retrieval methods are statistical methods that treat text as little more than a bag of words. However, attempts to improve retrieval performance through more sophisticated linguistic processing have been largely unsuccessful. Indeed, unless done carefully, such processing can degrade retrieval effectiveness.
Several factors contribute to the difficulty of improving on a good statistical baseline including: the forgiving nature but broad coverage of the typical retrieval task; the lack of good weighting schemes for compound index terms; and the implicit linguistic processing inherent in the statistical methods. Natural language processing techniques may be more important for related tasks such as question answering or document summarization.

1 Introduction

Imagine that you want to research a problem such as eliminating pests from your garden or learning the history of the city you will visit on your next holiday. One strategy is to gather recommendations for items to read; that is, to ask for references to documents that discuss your problem rather than to ask for specific answers. Computer systems that return documents whose contents match a stated information need have historically been called *information retrieval* (IR) systems, though lately they are more often called *document retrieval* or *text retrieval* systems to distinguish them from systems that support other kinds of information-seeking tasks.

Information retrieval systems search a collection of natural language documents with the goal of retrieving exactly the set of documents that pertain to a user's question. In contrast to database systems that require highly structured data and have a formal semantics, IR systems work with unstructured natural language text. And in contrast to expert systems, IR systems do not attempt to deduce or generate specific answers but return (pieces of) documents whose content is similar to the question. While IR systems have existed for over 40 years, today the World Wide Web search engines are probably the best-known

Pazienza (Ed.): Information Extraction, LNAI 1714, pp. 32–48, 1999.

examples of text retrieval systems. Other examples include systems that support literature searches at libraries, and patent- or precedent-searching systems in law firms. The underlying technology of retrieval systems—estimating the similarity of the content of two texts—is more broadly applicable, encompassing such tasks as information filtering, document summarization, and automatic construction of hypertext links.

Information retrieval can be viewed as a great success story for natural language processing (NLP): a major industry has been built around the automatic manipulation of unstructured natural language text. Yet the most successful general purpose retrieval methods rely on techniques that treat text as little more than a bag of words. Attempts to improve retrieval performance through more sophisticated linguistic processing have been largely unsuccessful, resulting in minimal differences in effectiveness at a substantially greater processing cost or even degrading retrieval effectiveness.

This paper examines why linguistically-inspired retrieval techniques have had little impact on retrieval effectiveness. A variety of factors are indicated, ranging from the nature of the retrieval task itself to the the fact that current retrieval systems already implicitly incorporate features the linguistic systems make explicit. The next section provides general IR background by describing both how current retrieval systems operate and the evaluation methodology used to decide if one retrieval run is better than another. Section 3 provides an overview of recent NLP and IR research including a case study of a particular set of NLP experiments to illustrate why seemingly good ideas do not necessarily lead to enhanced IR performance. The final section suggests some related tasks that may benefit more directly from advances in NLP.

2 Background

Text retrieval systems have their origins in library systems that were used to provide bibliographic references to books and journals in the library's holdings [1]. This origin has had two major influences on how the retrieval task is defined. First, retrieving (pointers to) documents rather than actual answers was the natural extension to the manual processes that were used in the libraries at the time, and this continues to be the main focus of the task. Second, retrieval systems are expected to handle questions on any subject matter included in a relatively large amount of text. This requirement for domain-independence and large amounts of text precluded knowledge-based approaches for text understanding from being incorporated into retrieval systems because the requisite knowledge structures were not available and the processing was too slow. Instead, the majority of information retrieval systems use statistical approaches to compute the similarity between documents and queries. That is, they use word counting techniques and assume that two texts are about the same topic if they use the same words.

A basic understanding of how these current retrieval systems work is required to appreciate how linguistic processing might affect their performance. This section provides a summary of the current practice in IR based on the results of an on-going series of evaluations known as the Text REtrieval Conference (TREC) workshops. The final part of the section describes common practices for retrieval system evaluation.

2.1 The Basics of Current IR Systems

Retrieval systems consist of two main processes, *indexing* and *matching*. Indexing is the process of selecting terms to represent a text. Matching is the process of computing a measure of similarity between two text representations.

In some environments human indexers assign terms, which are usually selected from a controlled vocabulary. A more common alternative is to use automatic indexing where the system itself decides on the terms based on the full text of the document. A basic automatic indexing procedure for English might proceed as follows:

1. split the text into strings of characters delimited by white space, considering such strings to be "words" (tokenization);
2. remove very frequent words such as prepositions and pronouns (removal of *stop words*); and
3. conflate related word forms to a common stem by removing suffixes (stemming).

The resulting word stems would be the terms for the given text.

In early retrieval systems, queries were represented as Boolean combinations of terms, and the set of documents that satisfied the Boolean expression was retrieved in response to the query. While this Boolean model is still in use today, it suffers from some drawbacks: the size of the retrieved set is difficult to control, and the user is given no indication as to whether some documents in the retrieved set are likely to be better than others in the set. Thus most retrieval systems return a ranked list of documents in response to a query. The documents in the list are ordered such that the documents the system believes to be most like the query are first on the list.

The vector-space model is another early retrieval model still in use today [2]. In this model, documents and queries are represented by vectors in T-dimensional space, where T is the number of distinct terms used in the documents and each axis corresponds to one term. Given a query, a vector system produces a ranked list of documents ordered by similarity to the query, where the similarity between a query and a document is computed using a metric on the respective vectors.

Other retrieval models exist, including several different probabilistic models and models based on word proximity. One of the findings of the TREC workshops is that retrieval systems based on quite different models exhibit similar retrieval effectiveness. That is, retrieval effectiveness is not strongly influenced by the specifics of the model used as long as the model incorporates appropriate term weighting. Term weighting, on the other hand, has been shown to have a primary effect on retrieval quality, with the best weights combining term frequency (*tf*), inverse document frequency (*idf*), and document length (*dl*) factors [3]. In this formulation, the *tf* factor weights a term proportionally to the number of times it occurs in the text, the *idf* factor weights a term inversely proportional to the number of documents in the collection that contain the term, and the *dl* factor compensates for widely varying document lengths.

2.2 The TREC Workshops

The relative merit of different retrieval approaches (for example, different weighting schemes) is evaluated using *test collections*, benchmark tasks for which the correct answers are known. Because retrieval performance is known to vary widely across queries, test collections need to contain a sufficient number of queries to make comparisons meaningful. Further, an observed difference in retrieval performance between two systems is generally considered valid only if it is repeatable across multiple collections. Thus statements regarding best practices in IR must be based on hundreds of retrieval runs. TREC provides the necessary infrastructure to support such comparisons [`http://trec.nist.gov`].

The TREC workshops are designed to encourage research on text retrieval for realistic applications by providing large test collections, uniform scoring procedures, and a forum for organizations interested in comparing results. Started in 1992, the conference is co-sponsored by the National Institute of Standards and Technology (NIST) and the Defense Advanced Research Projects Agency (DARPA). For each TREC, NIST provides a test set of documents and questions. Participants run their retrieval systems on the data, and return to NIST a list of the retrieved top-ranked documents. NIST pools the individual results, judges the retrieved documents for correctness, and evaluates the results. The TREC cycle ends with a workshop that is a forum for participants to share their experiences.

TREC's success depends on having a diverse set of participants. Since the relevance judgments (the "correct answers") are based on pooled results, the pools must contain the output from many different kinds of systems for the final test collections to be unbiased. Also, a variety of different candidate techniques must be compared to make general recommendations as to good retrieval practice. Fortunately, TREC has grown in both the number of participants and the number of different retrieval tasks studied since the first TREC. The latest TREC, TREC-7 held in November 1998, had 56 participating groups from 13 different countries and included representatives from the industrial, academic, and government sectors.

The first TREC conferences contained just two main tasks, *ad hoc* and *routing*. Additional subtasks known as "tracks" were introduced into TREC in TREC-4 (1995). The main ad hoc task provides an entry point for new participants and provides a baseline of retrieval performance. The tracks invigorate TREC by focusing research on new areas or particular aspects of text retrieval. To the extent the same retrieval techniques are used for the different tasks, the tracks also validate the findings of the ad hoc task. Figure 1 shows the number of experiments performed in each TREC, where the set of runs submitted for one track by one participant is counted as one experiment.

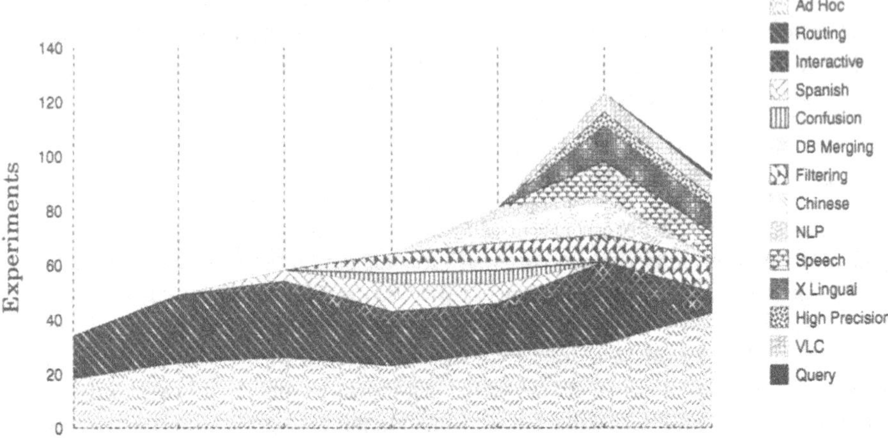

Fig. 1. Number of TREC experiments by TREC task

2.3 Best Practices

Enough different experiments have been run in TREC to support general conclusions about best practices for IR—retrieval techniques incorporated by most retrieval systems because they have been shown to be beneficial [3]. One such practice, term weighting, has already been mentioned as being critical to retrieval success.

Another primary factor in the effectiveness of retrieval systems is good query formulation. Of course, the best way of getting a good query is to have the user provide one. Unfortunately, users don't tend to provide sufficient context, usually offering a few keywords as an initial question. Retrieval systems compensate by performing *query expansion*, adding related terms to the query. There are several different ways such expansion can be accomplished, but the most commonly used method is through *blind feedback*. In this technique, a retrieval run consists of two phases. In the first phase, the original query is used to retrieve a list of documents. The top documents on the list are assumed to be relevant and are used as a source of discriminating terms; these terms are added to the query and the query is reweighted. The second phase uses the reformulated query to retrieve a second document list that is returned to the user.

Two other techniques, the use of passages and phrasing, are now used by most retrieval systems though they do not have as large an impact on the final results as weighting and query formulation do. Phrasing is the determination of compound index terms, i.e., an index term that corresponds to more than one word stem in the original text. Most frequently the phrases are word pairs that co-occur in the corpus (much) more frequently than expected by chance. Generally, both the individual word stems and the compound term are added to the query. Passages are subparts of a document. They are used as a means of finding areas of homogenous content within large documents that cover a variety of subjects.

2.4 Evaluating Retrieval System Effectiveness

Throughout this paper I assume it is possible to decide that one retrieval run is more effective than another. This subsection describes the evaluation methodology used to make this determination.

Retrieval experiments are performed using test collections. A test collection consists of a set of documents, a set of questions (called "topics" in TREC), and, for each question, a list of the documents that are relevant to that question, the *relevance assessments*. Relevance assessments are generally binary (a document is either relevant or not) and assumed to be exhaustive (if a document is not listed as being relevant, it is irrelevant).

A number of different effectiveness measures can be computed using the relevance assessments of a test collection. A very common method of evaluating a retrieval run is to plot *precision* against *recall*. Precision is the proportion of retrieved documents that are relevant, and recall is the proportion of relevant documents that are retrieved. While a perfect retrieval run will have a value of 1.0 for both recall and precision, in practice precision and recall are inversely related.

The effectiveness of individual queries varies greatly, so the average of the precision and recall values over a set of queries is used to compare different schemes. The precision of an individual query can be interpolated to obtain the precision at a standard set of recall values (for example, 0.0 – 1.0 in increments of .1). The precision at these recall points is then averaged over the set of queries in the test collection. The "3-point" average precision is used below as a single measure of retrieval effectiveness in a case study; this average is the mean of the precision values at each of 3 recall values (.2, .5, and .8).

Another single-valued measure called "(non-interpolated) average precision" was introduced in the TREC workshops and is used to discuss the TREC results below. The average precision for a single topic is the mean of the precision values obtained after each relevant document is retrieved. The mean average precision for a run consisting of multiple queries is the mean of the average precision scores of each of the queries in the run. In geometric terms, the average precision for a single query is the area underneath the uninterpolated recall-precision graph.

3 Current Applications of NLP to IR

Before discussing how NLP is used in IR, it is necessary to define what constitutes "natural language processing". The very fact that retrieval systems operate on natural language text and return useful results demonstrates that, at some level, text retrieval *is* natural language processing. IR systems must at least tokenize the text,[1] which is fairly trivial for English, but is more of a challenge

[1] Not all systems tokenize the text into words. Systems based on n-grams [6] use word fragments as index terms. Other systems such as the MultiText system [7] do not

in languages such as German (with its extensive use of compound forms) or Chinese (where there are very few syntactic clues to word boundaries). Many retrieval systems also perform stemming, a type of morphological processing.

Nonetheless, in common usage "NLP for IR" has the more specific meaning of using linguistically-inspired processing to improve text retrieval system effectiveness [4,5]. In most cases, the NLP has focused on improving the representation of text (either documents or queries) during indexing. Matching the resulting query and document representations then proceeds in the usual way, though special processing may be used to decide if two individual terms match. For example, if index terms are noun phrases, then a partial match may be made if two terms share a common head but are not identical.

This section reviews some of the recent research in applying NLP techniques to information retrieval indexing. The section begins by examining a particular experiment as a case study of the types of issues involved when incorporating NLP techniques within existing retrieval frameworks. It then looks at the research that has been undertaken in the context of the TREC program, especially the NLP track in TREC-5 (1996) [8].

3.1 A Case Study

The case study involves an investigation into using the semantic information encoded in WordNet, a manually-constructed lexical system developed by George Miller and his colleagues at Princeton University [9], to enhance access to collections of text. The investigation took place several years ago and is described in detail elsewhere [10,11]. It is summarized here to illustrate some of the pitfalls of linguistic processing.

WordNet is a system that reflects current psycholinguistic theories about how humans organize their lexical memories. The basic object in WordNet is a set of strict synonyms called a *synset*. By definition, each synset in which a word appears is a different sense of that word. Synsets are organized by the lexical relations defined on them, which differ depending on part of speech. For nouns (the only part of WordNet used in the experiment), the lexical relations include antonymy, hypernymy/hyponymy (*is-a* relation) and three different meronym/holonym (*part-of*) relations. The *is-a* relation is the dominant relationship, and organizes the synsets into a set of approximately ten hierarchies.

The focus of the investigation was to exploit the knowledge encoded in WordNet to ameliorate the effects synonyms and homographs have on text retrieval systems that use word matching. In the case of homographs, words that appear to be the same represent two distinct concepts, such as 'bank' meaning both the sides of a river and a financial institution. With synonyms, two distinct words represent the same concept, as when both 'board' and 'plank' mean a piece of wood. Homographs depress precision because false matches are made, while synonyms depress recall because true matches are missed. In principle,

---

index at all, but treat the entire document collection as one long string and define queries as arbitrary patterns over the string.

retrieval effectiveness should improve if matching is performed not on the words themselves, but on the concepts the words represent.

This idea of *conceptual indexing* is not new to IR. Controlled vocabularies generally have a canonical descriptor term that is to be used for a given concept. Concept matching has also been used successfully in limited domains by systems such as SCISOR [12] and FERRET [13]; in these systems, meaning structures are used to represent the concepts and sophisticated matching algorithms operate on the structures. Less knowledge-intensive approaches to concept matching have also been developed. For example, abstracting away from the particular words that happen to be used in a given text is the motivation behind latent semantic indexing [14]. The point of our investigation was to see if WordNet synsets could be used as concepts in a general-purpose retrieval system.

Successfully implementing conceptual indexing using synsets requires a method for selecting a single WordNet synset as the meaning for each noun in a text, i.e., a word sense disambiguation procedure. The disambiguation procedure used will not be described here. For this discussion, the important feature of the procedure is that it used the contents of a piece of text (document or query) and the structure of WordNet itself to return either one synset id or a failure indicator for each ambiguous noun in the text. The synset ids were used as index terms as described in the next paragraph.

The experiments used an extended vector space model of information retrieval that was introduced by Fox [15]. In this model, a vector is a collection of subvectors where each subvector represents a different aspect of the documents in the collection. The overall similarity between two extended vectors is computed as the weighted sum of the similarities of corresponding subvectors. That is, the similarity between query Q and document D is

$$\mathrm{sim}(Q,D) = \sum_{\text{subvector } i} \alpha_i \mathrm{sim}_i(Q_i, D_i)$$

where α_i reflects the importance of subvector i in the overall similarity between texts and sim_i is the similarity metric for vectors of type i. For the conceptual indexing experiments, document and query vectors each contained three subvectors: stems of words not found in WordNet or not disambiguated, synonym set ids of disambiguated nouns, and stems of the disambiguated nouns. The second and third subvectors are alternative representations of the text in that the same text word causes an entry in both subvectors. The noun word stems were kept to act as a control group in the experiment. When the weight of the synset id subvector is set to zero in the overall similarity measure, document and query texts are matched solely on the basis of word stems.

To judge the effectiveness of the conceptual indexing, the performance of the sense vectors was compared to the performance of a baseline run (see Table 1). In the baseline run, both document and query vectors consisted of just one subvector that contained word stems for all content words. The table gives the effectiveness of the baseline run and three different sense-based vector runs for five standard test collections. The five test collections are

CACM: 3204 documents on computer science and 50 queries,
CISI: 1460 documents on information science and 35 queries,
CRAN: 1400 documents on engineering and 225 queries,
MED: 1033 documents on medicine and 30 queries, and
TIME: 423 documents extracted from *Time Magazine* and 83 queries.

Each row in the table gives the average 3-point precision value obtained by the four different retrieval runs for a particular collection, where the average is over the number of queries in that collection. For each of the sense-based vector runs, the percentage change in 3-point precision over the standard run is also given. Thus, the entry in row 'MED', column '211' of the table indicates that the average precision for the MED collection when searched using sense-based vectors 211 (explained below) is .4777, which is a 13.6% degradation in effectiveness as compared to the average precision of .5527 obtained when using standard stem-based vectors.

Table 1. 3-point average precision for sense-based vector runs

	Baseline	110		211		101	
Collection	3-pt	3-pt	%	3-pt	%	3-pt	%
CACM	.3291	.1994	-39.4	.2594	-21.2	.2998	-8.9
CISI	.2426	.1401	-42.3	.1980	-18.4	.2225	-8.3
CRAN	.4246	.2729	-35.7	.3261	-23.2	.3538	-16.7
MED	.5527	.4405	-20.3	.4777	-13.6	.4735	-14.3
TIME	.6891	.6044	-12.3	.6462	-6.2	.6577	-4.6

The three sense-based vector runs differ in the way the subvectors were weighted when computing the overall similarity between documents and queries, and these weights are used to label the runs. The run labeled '110' gives equal weight to the non-noun word stems and the synset ids and ignores the noun word stems. This run represents a true conceptual indexing run. The run labeled '211' gives the non-noun word stems twice the weight given to each of the synset ids and the noun word stems. This run weights the non-noun stems twice to counterbalance the fact that both the noun stems and the noun senses are included. The final run ('101') is a control run— all of the word stems get equal weight and the synset ids are ignored. This is *not* equivalent to the baseline run since the overall similarity measure only counts a term match if the term occurs in the same subvector in both the query and document.

Clearly, the effectiveness of the sense-based vectors was worse than that of the stem-based vectors, sometimes very much worse. As is usually the case with retrieval experiments, examination of individual query results shows that some queries were helped by the conceptual indexing while others were hurt by it. For example, the retrieval effectiveness of MED query 20 was improved by the sense-based vectors. Query 20 requests documents that discuss the effects of 'somatotropin', a human growth hormone. Many of the relevant documents use the variant spelling 'somatotrophin' for the hormone and thus are not retrieved in the standard run. Since the synset that represents the hormone includes both spellings as members of the set, documents that use either spelling are indexed with the same synset identifier in the sense-based run and match the query. In contrast, the retrieval effectiveness of MED query 16 was severely degraded by the sense-based vectors. The query requests documents on separation anxiety in infant and preschool children. It retrieves 7 relevant documents in the top 15 for the standard run but only 1 relevant document in the top 15 for the '110' run. The problem is selecting the sense of 'separation' in the query. WordNet contains eight senses of the noun 'separation'. With few clues to go on in the short query text, the indexing procedure selected a sense of 'separation' that was not used in any document. The query's separation concept could therefore never match any document, and retrieval performance suffered accordingly.

In this particular set of experiments, almost all of the degradation in retrieval performance can be attributed to missing term matches between documents and queries when using sense-based vectors that are made when using standard word stem vectors. The missed matches have several causes: different senses of a noun being chosen for documents and queries when in fact the same sense is used; the inability to select any senses in some queries due to lack of context; and adjectives and verbs that conflate to the same stem as a noun in the standard run but are maintained as separate concepts in the sense-based runs. The importance of finding matches between document and query terms is confirmed by the degradation in performance of the control run '101' compared to the baseline run. The only major difference between the control run, which ignores the senses and just uses the word stems, and the baseline run, which also uses only word stems, is the introduction of subvectors in the '101' run. In the sense-based vectors, stems of words that are not nouns or nouns that are not in WordNet are in one subvector and stems of WordNet nouns are in the other subvector. The extended vector similarity measure matches a word stem in the document vector only if that word stem appears in the same subvector in the query. Therefore, adjectives and verbs that conflate to the same stem as a noun get counted as a match in the baseline run but do not match in the '101' run.

Of course, the fact that the conceptual indexing failed in this one experiment does not mean that concepts are inherently inferior to word stems. A disambiguation procedure that was able to resolve word senses more consistently between documents and queries would have improved the sense-based results above, as would an indexing procedure that could recognize concepts implied by words other than nouns. But the experiment does offer some broader insights into improving word-based retrieval through linguistically selected index terms.

Linguistic techniques must be essentially perfect to help. The state of the art in linguistic processing of domain-independent text (e.g., part-of-speech tagging, sense resolution, parsing, etc.) is such that errors still occur. Thus the effect of errors on retrieval performance must be considered when trying to use these techniques to overcome the deficiencies of word stem indexing. Unfortunately, in the particular case of word sense disambiguation, a common error (incorrectly resolving two usages of the same sense differently) is disastrous for retrieval effectiveness. Sanderson found that disambiguation accuracy of at least 90% was required just to avoid degrading retrieval effectiveness [16]. This is a very high standard of performance for current NLP technology.

Queries are difficult. Queries are especially troublesome for most NLP processing because they are generally quite short and offer little to assist linguistic processing. But to have any effect whatsoever on retrieval, queries must also contain the type of index terms used in documents, or at least have some way of interacting with the documents' index terms.

Nonlinguistic techniques implicitly exploit linguistic knowledge. Even if done perfectly, linguistic techniques may provide little benefit over appropriate statistical techniques because the statistical techniques implicitly exploit the same information the linguistic techniques make explicit. Again using sense disambiguation as an example, in practice homographs are not a major contributor to retrieval failure unless the query is extremely short (one word) or the searcher is interested in very high recall [17]. If a document has enough terms in common with a query to have a high similarity to the query, then the contexts in the two texts are similar and any polysemous words will likely be used in the same sense. In fact, the IR method of computing similarities among texts can be used to build a classifier to discriminate among word senses [18].

Term normalization might be beneficial. Term normalization, i.e., mapping variant spellings or formulations of the same lexical item to a common form, may be one area in which linguistic approaches improve on simple word stems. The use of *somatotropin/somatotrophin* is one example of this effect. Proper nouns are a more general class of lexical items that word stem approaches do not handle very well, but are regular enough to be accurately captured by more sophisticated techniques [19]. Although current IR test collections do not contain enough queries that depend on proper nouns to be able to quantify how much special processing helps, in other retrieval environments such as web search engines providing special processing for names is noticeably better.

3.2 TREC-5 NLP Track

Sense resolution is but one approach to using NLP to improve indexing. The NLP track in TREC-5 invited participants to try any NLP approach on the test collection consisting of almost 75,000 *Wall Street Journal* articles (240MB of text) and TREC topics 251–300. Four groups submitted runs to the track. While the track accepted both automatic and manual runs, only the automatic runs will be discussed here in keeping with the focus of the rest of the paper.

The MITRE group [20] had experience building trainable natural language algorithms for information extraction tasks by participating in the Message Understanding Conferences (MUC). However, TREC-5 was their first entry into TREC, and they were not able to complete all they had hoped to do by the time of the TREC-5 conference. The run they did submit to the NLP track consisted of pre- and post-processing steps applied to a basic SMART[2] statistical run. The preprocessing step aimed to automatically locate and remove from the query statement extraneous material that might mislead a stem-based search. The post-processing step aimed to re-order the ranked output of the SMART search based on learning which were the important keywords and phrases in the query and giving documents containing those terms higher ranks. As implemented for the track, neither process had any appreciable impact (either positive or negative) on the SMART results.

The other three entries in the NLP track tested syntactic phrasing (sometimes in conjunction with other NLP techniques) as a possible improvement over statistical phrases. As noted in Section 2.3, one of the findings of TREC is that phrasing in some form is generally useful. Most systems use statistical phrasing where a "phrase" is any pair of words that co-occur in documents sufficiently frequently. Generally the pair and both the individual word stems are used as index terms. Statistical phrases are clearly only a rough approximation to natural language phrases. Some frequently co-occurring pairs such as 'early fourth' are not phrases at all. Documents containing non-compositional collocations such as 'hot dog' and 'White House' are still (incorrectly) indexed by their component words. Phrases longer than two words are ignored. The internal structure of the phrase is also ignored so that 'college junior' is conflated with 'junior college'. The question is to what extent these problems affect retrieval.

The Xerox TREC-5 NLP track entry directly compared the effectiveness of retrieval runs using statistical phrasing vs. a specific kind of syntactic phrasing [21]. The syntactic phrasing was accomplished by using a light parser to perform a shallow syntactic analysis of text. Pairs of words that the parse found to be in one of the following relations were extracted as phrases: subject-verb, verb-direct object, verb-adjunct, noun modifying noun, adjective modifying noun, adverb modifying verb. Phrases that included a stop word as a phrase component were discarded. For each of the remaining phrases, the component words were stemmed and alphabetically sorted to form the final index term. Figure 2, derived from figures given in the Xerox paper, shows the phrases detected by the statistical and syntactic methods for an example query.

Using the mean average precision measure to evaluate the retrieval runs, the use of the syntactic phrases increased effectiveness 15% as compared to a baseline run with no phrases (from .200 to .231). Using the statistical phrases improved the mean average precision by only 7% over the same baseline (from .200 to .215), so the syntactic phrases did have a positive effect. But this gain came at a cost in processing time; indexing the 240MB document text took 36 hours longer using the parsing than it did using the statistical methods. Also, the syntactic phrasing was only beneficial when starting with the longer version

[2] SMART is a retrieval system based on the vector space model that was developed at Cornell University.

Original Text (non-stopwords in *italics*):
Where and for what *purpose* is *scuba diving* done *professionally*?

Statistical phrases (in WSJ corpus):
dive_scub (diving, scuba)

Xerox syntactic phrases:
dive_scub (diving, scuba)
dive_profess (diving, professionally)

Fig. 2. Phrases derived for an example query by both statistical and syntactic methods

of the TREC topics. When only the short version of the topics was used (e.g., a single sentence as shown in Figure 2) the syntactic phrasing run *degraded* the baseline effectiveness by 30%.

The the CLARITECH NLP track entry was also an evaluation of the use of syntactic phrases for document indexing [22]. The main goal of the study was to compare different kinds of syntactic phrases to each other, rather than compare syntactic phrases to statistical phrases. The syntactic phrases used by the CLARIT system are noun phrases, and the different types of phrases tested were full noun phrases (e.g., "heavy construction industry group"), adjacent subphrases in the noun phrase (e.g., "heavy construction industry"), and head modifier pairs (e.g, "construction industry", "industry group", "heavy construction").

Four different CLARIT runs were made: a base case consisting of only single words; single words plus head modifier pairs; single words plus head modifier pairs plus full noun phrases; and single words plus all types of phrases. The most effective run was the run that included single words plus head modifier pairs only, which increased mean average precision by 13% over the base case of words only (from .183 to .206). A second set of runs performed after TREC-5 used a more effective query weighting scheme that improved all the runs. With this weighting scheme, the head modifier pairs run was still the most effective, with an increase in mean average precision of 9% over the base case of no phrases (from .221 to .240). These results all used the long version of the topics. Even when using the long version, CLARITECH noted that they did not see as much of an effect on retrieval performance using phrases as expected because the queries contained so few phrases. They also noted that appropriately weighting phrases is an important factor in phrase-based indexing.

The focus of the GE-led TREC group has been on NLP techniques for information retrieval since TREC began [23,5]. Because their earlier experiments demonstrated that the NLP techniques worked significantly better with longer query statements, much of their TREC-5 work was an investigation into performance of their system when the topic statements were expanded with large amounts of hand-selected document text. Such expansion significantly improves the performance of both statistical and NLP runs, though the NLP runs may get somewhat more of a boost.

TREC-5 was also the year the GE group introduced a stream architecture. In this architecture different independent processes produce index terms for a text and a combination mechanism resolves the various candidate index term sets into one final set. The stream architecture provides a convenient testbed to investigate the relative contributions of the different streams. The group implemented a variety of statistical and linguistic streams including word stems; head modifier pairs (derived from verb object and subject verb combinations in addition to noun phrases); unnormalized noun groups; and names. Similar to the CLARITECH findings, the results of the stream architecture experiments suggested that having some phrases is an improvement over no phrases, but simpler phrases (in this case the unnormalized noun groups) work better than more complicated phrases.

The TREC-5 NLP track participants found the same types of difficulties in trying to improve on statistical IR system effectiveness as were encountered in the case study. Queries are short and therefore don't offer much opportunity to perform processing that will significantly affect retrieval. Large degradation in performance is possible unless the NLP works very well and the term weighting is not disturbed. The statistical phrases capture most of the salient information that can be exploited by syntactic phrases. These are the issues that need to be addressed to improve retrieval effectiveness through linguistic processing.

4 Summary

The explosive growth in the number of full-text, natural language documents that are available electronically makes tools that assist users in finding documents of interest indispensable. Information retrieval systems address this problem by matching query language statements (representing the user's information need) against document surrogates. Intuitively, natural language processing techniques should be able to improve the quality of the document surrogates and thus improve retrieval performance. But to date explicit linguistic processing of document or query text has afforded essentially no benefit for general-purpose (i.e., not domain specific) retrieval systems as compared to less expensive statistical techniques.

The question of statistical vs. NLP retrieval systems is miscast, however. It is not a question of either one or the other, but rather a question of how accurate an approximation to explicit linguistic processing is required for good retrieval performance. The techniques used by the statistical systems are based on linguistic theory in that they are effective retrieval measures precisely because they capture important aspects of the way natural language is used. Stemming is an approximation to morphological processing. Finding frequently co-occurring word pairs is an approximation to finding collocations and other compound structures. Similarity measures implicitly resolve word senses by capturing word forms used in the same contexts. Current information retrieval research demonstrates that more accurate approximations cannot yet be reliably exploited to improve retrieval.

So why should relatively crude approximations be sufficient? The task in information retrieval is to produce a ranked list of documents in response to a query. There is no evidence that detailed meaning structures are necessary to accomplish this task. Indeed, the IR literature suggests that such structures are not required. For example, IR systems can successfully process documents whose contents have been garbled in some way such as by being the output of OCR processing [24,25] or the output of an automatic speech recognizer [26]. There has even been some success in retrieving French documents with English queries by simply treating English as misspelled French [27]. Instead, retrieval effectiveness is strongly dependent on finding all possible (true) matches between documents and queries, and on an appropriate balance in the weights among different aspects of the query. In this setting, processing that would create better linguistic approximations must be essentially perfect to avoid causing more harm than good.

This is not to say that current natural language processing technology is not useful. While information retrieval has focused on retrieving documents as a practical necessity, users would much prefer systems that are capable of more intuitive, meaning-based interaction. Current NLP technology may now make these applications feasible, and research efforts to address appropriate tasks are underway. For example, one way to support the user in information-intensive tasks is to provide summaries of the documents rather than entire documents. A recent evaluation of summarization technology found statistical approaches quite effective when the summaries were simple extracts of document texts [28], but generating more cohesive abstracts will likely require more developed linguistic processing. Another way to support the user is to generate actual answers. A first test of systems' ability to find short text extracts that answer fact-seeking questions will occur in the "Question-Answering" track of TREC-8. Determining the relationships that hold among words in a text is likely to be important in this task.

Acknowledgements

My thanks to Donna Harman and Chris Buckley for improving this paper through their comments.

References

1. Sparck Jones, K., Willett, P. (eds.): Readings in Information Retrieval. Morgan Kaufmann, San Franciso (1997)
2. Salton, G. Wong, A., Yang, C.S.: A Vector Space Model for Automatic Indexing. Communications of the ACM. **18** (1975) 613–620

3. Sparck Jones, K.: Further Reflections on TREC. Information Processing and Management. (To appear.)
4. Sparck Jones, K.: What is the Role of NLP in Text Retrieval? In: Strzalkowski, T. (ed.): Natural Language Information Retrieval. Kluwer (In press.)
5. Perez-Carballo, J., Strzalkowski, T.: Natural Language Information Retrieval: Progress Report. Information Processing and Mangement. (To appear.)
6. D'Amore, R.J., Mah, C.P.: One-Time complete Indexing of Text: Theory and Practice. Proceedings of the Eighth Annual International ACM SIGIR Conference on Research and Development in Information Retrieval. ACM Press (1985) 155–164
7. Cormack, G.V., Clarke, C.L.A., Palmer, C.R., To, S.S.L.: Passage-Based Query Refinement. Information Processing and Management. (To appear.)
8. Strzalkowski, T.: NLP Track at TREC-5. Proceedings of the Fifth Text REtrieval Conference (TREC-5). NIST Special Publication 500-238 (1997), 97–101. Also at `http://trec.nist.gov/pubs.html`
9. Fellbaum, C. (ed.): WordNet: An Electronic Lexical Database. MIT Press (1998)
10. Voorhees, E.M.: Using WordNet to Disambiguate Word Senses for Text Retrieval. Proceedings of the Sixteenth Annual International ACM SIGIR Conference on Research and Development in Information Retrieval. ACM Press (1993) 171–180
11. Voorhees, E.M.: Using WordNet for Text Retrieval. In: Fellbaum, C. (ed.): WordNet: An Electronic Lexical Database. MIT Press (1998) 285–303
12. Rau, L.F.: Conceptual Information Extraction and Retrieval from Natural Language Input. In: Sparck Jones, K., Willett, P. (eds.): Readings in Information Retrieval. Morgan Kaufmann, San Franciso (1997) 527–533
13. Mauldin, M.L.: Retrieval Performance in FERRET. Proceedings of the Fourteenth Annual International ACM-SIGIR Conference on Research and Development in Information Retrieval. ACM Press (1991) 347–355
14. Deerwester, S., Dumais, S.T., Furnas, G.W., Landauer, T.K., Harshman, R.: Indexing by Latent Semantic Analysis. Journal of the American Society for Information Science. **41** (1990) 391–407
15. Fox, E.A.: Extending the Boolean and Vector Space Models of Information Retrieval with P-Norm Queries and Multiple Concept Types. Unpublished doctoral dissertation, Cornell University, Ithaca, NY. University Microfilms, Ann Arbor, MI.
16. Sanderson, M.: Word Sense Disambiguation and Information Retrieval. Proceedings of the Seventeenth Annual International ACM-SIGIR Conference on Research and Development in Information Retrieval. Springer-Verlag (1994) 142–151
17. Krovetz, R., Croft, W.B.: Lexical Ambiguity in Information Retrieval. ACM Transactions on Information Systems. **10** (1992) 115–141
18. Leacock, C., Towell, G., Voorhees, E.M.: Towards Building Contextual Representations of Word Senses Using Statistical Models. In: Boguraev, B., Pustejovsky, J. (eds.): Corpus Processing for Lexical Acquisition. MIT Press (1996) 98–113
19. Paik, W., Liddy, E.D., Yu, E., Mckenna, M.: Categorizing and Standardizing Proper Nouns for Efficient Information Retrieval. In: Boguraev, B., Pustejovsky, J. (eds.): Corpus Processing for Lexical Acquisition. MIT Press (1996) 61–73
20. Burger, J.D., Aberdeen, J.S., Palmer, D.D.: Information Retrieval and Trainable Natural Language Processing. Proceedings of the Fifth Text REtrieval Conference (TREC-5). NIST Special Publication 500-238 (1997), 433–435. Also at `http://trec.nist.gov/pubs.html`
21. Hull, D.A., Grefenstette, G., Schulze, B.M., Gaussier, E., Schütze, H., Pedersen, J.O.: Xerox TREC-5 Site Report: Routing, Filtering, NLP, and Spanish Tracks.

Proceedings of the Fifth Text REtrieval Conference (TREC-5). NIST Special Publication 500-238 (1997), 167–180. Also at http://trec.nist.gov/pubs.html
22. Zhai, C., Tong, X., Milić-Frayling, N., Evans, D.A.: Evaluation of Syntactic Phrase Indexing—CLARIT NLP Track Report. Proceedings of the Fifth Text REtrieval Conference (TREC-5). NIST Special Publication 500-238 (1997), 347–357. Also at http://trec.nist.gov/pubs.html
23. Strzalkowski, T., Guthrie, L., Karlgren, J., Leistensnider, J., Lin, F., Perez-Carballo, J., Straszheim, T., Wang, J., Wilding, J.: Natural Language Information Retrieval: TREC-5 Report. Proceedings of the Fifth Text REtrieval Conference (TREC-5). NIST Special Publication 500-238 (1997), 291–313. Also at http://trec.nist.gov/pubs.html
24. Taghva, K., Borsack, J., Condit, A.: Results of Applying Probabilistic IR to OCR Text. Proceedings of the Seventeenth Annual International ACM-SIGIR Conference on Research and Development in Information Retrieval. Springer-Verlag, (1994) 202–211
25. Kantor, P.B., Voorhees, E.M.: Report on the TREC-5 Confusion Track. Proceedings of the Fifth Text REtrieval Conference (TREC-5). NIST Special Publication 500-238 (1997), 65–74. Also at http://trec.nist.gov/pubs.html
26. Garofolo, J., Voorhees, E.M., Auzanne, C.G.P., Stanford, V.M., Lund, B.A.: 1998 TREC-7 Spoken Document Retrieval Track Overview and Results. Proceedings of the Seventh Text REtrieval Conference (TREC-7). (In press.) Also at http://trec.nist.gov/pubs.html
27. Buckley, C., Mitra M., Walz, J., Cardie, C.: Using Clustering and SuperConcepts Within SMART: TREC 6. Proceedings of the Sixth Text REtrieval Conference (TREC-6). NIST Special Publication 500-240 (1998), 107–124. Also at http://trec.nist.gov/pubs.html
28. Mani, I., House, D., Klein, G., Hirschman, L., Obrst, L., Firmin, T., Chrzanowski, M., Sundheim, B.: The TIPSTER SUMMAC Text Summarization Evaluation Final Report. MITRE Technical Report MTR 98W0000138. McLean, Virginia (1998). Also at http://www.nist.gov/itl/div894/894.02/related_projects/tipster_summac/final_rpt.html

From Speech to Knowledge

Verónica Dahl

Simon Fraser University,
Burnaby B.C. V5A 1S6,Canada,
veronica@cs.sfu.ca,
http://www.cs.sfu.ca/people/Faculty/Dahl

Abstract. In human communication, assumptions play a central role. Linguists and logicians have uncovered their many facets. Much of AI work is also concerned with the study of assumptions in one way or another. Work on intuitionistic and linear logic has provided formally characterized embodiments of assumptions which have been influential on logic programming (e.g. [9,22,14]).
In this article we examine some uses of assumptive logic programming for speech-driven database creation and consultation, for speech driven robot control, and for web access through language.
This type of research can help relieve health problems related to the present typing/screen model of computer use. It can also partially address the need to integrate voice recognition, voice synthesis, and AI, along the route towards making computers into true extensions of our human abilities- extensions that adapt to our biology, rather than requiring our bodies to adapt.

1 Introduction

More than twenty years have elapsed since the first efforts towards declarative programming catapulted computing sciences from the old number-crunching paradigm into a new era paradigm of inferential engines. An era in which we no longer measure efficiency in terms of calculations per second, but in terms of inferences per second- a fantastic qualitative leap.

Logic programming, at the heart of this revolution in Computing Sciences, has been responsible for many beautiful incarnations, particularly in Artificial Intelligence, of the idea of programming through logic. Notable among them, natural language processing applications have blossomed around the axis of parsing-as-deduction (an expression coined by Fernando Pereira), ever since Alain Colmerauer developed the first logic grammar formalism, Metamorphosis Grammars [10].

These applications mostly span either language-to-language translation (e.g. French to English), with some meaning representation formalism mediating between the source language and the target language, or language-to-query translation, e.g. for using human languages as database front ends.

Pazienza (Ed.): Information Extraction, LNAI 1714, pp. 49–75, 1999.

The latter kind of applications exploit a natural closeness between the logic programming style of queries and human language questions. Consider for instance representing the query "Find the names of employees who work for First Bank Corporation" as a Datalog or as a Prolog query:

```
query(X):- works(X,'First Bank Corporation').
```

versus its SQL equivalent

```
select employee_name
from works
where company-name= "First Bank Corporation"
```

or its QUEL equivalent

```
range of t is works
retrieve (t.person-name)
where t.company-name= "First Bank Corporation"
```

Traditional database query languages are in fact closer to computer programs than to human language questions: notions irrelevant to the question itself need to be explicitly represented, such as the range of a tuple variable, or operations such as selecting. In contrast, logic programming based queries are almost readable by people with little background of either logic programming or database theory.

While written text has long been used for database consultation (e.g. [15]), its use for representing knowledge itself lags behind. Database updates through language have been studied (e.g.[17]), but database creation through language has not, to the best of our knowledge, been attempted yet.

This is partly because creating knowledge bases through human language presents more difficulties than thus consulting it or updating it, and partly because the availability of reasonably efficient speech analysis and synthesis software is relatively new. Typing in the human language sentences necessary to create a knowledge base is probably as time consuming, and perhaps more error-prone, as typing in the information itself, coded in one of the current knowledge representation formalisms. With a good speech analyzer, however, dictating natural language sentences that represent a given corpus of knowledge becomes a much more attractive task.

The field of speech analysis and recognition has in fact been slowly reaching maturity, to the point in which very effective speech software is now available at relatively low cost. For instance, products such as Microsoft speech agent or Dragon Co.'s Naturally Speaking software can recognize a person's speech modalities after about a half hour of training. That person can then dictate into a microphone, including punctuation marks, as s/he would dictate to a secretary, and see the written form or his or her utterances appear on the screen, being placed into a text file or being used as commands to the computer. Speech editing facilities are of course available (e.g. for correcting mistakes made by the speaker or by the speech software).

Impressive as it is, speech software has not yet been properly put together with artificial intelligence. Virtual Personalities Inc.'s verbal robots (verbots) come about the closest, but they mimic Weizembaum's Eliza style of "understanding", abounding in default responses such as "What does that suggest to you?", "I see", etc.

Yet AI technology is also mature enough for many of its applications to be profitably augmented with speech capabilities. Also, hardware technology is swiftly moving towards networks of wireless, portable, small personal computers that have little to envy our previous "big" computers in terms of power.

The pieces of the puzzle are laid down to now attempt more human like communication with computers- computers in a wide sense, including robots, virtual worlds, and the Internet. Industry is already identifying the need to integrate "voice recognition software so that the computer can listen to you, voice synthesis so it can talk back to you, and AI programs to guess what you really want" (Newsweek, March 1998: interview to Bill Gates).

In this article we examine some applications of logic programming that in our view, should be explored along the route towards making computers into true extensions of our human abilities- extensions that adapt to our biology, rather than requiring our bodies to adapt.

Our presentation style is intuitive rather than formal, since we assume little previous knowledge of logic grammars, language processing, or logic programming. Technical details can be found in the references given. Readers familiar with logic programming can skim through section 2, noticing only our notation conventions.

Section 2 describes our logic programming tools, and at the same time shows step-by-step the construction of a (simplistic but adequate for exemplifying purposes) first prototype grammar for gleaning knowledge from natural language sentences, based on assumptive logic programming. The resulting data bases may include general rules as well as facts. Section 3 proposes a more detailed approach to the creation of knowledge bases (this section partially overlaps with [16]), and introduces a new type of assumption reasoning for dealing with discourse.

Section 4 discusses other types of knowledge bases that can be driven through speech: concept-based retrieval, robot control, generating animations and controlling virtual worlds. Finally, we present our concluding remarks. A sample session from a more encompassing database creation prototype than the one developed in 2 is shown in Appendices I and II. Appendix III shows a sample interaction with a Spanish consultable virtual world.

2 A First Prototype for Creating and Consulting Knowledge Bases

2.1 Definite Clause Grammars

The Basic Formalism Imagine rewrite grammar rules that can include variables or functional symbols as arguments, so that rewriting involves unification. What you have is called metamorphosis grammars [10], or DCGs [8]. Through them, you can for instance declare a noun phrase to be constituted by a name, or by a quantifier, an adjective, and a noun (we take notational liberties for consistency throughout this paper. ":-" stands for "rewrite into".):

```
noun_phrase:- name.
noun_phrase:- quant, adj, noun.
```

More usefully, we can augment the grammar symbols with arguments which automate the construction of meaning representation:

```
noun_phrase(X,true) :- name(X).
noun_phrase(X,(A,N)):- quant, adj(X,A), noun(X,N).
```

Variables are capitalized. The first rule, for instance, commands the rewrite of any symbol matching *noun_phrase*$(X, true)$ into *name*(X) (where X has been matched in the same way). Variables names are, as in Prolog, local to the clause (rule) in which they appear (since they are implicitly universally quantified within it).

The second argument of "noun_phrase" constructs the noun phrase's "meaning". In the case of a complex noun phrase, this meaning is composed by the meanings of the adjective (A) , and the noun (N) (both of which will involve X, as we shall next see). In the case of a simple noun phrase (a name), its meaning is "true"- a primitive Prolog predicate which is always satisfied.

Words are preceded by "#", and "or" can be represented as ";" (thus the quantifier rule below shows six alternative quantifying words). Proper names must be written in lower case. We can make up rewrite rules for the remaining grammar symbols as well, e.g.:

```
name(rahel):- #rahel.
name(estha):- #estha.

quant:- #the; #a; #an; #some; #all; #every.

adj(X,wise(X)):- #wise.
adj(X,true).

noun(X,owl(X)):- #owl.
```

Notice that adjectives are optional- if not present, the trivial representation "true" is generated. Here are some noun phrases and their representations as obtained by the above grammar:

```
the wise owl              (wise(X),owl(X))
an owl                    (true,owl(X))
rahel                     rahel
```

Querying Logic Databases From representations such as the above we can, for instance, directly query a Prolog database about the subject domain (e.g. owls), and obtain the answers automatically.

For instance, to ask for a wise owl, we would write the representation of that noun phrase as a Prolog query:

```
?- wise(X),owl(X).
```

Prolog will respond with X=owsa with respect to a database in which owsa has been defined to be wise and to be an owl, e.g.:

```
wise(owsa).
owl(owsa).
```

Initializing Knowledge Bases We could also *create* a database of knowledge from such representations. Let us first add verb phrases, and compose sentences from noun phrases and verb phrases, e.g. through the rules:

```
verb(X,Y,saw(X,Y)):- #saw.
verb(X,Y,likes(X,Y)):- #likes.

verb_phrase(X,Head,VP):- verb(X,Y,Head),noun_phrase(Y,VP).

sentence((Head,NP,VP)):- noun_phrase(X,NP),verb_phrase(X,Head,VP).
```

Anonymous variables (i.e., variables which only appear once in a rule and thus do not need a specific name) are noted "_".

To analyze a string from a given start symbol, we simply query the primitive predicate analyze(Symbol), and follow the prompts, e.g.:

```
?- analyze(sentence(S)).

Enter the string to be analyzed, followed by a return: estha saw
the wise owl

S=saw(estha,_x16074),wise(_x16074),owl(_x16074)
```

Notice that in the sentence's representation S we have all the elements needed to create a Prolog rule representing to a data base the knowledge that Estha saw the wise owl. We merely need to rearrange its components in Prolog rule fashion:

```
saw(estha,X):- wise(X),owl(X).
```

where ":-" now is read as "if": if X is wise and an owl, then estha saw it.

Assumption Grammars for Relating Long-distant Constituents Now suppose you want to add a relative clause to the complex noun phrase rule:

```
noun_phrase(X,(A,N,R)):- quant, adj(X,A), noun(X,N), #that,
  relative(X,R).
```

For noun phrases in which it is the subject that is missing (to be identified with the relative's antecedent), the relative clause reduces to a verb phrase, so we could simply write instead:

```
noun_phrase(X,(A,N,H,VP)):- quant, adj(X,A), noun(X,N), #that,
           verb_phrase(X,H,VP).
```

This rule makes X (the representation of the relative's antecedent) the subject of the relative clause's verb phrase. We can now test, for instance, the sentence:

```
estha saw the owl that likes rahel
```

from which we obtain:

```
X=saw(estha,_x19101),true,owl(_x19101),likes(_x19101,rahel),true
```

However, extrapolating this technique to relatives from which another noun phrase than the subject is missing (e.g., "the owl that rahel saw", or "the owl that rahel gave a scolding to") would necessitate passing the antecedent X, which needs to be identified with the missing noun phrase, all the way to the place where the noun phrase is missing. This is inconvenient because it imposes the addition of X into symbols that have no direct business with it, since they merely act as transfer entities for X.

It would be convenient to have a way of hypothesizing a potential relative's antecedent as such in a more global fashion, and then using it wherever it is required (i.e., where a noun phrase is expected and cannot be found).

This is exactly what we can do with assumption grammars, in which a hypothesis- a (linear) assumption [1]- is noted as a Prolog predicate preceded by

[1] Linear assumptions [9] can be consumed only once, whereas intuitionistic assumptions can be consumed any number of times.

"+", and its use (consumption) is noted "-". An assumption is available during the continuation of the present computation, and vanishes upon backtracking.

So, for instance, we can define a relative as a sentence with a missing noun phrase preceded by a relative pronoun, through the grammar rule:

```
relative(X,R):- #that, +missing_np(X), sent(R).
```

The appropriate antecedent (i.e. the variable to be bound with X- remember that variables are implicitly quantified within each rule, so variables of the same name in different rules are a priori unrelated) can then transmitted to the relative clause through the noun phrase rule:

```
noun_phrase(X,(A,N,R)):- quant, adj(X,A), noun(X,N),
  relative(X,R).
```

and the missing noun phrase is associated with this antecedent through consumption at the point in which it is shown missing (i.e., as the last noun phrase rule, to be tried after all others have failed):

```
 noun_phrase(X,true) :- -missing_np(X).
```

Finally, we allow for noun phrases with no relative clauses:

```
relative(_,true).
```

A sentence such as "the owl that estha saw likes rahel"
now yields the representation:

```
S=likes(_x19102,rahel),(true,owl(_x19102),saw(estha,_x19102),true,
true),true
```

The spurious "true" predicates disappear upon writing these results into a file.

Again, from such a representation we can then construct the Prolog database definition:

```
likes(A,rahel):- owl(A),saw(estha,A).
```

3 A More Detailed Approach to Knowledge Base Creation

Going beyond our first prototype for knowledge base creation and consultation involves decisions such as what language subset is going to be covered, how exactly is it going to be represented, etc.

In this section we propose one possible approach, and we argue that a simple higher level extension of LP, timeless assumptions, greatly facilitates the task of going from discourse to databases. More research is needed to provide a thorough proof of concept.

3.1 Underlying Conventions

Let us examine what kinds of English descriptions we shall admit, and what kinds of representations for database relations should be extracted automatically from them.

The Natural Language Subset Our subset of language consists of sentences in the active voice, where relation words (nouns, verbs and adjectives) correspond to database predicates, and their complements to arguments of these predicates. For instance, "John reads Ivanhoe to Mary" generates the Prolog assertion

reads(john,ivanhoe,mary).

Vocabulary reasonably common to all databases belongs to the static part of our system (e.g. articles, prepositions, common verbs such as "to be", etc.), and vocabulary specific to each application (e.g. proper names, nouns, verbs proper of the application, etc.) is entered at creation time, also through spoken language, with menu-driven help from the system.

In the interest of ease of prototyping, we shall first only use universal quantifiers (as in the clausal form of logic), whether explicit or implicit, and only the restrictive type of relative clauses (i.e., those of the form "(All) ... that...", where the properties described by the relative clause restrict the range of the variable introduced by the quantifier "all". Such relatives, as we have seen, translate into additional predicates in the clause's body, as in:

```
People like cats that purr.
```

for which a possible translation is

```
like(P,C):- person(P), cat(C), purrs(C).
```

It is easy to include alternative lexical definitions in the language processing module of our system, so that all words for a given concept, say "people" and "persons", translate into a single database relation name (say, "people"). Thus we can allow the flexibility of synonyms together with the programming convenience of having only one constant for each individual- no need for equality axioms and their related processing overhead.

Semantic Types It is useful to have information about semantic types. For instance, we may have informed the database that people like animals, and may not have explicitly said that people like cats that purr. But if we knew that cats are animals, we could easily infer that people like cats and that they like cats that purr, given the appropriate query.

If we wanted to reject semantically anomalous input, much of this could be done through simply checking type compatibility between, say, the expected argument of a predicate, and its actual argument. For instance, if "imagine" requires a human subject, and appears in a sentence with a non-human subject, the user can be alerted of the anomaly and appropriate action can be taken. Variables can be typed when introduced by a natural language quantifier, and constants can be typed in the lexicon, when defining proper names. The notation used to represent a semantic type can reflect the relevant set inclusion relationships in the type hierarchy.

Much effort has been devoted to efficient encodings of type hierarchies. A recent survey and breakthrough results for logic programming are presented in [12]. These results can be transfered to a menu-driven module of our system which will question the user about a topmost class in the database's domain, its subsets, etc., and accordingly construct the class hierarchy encoded in such a way that set inclusion relationships are decidable with little more than unification.

Set-orientation Our logic programming representation of a database should be set-oriented. That is, rather than having n clauses for representing a unary property that n individuals satisfy, we can have one clause for the entire set (e.g. biblical([adam,eve]). Database primitives for handling relations on sets are provided.

Intensionally as well as extensionally represented sets should be allowed, in two ways. First, having semantic types associated to each variable and constant makes it possible to give intensional replies rather than calculating an extensionally represented set. For instance, we can reply "all birds" to the question of which birds fly if the database expresses that all entities of type bird fly, rather than checking the property of flying on each individual bird (assuming we even were to list all birds individually). We can even account for exceptions, e.g. by replying: "All birds except penguins". The user can always choose to request an extensional reply if the first, intensional answer is not enough.

Secondly, we have found it useful in some cases to represent sets of objects as a type and an associated cardinality (e.g., in a query such as "How many cars are in stock?", we do not really want to have a name for each of the cars, being only interested in the numbers of (indistinguishable) entities of type car.

Events In order to correctly relate information about the same event given in different sentences of a discourse, we translate n-ary relations into sets of binary ones linked by an event number. For instance, if we input the sentence:

"John gave Rover to Mary."
instead of generating the ternary relation:

```
gave(john,rover,mary)
```

the analyzer can generate a representation that keeps track of the event, or information number within the discourse, through the three assertions[2]:

```
gave(1,who,john).
gave(1,what,rover).
gave(1,to,mary).
```

This method roughly corresponds to event logics, dating as far back as 1979 [11]. It provides us with a simple way to be flexible as to the number of arguments in a relation. Notice that the event number is not necessarily the same as the sentence number. If our next sentence is

```
"This happened in 1998"
```

then the system needs to recognize the event described in the previous sentence as the one referred to by "this", and add the following clause to the database:

```
gave(1,when,1998).
```

In order for our natural language analyzer to be able to effect such translations, it needs information about semantic types of each argument of a relation. This can be given in the lexicon, specifically in the definitions of nouns, verbs and adjectives, since these words typically correspond to predicates in a database. Lexical definitions for these can either be input once and for all for a given domain, or elicited from the user in menu-driven fashion. The latter option has the attraction of providing extensibility to the system, which can then admit new words into its vocabulary.

3.2 From Sentences to Discourse-Timeless Assumptions

While it is certain that we must restrict the range of natural language accepted by our speech applications, we should seek naturalness and allow not only isolated sentences or queries, but the flexibility of discourse and paraphrase as well.

Determining which entities co-specify (i.e., refer to the same individual) is one of the most important problems in understanding discourse. For instance, if a user enters the information: "John Smith works in the toy department. It does not meet fire safety standards. His country's laws are not enough to protect him", the system translating this input into a knowledge base needs to identify

[2] In fact, semantic types can also be generated at language analysis stage, but we overlook them here for simplicity.

"it" with the toy department mentioned, and "his" and "him" as relating to John Smith.

A thorough treatment of co-specification is a complex and widely studied issue, involving not only syntactic but also semantic, pragmatic and contextual notions (consider for instance "Don't step on it", referring to a snake just seen, or "John kicked Sam on Monday and it hurt", where "it" refers to an abstract proposition rather than a concrete individual).

A discussion of possible treatments of co-specification is beyond the scope of this article, but we shall introduce a methodology -timeless assumptions- for facilitating the detection of co-specification. This basic technique can be adapted to incorporate different criteria for co-specification determination.

Timeless assumptions allow us to consume assumptions after they are made (as before), but also, when a program requires them to be consumed at a point in which they have not yet been made, they will be assumed to be "waiting" to be consumed, until they are actually made (the Prolog cut, noted "!", is a control predicate preventing the remaining clauses from being considered upon backtrack):

```
% Assumption:

% the assumption being made was expected by a previous consumption
=X:- -wait(X), !.
% if there is no previous expectation of X, assume it linearly
=X:- +X.

% Consumption:

% uses an assumption, and deletes it if linear
=-X:- -X, !.
% if the assumption has not yet been made,
% adds its expectation as an assumption
=-X:- +wait(X).
```

With these definitions it no longer matters whether an assumption is first made and then consumed, or first "consumed" (i.e., put in a waiting list until when it is actually made) and then made.

We can use timeless assumptions for instance to build a logic programmed database directly from:

```
The blue car stopped. Two people came out of it.
```

or:

```
Two people came out of it after the blue car stopped.
```

To cover both cases, we could timelessly assume an object of description D for each noun phrase represented by a variable X and with features F that appears in the discourse:

```
=object(X,F,D).
```

When encountering a pronoun with matching features F', in a sentence that further describes the referred object as D', replace the timeless assumption by one which adds D' to what is known of X. With some notational license:

```
=object(X,F,D&D').
```

Once the discourse ends, we can firm the assumption into a regular database clause.

Of course, there will be cases of unresolvable ambiguity, in which even the most informed co-specification resolution criteria will fail (as it will in human communication). And introducing the complexities of discourse into a system that depends on it fully for gathering information its is no small a challenge. But the availability of a time-independent assumption mechanism can greatly help. Timeless assumptions have also proved useful for treating other linguistic phenomena such as coordination [14]

4 Further Applications Amenable to Speech

As we hope to have shown in previous sections, the database field is one of the main candidates for speech interactions through logic, being sufficiently studied, and given that it also includes logic-based incarnations such as Datalog.

Other applications, while less studied, are emerging as good candidates too. For instance, the new need for processing massive amounts of web data which are mostly expressed in natural language opens up several interesting possibilities. In this section we briefly discuss current research which sets the stage for speech interactions to be also incorporated into them.

4.1 Speech Driven Robot Control

Controlling Mobile Mini-robots Using speech to control robots is also an interesting application of natural language processing through logic: since robots' worlds are fairly restricted, commands tend to be relatively simple and fairly devoid of the ambiguity that plagues other natural language applications.

Preliminary work has been done jointly with Marie-Claude Thomas and Andrew Fall to control a simple world of mini robots through natural language commands [4,5]. These robots move in an enclosed room, avoiding obstacles through sensors. They know about time units, they can detect features such as room temperature and humidity, move to sources of light, avoid obstacles, and recharge themselves through sources of light positioned within the room.

Natural language commands translate into a specially developed formal logic system. This high degree of formalization is currently believed necessary in robotics, and allows us in particular great economy: the syntax of our logic system is the representation language for commands, and its semantics is the high level execution specification, resulting in several calls to Prolog and C routines.

Natural language commands are of the form exemplified below:

- Go to the nearest source of light in ten minutes.
- Go to point P taking care that the temperature remains between X and Y degrees.
- Let robot A pass.
- Give X to robot B.
- Stop as soon as the humidity exceeds H.

Imperative sentences with an implicit subject, which are rare in other applications, are common here. Complements are typically slots to be filled in mostly by constants.

Our approach combines the two current main approaches in robotics: a high-level deductive engine generates an overall plan, while dynamically consulting low level, distributed robotics programs which interface dynamically with the robot's actions and related information.

Obviously, adding a speech component to such systems would enhance them greatly. Mobile computers and wireless networks, as well as already available speech software which can be adapted, will help towards the goal of transporting these specialized robots to wherever they are needed, while communicating with them in more human terms.

Controlling Virtual, Visual World Robots Another interesting family of Internet applications of speech is that of robots that operate in virtual, visual worlds. For instance, Internet-based VRML animations have been generated through English-controlled partial order planners [3]. The next step is for such systems to accept speech rather than written input.

This research, done in collaboration with Andrea Schiel and Paul Tarau, presents a proof-of-concept Internet-based agent programmed in BinProlog which receives a natural language description of a robot's goal in a blocks world, and generates the VRML animation of a sequence of actions by which the robot achieves the stated goal. It uses a partial order planner.

The interaction storyboard is as follows: The user types in an NL request via an HTML form, stating a desirable final state to be achieved. This is sent over the Internet to a BinProlog based CGI script working as a client connected to the multi-user World-State server. The NL statement is used to generate an expression of the goal as a conjunction of post-conditions to be achieved. The goal is passed to the planner module, also part of the CGI script. The plan materializes as a VRML animation, ending in a visual representation of the final state to be sent back as the result of the CGI script, as well as in an update of the WorldState database.

Our analyzer, based on Assumption Grammars, can deal with multisentential input and with anaphora (e.g. relating pronouns to antecedents in previous sentences). Pronoun resolution involves intuitionistic rather than linear assumptions (since an antecedent can be referred to by a pronoun more than once).

The results we prototyped for the blocks world can be transposed to other domains, by using domain-tailored planners and adapting the NL grammar to those specific domains. A more interesting extension is the development of a single agent to produce VRML animations from NL goals with respect to different applications of planning. This might be achieved by isolating the domain-specific knowledge into an application-oriented ontology; adapting a partial order planner to consult this ontology modularly; and likewise having the grammar examine the hierarchy of concepts in order to make sense of domain-oriented words.

4.2 Web Access Through Language

The intersection between logic programming and the Internet is a very new but rapidly growing field. Recent logic-based web applications have been presented [18,20], and a special issue of the Journal of Logic Programming on this subject is currently under preparation.

Among the exciting new applications that these interactions are making possible, concept-based retrieval and virtual worlds stand out as particularly promising for long-distance interactions, distributed work, and interactive teaching through the web [6]. Endowing these budding applications with access through language, and in particular speech, would greatly enhance their capabilities. In particular, multilingual access to virtual worlds over the Internet would help remove geographic and language barriers to cooperation. Preliminary work in this direction is [2].

Speech Driven Virtual World Communication This research implements a Bin-Prolog based virtual world running under Netscape and Explorer, called LogiMOO, with a multilingual and extensible natural language front end [13], which will also be endowed with a speech as well as a visual component. It allows (written at present) communication between distant users in real time, hiding the complexities of the distributed communication model through the usual metaphors: places (starting from a default lobby), ports, ability to *move* or *teleport* from one place to another, a *wizard* resident on the server, *ownership* of objects, the ability to *transfer* ownership and a built-in notifier agent watching for messages as a background thread.

LogiMOO makes use of linear and intuitionistic assumption techniques, and is based on a set of embeddable logic programming components which interoperate with standard Web tools. Immediate evaluation of world knowledge by the parser yields representations which minimize the unknowns, allowing us to deal with advanced natural language constructs like anaphora and relativization efficiently. We take advantage of the simplicity of our controlled language to provide as well an easy adaptation to other natural languages than English, with English-like representations as a universal interlingua.

The peculiar features of the world to be consulted- a virtual world- induced novel parsing features which are interesting in themselves: flexible handling of dynamic knowledge, immediate evaluation of noun phrase representations, allowing us to be economic with representation itself, inference of some basic syntactic categories from the context, a treatment of nouns as proper nouns, easy extensibility within the same language as well as into other natural languages.

Speech Driven Concept Based Retrieval As anyone knows who has tried to query the Internet through the existing search engines, there is a glaring need for intelligent access to that fantastic but frustratingly mechanical repository of world knowledge that the Internet has become. From this perspective alone, logic should play a major role, given that deduction is obviously needed to make enough sense of a query as to minimize noise (the number of irrelevant documents obtained for a given query to a search engine) and silence (the number of failures to find any relevant documents that do exist).

For instance, within a forestry domain of interest, we can use a taxonomy of forestry-related concepts, which allows the search engine to specialize or generalize given concepts (e.g. going from "water" to "lakes", or vice versa), and to use the contextual information provided by forestry domains in order to avoid nonsensical answers. Search engines that base their search on keywords rather than semantics, in contrast, have been known to respond for instance to a query for documents related to "clear cuts near water" with "Complete poetical works from William Wordsworth", among a list of other equally wrong associations.

Concept-based search engines are starting to appear, but to our knowledge there are none yet that go much beyond a shallow use of keywords and concept classifications. Full meaning extraction and comparison, however, can only be done once the subtleties of natural language semantics are taken into account. A challenging task, but again, one for which logic programming is particularly suited. Assumption Grammars have been proposed, in conjunction with other techniques from Artificial Intelligence and Databases (concept hierarchies, multi-layered databases and intelligent agents) for intelligently searching information pertaining to a specific industry on the web [7].

5 Concluding Remarks

Computers have become so ubiquitous, that it is high time to develop alternative computer work modes than the present typing/screen based model. We are the first generation with exponents that have spent twenty or thirty years working in front of a computer terminal, and the ill effects are all too visible around us: tendonitis; eye, neck and back strain; Carpal Tunnel syndrome...

Speech-driven knowledge base creation and consultation, just as speech driven robot control or programming, and web access through language, could bring relief from such problems. They can also partially address the present need to integrate voice recognition software, voice synthesis, and AI programs.

In this article we have proposed some emerging approaches towards such ends. However, putting all the pieces of the puzzle together will require careful crafting. Within the logic-based database field, some recent developments could prove most valuable towards this objective, like the uses of Inductive Logic Programming to automate the construction of natural language interfaces for database queries [19].

Logic grammar formalisms have been developed moreover with linguistic ease of expression in mind. In helping linguists write executable grammars in terms that are not too removed from their own, we might by the way be able to tap on linguistic expertise that might be most valuable for our own language processing applications.

The availability of powerful while mobile computers and applications (e.g. [21] also adds unprecedented potential to speech interfacing software, for instance for business people or academics who often travel, and who could therefore make the most of such results if they were portable. Finally, our experience with the circumscribed domain of database creation could prove useful as a first step towards an even more daring application, that of programming through natural language.

Efforts are under way for a EU/NorthAmerica Compulog Network of Centres of Excellence to launch a cooperation around NL projects using logic programming, presently coordinated jointly by Dr. Pearce and the author. With the present article we hope to stimulate further interaction along these lines, both in a geographic sense and across areas.

6 Appendix I: Sample Database Creation and Consultation Session

In the following sample creation session, user input is prompted by ">"

```
?- go.

Enter information for the database one sentence at a time
When you are done, say stop


> anne is a person

I am adding the clause:
  person(anne)


> garfield is a cat
```

```
I am adding the clause:
  cat(garfield)


> garfield purrs

I am adding the clause:
  purrs(garfield)


> earth is the mother of anne

I am adding the clause:
  mother_of(earth,anne)


> anne is canadian

I am adding the clause: canadian(anne)


> people like cats that purr

I am adding the clause:
  likes(_x38299,_x38336):-
    (person(_x38299),true),cat(_x38336),purrs(_x38336),true


> the mother of anne likes cats that purr

I am adding the clause:
  likes(_x39082,_x39147):-
    (mother_of(_x39082,anne),true,true),cat(_x39147),
    purrs(_x39147),true


> eve and adam like paradise

I am adding the clause:
  likes([eve,adam],paradise)


> peter is angry with rover

I am adding the clause:
```

```
  angry_with(peter,rover)


> the mother of anne gives rover to peter

I am adding the clause:
  gives(_x37230,rover,peter):-
    (mother_of(_x37230,anne),true,true),true


> anne is intelligent

I am adding the clause:
  intelligent(anne)


> a person that likes cats that purr is intelligent

I am adding the clause:
  intelligent(_x38073):-
    person(_x38073),likes(_x38073,_x38193);cat(_x38193),
    purrs(_x38193),true


> stop

You can consult the database by typing "answer."
yes
?- answer.


> who is intelligent

Representation of the query:
question(_x2599,(intelligent(_x2599),true))
Answer: anne


> who likes cats that purr

Representation of the query:
question(_x2889,(likes(_x2889,_x2948),cat(_x2948),purrs(_x2948),
true))
Answer: anne
Answer: earth
```

```
> who is angry with rover

Representation of the query:
question(_x3169,(angry_with(_x3169,rover),true))
Answer: peter


> who gives rover to peter

Representation of the query:
question(_x3459,(gives(_x3459,rover,peter),true))
Answer: earth


> earth gives rover to who

Representation of the query:
question(_x3749,(gives(earth,rover,_x3749),true))
Answer: peter


> earth gives who to peter

Representation of the query:
question(_x4039,(gives(earth,_x4039,peter),true))
Answer: rover


> who likes paradise

Representation of the query:
question(_x4257,(likes(_x4257,paradise),true))
Answer: [eve,adam]


> who likes garfield

Representation of the query:
question(_x4643,(likes(_x4643,garfield),true))
Answer: anne
Answer: earth
```

```
> stop
Goodbye
```

N.B. The mother of anne (earth) is not identified as one of the answers on who is intelligent because She has not been declared to be a person.

7 Appendix II - The Database Created Through the Session in Appendix I

```
% dyn_compiled: person/1:
person(anne).


% dyn_compiled: cat/1:
cat(garfield).


% dyn_compiled: purrs/1:
purrs(garfield).


% dyn_compiled: mother_of/2:
mother_of(earth,anne).


% dyn_compiled: canadian/1:
canadian(anne).


% likes/2:
likes(A,B) :-
        person(A),
        true,
        cat(B),
        purrs(B).
likes(A,B) :-
        mother_of(A,anne),
        true,
        true,
```

```
        cat(B),
        purrs(B).
likes([eve,adam],paradise).


% angry_with/2:
angry_with(peter,rover).


% gives/3:
gives(A,rover,peter) :-
        mother_of(A,anne),
        true,
        true.


% intelligent/1:
intelligent(anne).
intelligent(A) :-
        person(A),
        likes(A,B),
        cat(B),
        purrs(B).
```

8 Appendix III - Sample Interaction with a Spanish Consultable Virtual World Through LogiMOO

This Spanish session illustrates among other things flexibility re. nouns., within a controlled English coverage. Since the virtual world admits the crafting of new objects,and we do not want to restrict the user to crafting only those objects whose vocabulary is known, the system assumes from context that an unknown word is a noun, and proceeds to translate it as itself. Thus we get a definite "Spanglish" flavour in the internal representations obtained, but for the purposes of reacting to the Spanish commands, this does not matter much. Ultimately, a bilingual dictionary consultation on line should generate the translation, perhaps in consultation with the user as to different possible translations. Other shortcuts are also taken (e.g. guest room translates into the single identifier guest_room, clitic pronouns are in an unnatural position, etc).

The Spanish interactions shown translate into:

I am Paul. Dig a guest room. Go there. Dig a kitchen. Go to the hall. Look. I am the wizard. Where am I? Dig the bedroom. Go there. Dig a kitchen, open a port to the south of the kitchen, go there, open a port to the north of the bedroom. Go there. Build a portrait. Give it to the wizard. Look. I am Diana. Build a car. Where is the car? Build a Gnu. Who has it? Where is the Gnu? Where am I? Give the wizard the Gnu that I built. Who has it?

```
test_data("Yo soy Paul.").
test_data("Cave una habitacion_huespedes.
 Vaya alli. Cave una cocina.").

test_data("Vaya al vestibulo. Mire.").

test_data("Yo soy el brujo.
 Donde estoy yo?").

test_data("Cave el dormitorio. Vaya alli.
 Cave una cocina, abra una puerta alsur de
 la cocina, vaya alli, abra una puerta
 alnorte del dormitorio. Vaya alli.
 Construya un cuadro. Dese lo al brujo.
 Mire.").

test_data("Yo soy Diana. Construya un
 automovil. Donde esta el automovil?").

test_data("Construya un Gnu. Quien tiene
 lo? Donde esta el Gnu? Donde estoy yo?").

test_data("Dele al brujo el Gnu que yo
 construi. Quien tiene lo?").

/* TRACE:

==BEGIN COMMAND RESULTS==
TEST: Yo soy Paul.
WORDS: [yo,soy,paul,.]
SENTENCES: [yo,soy,paul]

==BEGIN COMMAND RESULTS==
login as: paul with password: none
your home is at http://199.60.3.56/~veronica

SUCCEEDING(iam(paul))

==END COMMAND RESULTS==

TEST: Cave una habitacion_huespedes.
 Vaya alli. Cave una cocina.
```

```
WORDS: [cave,una,habitacion_huespedes,.,
 vaya,alli,.,cave,una,cocina,.]
SENTENCES: [cave,una,habitacion_huespedes]
 [vaya,alli] [cave,una,cocina]

==BEGIN COMMAND RESULTS==
SUCCEEDING(dig(habitacion_huespedes))
you are in the  habitacion_huespedes
SUCCEEDING(go(habitacion_huespedes))
SUCCEEDING(dig(cocina))

==END COMMAND RESULTS==

TEST: Vaya al vestibulo. Mire.
WORDS: [vaya,al,vestibulo,.,mire,.]
SENTENCES: [vaya,al,vestibulo] [mire]

==BEGIN COMMAND RESULTS==
you are in the  lobby
SUCCEEDING(go(lobby))
user(veronica,none,'http://...').
user(paul,none,'http://...').
login(paul).
online(veronica).
online(paul).
place(lobby).
place(habitacion_huespedes).
place(cocina).
contains(lobby,veronica).
contains(lobby,paul).
SUCCEEDING(look)

==END COMMAND RESULTS==

TEST: Yo soy el brujo. Donde estoy yo?
WORDS: [yo,soy,el,brujo,.,donde,estoy,yo,?]
SENTENCES: [yo,soy,el,brujo]
 [donde,estoy,yo]

==BEGIN COMMAND RESULTS==
login as: wizard with password: none
your home is at http://199.60.3.56/~veronica

SUCCEEDING(iam(wizard))
you are in the  lobby
SUCCEEDING(whereami)

==END COMMAND RESULTS==

TEST: Cave el dormitorio. Vaya alli. Cave
```

```
 una cocina, abra una puerta alsur de la
 cocina, vaya alli, abra una puerta alnorte
 del dormitorio. Vaya alli. Construya un
 cuadro. Dese lo al brujo. Mire.
WORDS: [cave,el,dormitorio,.,vaya,alli,.,
 cave,una,cocina,(,),abra,una,puerta,alsur,
 de,la,cocina,(,),vaya,alli,(,),abra,una,
 puerta,alnorte,del,dormitorio,.,vaya,alli,
 .,construya,un,cuadro,.,dese,lo,al,brujo,.,
 mire,.]
SENTENCES: [cave,el,dormitorio] [vaya,alli]
 [cave,una,cocina] [abra,una,puerta,alsur,
 de,la,cocina] [vaya,alli] [abra,una,puerta,
 alnorte,del,dormitorio] [vaya,alli]
 [construya,un,cuadro] [dese,lo,al,brujo]
 [mire]

==BEGIN COMMAND RESULTS==
SUCCEEDING(dig(bedroom))
you are in the  bedroom
SUCCEEDING(go(bedroom))
SUCCEEDING(dig(cocina))
SUCCEEDING(open_port(south,cocina))
you are in the  cocina
SUCCEEDING(go(cocina))
SUCCEEDING(open_port(north,bedroom))
you are in the  bedroom
SUCCEEDING(go(bedroom))
SUCCEEDING(craft(cuadro))
logimoo:<wizard># 'wizard:I give you cuadro'
SUCCEEDING(give(wizard,cuadro))
user(veronica,none,'http://...').
user(paul,none,'http://...').
user(wizard,none,'http://...').
login(wizard).
online(veronica).
online(paul).
online(wizard).
place(lobby).
place(habitacion_huespedes).
place(cocina).
place(bedroom).
contains(lobby,veronica).
contains(lobby,paul).
contains(bedroom,wizard).
contains(bedroom,cuadro).
port(bedroom,south,cocina).
port(cocina,north,bedroom).
has(wizard,cuadro).
crafted(wizard,cuadro).
```

```
SUCCEEDING(look)

==END COMMAND RESULTS==

TEST: Yo soy Diana. Construya un automovil.
 Donde esta el automovil?
WORDS: [yo,soy,diana,.,construya,un,
 automovil,.,donde,esta,el,automovil,?]
SENTENCES: [yo,soy,diana]
 [construya,un,automovil]
 [donde,esta,el,automovil]

==BEGIN COMMAND RESULTS==
login as: diana with password: none
your home is at http://199.60.3.56/~veronica

SUCCEEDING(iam(diana))
SUCCEEDING(craft(automovil))
automovil is in lobby
SUCCEEDING(where(automovil))

==END COMMAND RESULTS==

TEST: Construya un Gnu. Quien tiene lo?
 Donde esta el Gnu? Donde estoy yo?
WORDS: [construya,un,gnu,.,quien,tiene,
 lo,?,donde,esta,el,gnu,?,donde,estoy,yo,?]
SENTENCES: [construya,un,gnu]
 [quien,tiene,lo] [donde,esta,el,gnu]
 [donde,estoy,yo]

==BEGIN COMMAND RESULTS==
SUCCEEDING(craft(gnu))
diana has gnu
SUCCEEDING(who(has,gnu))
gnu is in lobby
SUCCEEDING(where(gnu))
you are in the  lobby
SUCCEEDING(whereami)

==END COMMAND RESULTS==

TEST: Dele al brujo el Gnu que yo construi.
 Quien tiene lo?
WORDS: [dele,al,brujo,el,gnu,que,yo,
 construi,.,quien,tiene,lo,?]
SENTENCES: [dele,al,brujo,el,gnu,que,yo,
 construi] [quien,tiene,lo]

==BEGIN COMMAND RESULTS==
```

```
logimoo:<diana># 'wizard:I give you gnu'
SUCCEEDING(give(wizard,gnu))
wizard has gnu
SUCCEEDING(who(has,gnu))

==END COMMAND RESULTS==

SUCCEEDING(test)

==END COMMAND RESULTS==
*/
```

References

1. V. Dahl, P. Tarau, P. Accuosto, S. Rochefort, and M. Scurtescu. Assumption Grammars for Knowledge Based Systems. *Informatica* 22(4), pages 435–444, 1998.
2. V. Dahl, P. Tarau, S. Rochefort, and M. Scurtescu. A Spanish Interface to LogiMoo- towards multilingual virtual worlds. *Informatica*, volume 2, june 1999.
3. A. Schiel, V. Dahl and P. Tarau. *Generating Internet Based VRML Animations through Natural Language Controlled Partial Order Planners* Technical Report, Simon Fraser University, 1998.
4. V. Dahl, A. Fall and M.C. Thomas. Driving Robots through natural language. *Proceedings 1995 International Conference on Systems, Man and Cybernetics*, pages 1904–1908, july 1995.
5. M. C. Thomas, V. Dahl and A. Fall. Logic Planning in robotics. *Proceedings 1995 International Conference on Systems, Man and Cybernetics*, pages 2951–2955, july 1995.
6. S. Rochefort, V. Dahl and P. Tarau. A Virtual Environment for Collaborative Learning. *Proc. World Multiconference on Systemics, Cybernetics and Informatics (SCI'98) and 4th International Conference on Information Systems Analysis and Synthesis (ISAS'98)*, Orlando, Florida, 1998.
7. O.R. Zaiane, A. Fall, S. Rochefort, V. Dahl and P. Tarau. On-Line Resource Discovery using Natural Language. *Proc. RIAO'97 , Computer-Assisted Searching on the Internet*, pp. 336–355, McGill University, Montreal, June 1997.
8. F.C.N. Pereira and D.H.D. Warren. Definite Clause Grammars for Language Analysis - A survey of the formalism and a Comparison with Transition Networks. *Artificial Intelligence*, vol. 13, pages 231–278, 1980.
9. R. Pareschi and D. Miller. *Extending definite clause grammars with scoping constructs*, pages 373–389. Warren, David H. D. and Szeredi, P. (eds.) International Conference in Logic Programming, MIT Press, 1990.
10. A. Colmerauer. Metamorphosis Grammars. *Lecture Notes in Computer Science* 63, pages 133–189, Springer-Verlag, 1978.
11. R.A.K. Kowalski. *Logic for Problem Solving*. North-Holland, 1979.
12. A. Fall. The foundations of taxonomic encoding. *Computational Intelligence*, 14(4):1–45, 1998.
13. P. Tarau, K. De Boschere, V. Dahl, and S. Rochefort. LogiMOO: an Extensible Multi-User Virtual World with Natural Language Control *Journal of Logic Programming*, 38(3), pages 331–353, 1999.

14. V. Dahl, P. Tarau and R. Li. Assumption Grammars for Processing Natural Language. *Proceedings International Conference on Logic Programming'97*, pages 256–270, 1997.
15. V. Dahl. Logical Design of Deductive, Natural Language Consultable Data Bases. *Proc. V Int. Conf. on Very Large Databases, Rio de Janeiro*, pages 24–31, 1979.
16. V. Dahl. The logic of language. In K. Apt, V. Marek and D.S. Warren (eds.), *The Logic Programming Paradigm: A 25 year perspective*, pages 429–451, Springer-Verlag, 1999.
17. J. Davison. A Natural Language Interface for Performing Database Updates. *ICDE*, pages 69–76, 1984.
18. P. Tarau, K. De Bosschere and M. Hermenegildo (eds.). *Proc. of the 2nd International Workshop on Logic Programming Tools for Internet Applications*, ICLP'97, 1997.
19. J.M. Zelle and R. J. Mooney. Learning to Parse Database Queries using Inductive Logic Programming. *Proc. Thirteenth National Conference on Artificial Intelligence*, pages 1050–1055, 1996.
20. S.W. Loke. *Adding Logic Programming Behaviour to the World Wide Web* PhD Thesis, Univ. of Melbourne, Australia, 1998.
21. K.A. Bharat and L. Cardelli. Migratory applications. *Proc. 8th Annual ACM Symposium on User Interface Software and Technology*, 1995.
22. D.A. Miller and G Nadathur. Some uses of higher -order logic in computational linguistics. In *Proceedings of the 24th Annual Meeting of the Association for Computational Linguistics*, pages 247–255, 1986.

Relating Templates to Language and Logic

John F. Sowa

Westchester Polytechnic Univ. USA
sowa@west.poly.edu
http://west.poly.edu

Abstract. Syntactic theories relate sentence structure to the details of morphemes, inflections, and word order. Semantic theories relate sentences to the details of formal logic and model theory. But many of the most successful programs for information extraction (IE) are based on domain-dependent templates that ignore the details at the center of attention of the major theories of syntax and semantics. This paper shows that it is possible to find a more primitive set of operations, called the canonical formation rules, which underlie both the template-filling operations of IE and the more formal operations of parsers and theorem provers. These rules are first stated in terms of conceptual graphs and then generalized to any knowledge representation, including predicate calculus, frames, and the IE templates. As a result, the template-filling operations of IE become part of a more general set of operations that can be used in various combinations to process knowledge of any kind, including linguistic knowledge, at any level of detail.

1 Relating Different Language Levels

Since the 1960s, many theoretical and computational linguists have assumed that language processing, either in the human brain or in a computer program, is best performed by an integrated system of modules that operate on different language levels: phonology, morphology, syntax, semantics, pragmatics, and general world knowledge. Chomsky and his students started from the bottom and defined syntactic structures for the first three levels. Richard Montague and his colleagues started in the middle with symbolic logic for the semantic level and worked downward into syntax and upward to pragmatics. Roger Schank and his students started from the top with a variety of knowledge representations: conceptual dependencies, scripts, MOPs (memory organization packets), TOPs (thematic organization packets), and problem-dependent representations for case-based reasoning about general world knowledge. Although these schools of thought shared some common views about the existence of different language levels, their theoretical foundations and notations were so radically different that collaboration among them was impossible, and adherents of different paradigms ignored each other's work.

During the 1980s, Prolog demonstrated that a general logic-based approach could be fast enough to handle every level from phonology to world knowledge.

Pazienza (Ed.): Information Extraction, LNAI 1714, pp. 76–94, 1999.

Prolog-like unification grammars for the lower levels could be integrated with deductive reasoning and possible-world semantics for the higher levels. In one form or another, logic would be the underlying mechanism that supported every level of language processing. Various notations for different subsets of logic were developed: feature structures, description logics, discourse representation structures, conceptual graphs, SNePS (semantic network processing system), and many variations of predicate calculus. Although these systems used different notations, their common basis in logic made it possible for techniques developed for any one of the systems to be adapted to most if not all of the others.

During the 1990s, however, the MUC series of message understanding conferences and the ARPA Tipster project showed that the integrated systems designed for detailed analysis at every level are too slow for information extraction. They cannot process the large volumes of text on the Internet fast enough to find and extract the information that is relevant to a particular topic. Instead, competing groups with a wide range of theoretical orientations converged on a common approach: domain-dependent templates for representing the critical patterns of concepts and a limited amount of syntactic processing to find appropriate phrases that fill slots in the templates [7].

The group at SRI International ([1],[8]) found that TACITUS, a logic-based text-understanding system was far too slow. It spent most of its time on syntactic nuances that were irrelevant to the ultimate goal. They replaced it with FASTUS, a finite-state processor that is triggered by key words, finds phrase patterns without attempting to link them into a formal parse tree, and matches the phrases to the slots in the templates. Cowie [3] observed that the FASTUS templates, which are simplified versions of a logic-based approach, are hardly distinguishable from the sketchy scripts that De Jong ([4],[5]) developed as a simplified version of a Schankian approach.

Although IE systems have achieved acceptable levels of recall and precision on their assigned tasks, there is more work to be done. The templates are hand-tailored for each domain, and their success rates on homogeneous corpora evaporate when they are applied to a wide range of documents. The high performance of template-based IE comes at the expense of a laborious task of designing specialized templates. Furthermore, that task can only be done by highly trained specialists, usually the same researchers who implemented the system that uses the templates.

A practical IE system cannot depend on the availability of human consultants for routine customization. It should automatically construct new templates from information supplied by users who have some familiarity with the domain, but no knowledge of how the IE system works. But the laborious task of deriving customized templates for a new domain is very different from the high-speed task of using the templates. Whereas the extraction task does shallow processing of large volumes of text, the customization task requires detailed understanding of the user's questions and the context in which they are asked. It depends on all the syntactic, semantic, pragmatic, and logical nuances that are ignored in the high-speed search and extraction task.

Ultimately, a practical IE system must be able to perform detailed text understanding, but on a much smaller amount of information than the search and extraction task. When deriving customized templates, the system must focus on specific information about the user's requirements. The customization task must do more than translate a single query into SQL. It may start with a query, but it must continue with a clarification dialog to resolve ambiguities and fill in background knowledge. But linking the customization stage with the extraction stage requires a common semantic framework that can accommodate both.

The purpose of this paper is to show how the IE templates fit into a larger framework that links them to the more detailed issues of parse trees, discourse structures, and formal semantics. This framework is related to logic, but not in the same way as the logic-based systems of the 1980s. Instead, it depends on a small set of lower-level operations, called the canonical formation rules, which were originally developed in terms of conceptual graphs [12]. But those operations can be generalized to any knowledge representation language, including predicate calculus, frames, and IE templates. This paper presents the canonical formation rules, and relates them to conceptual graphs (CGs), predicate calculus, frames, and templates. The result is not a magic solution to all the problems, but a framework in which they can be addressed.

2 Canonical Formation Rules

All operations on conceptual graphs are based on combinations of six *canonical formation rules*, each of which performs one basic graph operation. Logically, each rule has one of three possible effects: it makes a CG more specialized, it makes a CG more generalized, or it changes the shape of a CG, but leaves it logically equivalent to the original. All the rules come in pairs: for each specialization rule, there is an inverse generalization rule; and for each equivalence rule, there is an inverse equivalence rule that transforms a CG to its original shape. These rules are fundamentally graphical: they are easier to show than to describe.

The first two rules, which are illustrated in Fig. 1, are *copy* and *simplify*. At the top is a conceptual graph for the sentence "The cat Yojo is chasing a mouse". The boxes are called *concepts*, and the circles are called *conceptual relations*. In each box is a *type label*, such as Cat, Chase, and Mouse. In the concept [Cat: Yojo], the *type field* is separated by a colon from the *referent field*, which contains the name of a specific cat named Yojo. The agent (Agnt) relation links the concept of chasing to the concept of the cat Yojo, and the theme (Thme) relation links it to the concept of a mouse.

The down arrow in Fig. 1 represents the copy rule. One application of the rule copies the Agnt relation, and a second application copies the subgraph
→ (Thme) → [Mouse] .
The dotted line connecting the two [Mouse] concepts is a *coreference link* that indicates that both concepts refer to the same individual. The copies in the bottom graph are redundant, since they add no new information. The up ar-

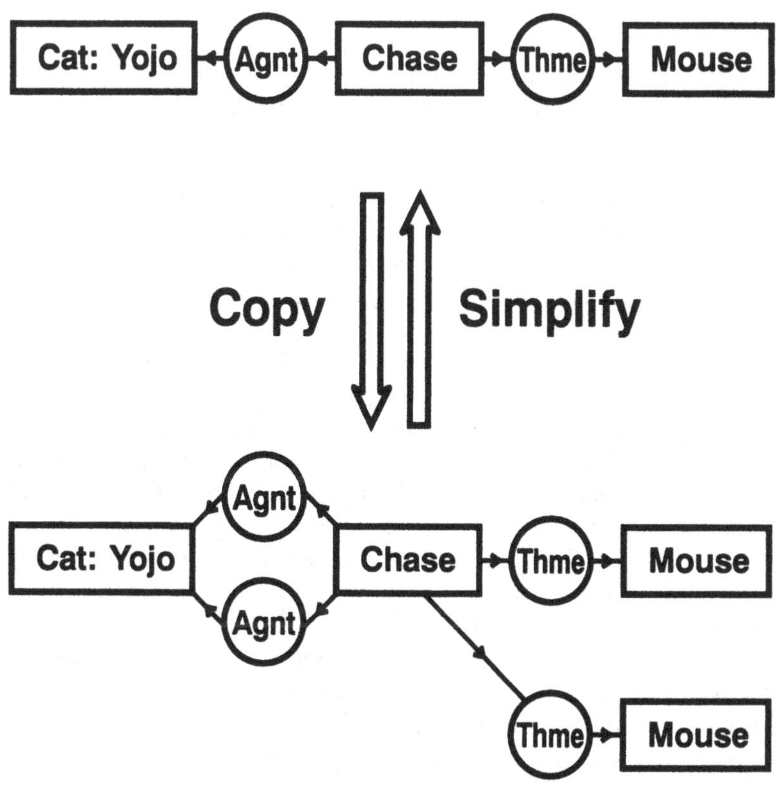

Fig. 1. Copy and simplify rules

row represents two applications of the simplify rule, which performs the inverse operations of erasing redundant copies. The copy and simplify rules are called *equivalence rules* because any two CGs that can be transformed from one to the other by any combination of copy and simplify rules are logically equivalent.

The two formulas in predicate calculus that are derived from the CGs in Fig. 1 are also logically equivalent. In typed predicate calculus, each concept of the top CG maps to a quantified variable whose type is the same as the concept type. If no other quantifier is written in the referent field, the default quantifier is the existential $\exists$. The top CG maps to the following formula:

$$(\exists x\text{:Cat})(\exists y\text{:Chase})(\exists z\text{:Mouse})$$
$$\quad(\text{name}(x,\text{'Yojo'}) \wedge \text{agnt}(y,x) \wedge \text{thme}(y,z)),$$

which is true or false under exactly the same circumstances as the formula that corresponds to the bottom CG:

$(\exists x{:}\text{Cat})(\exists y{:}\text{Chase})(\exists z{:}\text{Mouse})(\exists w{:}\text{Mouse})$
$(\ \text{name}(x,\text{'Yojo'}) \wedge \text{agnt}(y,x) \wedge \text{agnt}(y,x) \wedge \text{thme}(y,z) \wedge$
$\text{thme}(y,w) \wedge (z = w)\ )$

By the inference rules of predicate calculus, the redundant copy of agnt(y,x) can be erased. The equation $z = w$, which corresponds to the coreference link between the two [Mouse] concepts, allows the variable w to be replaced by z. After the redundant parts have been erased, the simplification of the second formula transforms it back to the first.

Fig. 2 illustrates the restrict and unrestrict rules. At the top is a CG for the sentence "A cat is chasing an animal." By two applications of the restrict rule, it is transformed to the CG for "The cat Yojo is chasing a mouse." The first step is a *restriction by referent* of the concept [Cat], which represents some indefinite cat, to the more specific concept [Cat: Yojo], which represents an individual cat named Yojo. The second step is a *restriction by type* of the concept [Animal] to a concept of the subtype [Mouse]. Two applications of the unrestrict rule perform the inverse transformation of the bottom graph to the top graph. The restrict rule is called a *specialization rule*, and the unrestrict rule is a *generalization rule*. The more specialized graph implies the more general one: if the cat Yojo is chasing a mouse, it follows that a cat is chasing an animal.

Equivalent operations can be performed on the corresponding formulas in predicate calculus. The top graph corresponds to the formula

$(\exists x{:}\text{Cat})(\exists y{:}\text{Chase})(\exists z{:}\text{Mouse})\ (\text{agnt}(y,x) \wedge \text{thme}(y,z)),$

Restriction by referent adds the predicate name(x,'Yojo'), and restriction by type replaces the type label Animal with Mouse:

$(\exists x{:}\text{Cat})(\exists y{:}\text{Chase})(\exists z{:}\text{Mouse})$
$(\text{name}(x,\text{'Yojo'}) \wedge \text{agnt}(y,x) \wedge \text{agnt}(y,x) \wedge \text{thme}(y,z))$

By the rules of predicate calculus, this formula implies the previous one.

Fig. 3 illustrates the *join* and *detach* rules. At the top are two CGs for the sentences "Yojo is chasing a mouse" and "A mouse is brown." The join rule overlays the two identical copies of the concept [Mouse] to form a single CG for the sentence "Yojo is chasing a brown mouse." The detach rule performs the inverse operation. The result of join is a more specialized graph that implies the one derived by detach.

In predicate calculus, join corresponds to identifying two variables, either by an equality operator such as $z = w$ or by a substitution of one variable for every occurrence of the other. The conjunction of the formulas for the top two CGs is

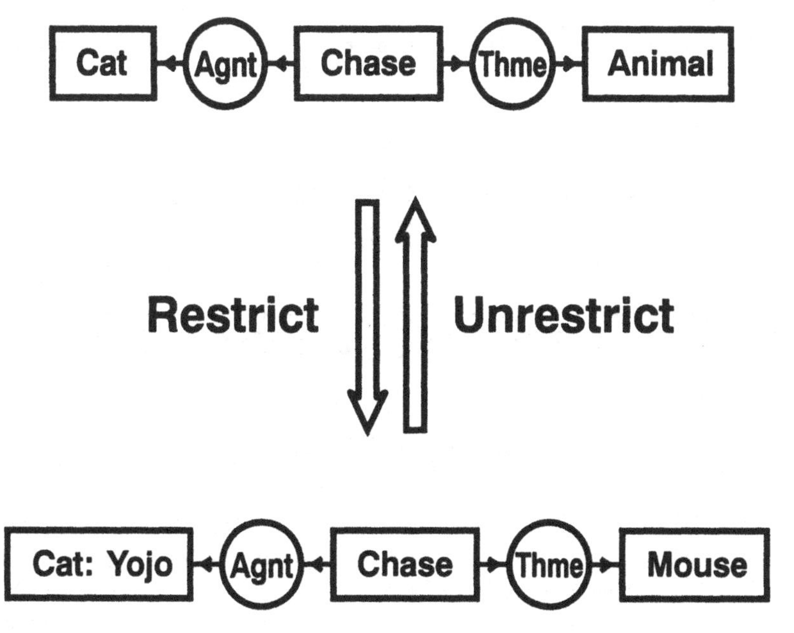

Fig. 2. Restrict and unrestrict rules

$((\exists x\text{:Cat})(\exists y\text{:Chase})(\exists z\text{:Mouse})\ (\text{name}(x,\text{'Yojo'}) \wedge \text{agnt}(y,x) \wedge \text{thme}(y,z)) \wedge$
$((\exists w\text{:Mouse})\ (\exists v\text{:Brown})\ \text{attr}(w,v))$

After substituting z for all occurrences of w and deleting redundancies,

$(\exists x\text{:Cat})\ (\exists y\text{:Chase})(\exists z\text{:Mouse})(\exists v\text{:Brown})$
$(\text{name}(x,\text{'Yojo'}) \wedge \text{agnt}(y,x) \wedge \text{thme}(y,z) \wedge \text{attr}(w,v))$

By the rules of predicate calculus, this formula implies the previous one.

Although the canonical formation rules are easy to visualize, the formal specifications require more detail. They are most succinct for the *simple graphs*, which are CGs with no contexts, no negations, and no quantifiers other than existentials. The following specifications, stated in terms of the abstract syntax, can be applied to a simple graph u to derive another simple graph w.

1. *Equivalence rules.* The copy rule copies a graph or subgraph. The simplify rule performs the inverse operation of erasing a copy. Let v be any subgraph of a simple graph u; v may be empty or it may be all of u.
   - *Copy.* The copy rule makes a copy of any subgraph v of u and adds it to u to form w. If c is any concept of v that has been copied from a concept d in u, then c must be a member of exactly the same coreference sets as d. Some conceptual relations of v may be linked to concepts of u that

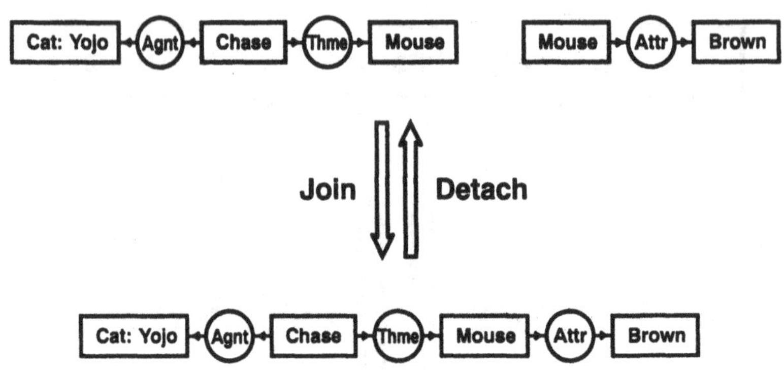

Fig. 3. Join and detach rules

are not in v; the copies of those conceptual relations must be linked to exactly the same concepts of u.

 - *Simplify.* The simplify rule is the inverse of copy. If two subgraphs v_1 and v_2 of u are identical, they have no common concepts or conceptual relations, and corresponding concepts of v_1 and v_2 belong to the same coreference sets, then v_2 may be erased. If any conceptual relations of v_1 are linked to concepts of u that are not in v_1, then the corresponding conceptual relations of v_2 must be linked to exactly the same concepts of u, which may not be in v_2.

2. *Specialization rules.* The restrict rule specializes the type or referent of a single concept node. The join rule merges two concept nodes to a single node. These rules transform u to a graph w that is more specialized than u.
   - *Restrict.* Any concept or conceptual relation of u may be *restricted by type* by replacing its type with a subtype. Any concept of u with a blank referent may be *restricted by referent* by replacing the blank with some other existential referent.
   - *Join.* Let c and d be any two concepts of u whose types and referents are identical. Then w is the graph obtained by deleting d, adding c to all coreference sets in which d occurred, and attaching to c all arcs of conceptual relations that had been attached to d.
3. *Generalization rules.* The unrestrict rule, which is the inverse of restrict, generalizes the type or referent of a concept node. The detach rule, which is the inverse of join, splits a graph in two parts at some concept node. The last two rules transform u to a graph w that is a generalization of u.
   - *Unrestrict.* Let c be any concept of u. Then w may be derived from u by unrestricting c either by type or by referent: unrestriction by type replaces the type label of c with some supertype; and unrestriction by referent erases an existential referent to leave a blank.

- *Detach.* Let c be any concept of u. Then w may be derived from u by making a copy d of c, detaching one or more arcs of conceptual relations that had been attached to c, and attaching them to d.

Although the six canonical formation rules have been explicitly stated in terms of conceptual graphs, equivalent operations can be performed on any knowledge representation. The equivalents for predicate calculus were illustrated for Figs. 1, 2, and 3. Equivalent operations can also be performed on frames and templates: the copy and simplify rules are similar to the CG versions; restrict corresponds to filling slots in a frame or specializing a slot to a subtype; and join corresponds to inserting a pointer that links slots in two different frames or templates.

For nested contexts, the formation rules depend on the level of nested negations. A positive context (sign +) is nested in an even number negations (possibly zero). A negative context (sign -) is nested in an odd number of negations.

- *Zero negations.* A context that has no attached negations and is not nested in any other context is defined to be positive.
- *Negated context.* The negation relation (Neg) or its abbreviation by the ∼ or ¬ symbol reverses the sign of any context it is attached to: a negated context contained in a positive context is negative; a negated context contained in a negative context is positive.
- *Scoping context.* A context c with the type label SC and no attached conceptual relations is a scoping context, whose sign is the same as the sign of the context in which it is nested.

Let u be a conceptual graph in which some concept is a context whose designator is a nested conceptual graph v. The following canonical formation rules convert u to another CG w by operating on the nested graph v, while leaving everything else in u unchanged.

1. *Equivalence rules.*
   - If v is a CG in the context C, then let w be the graph obtained by performing a copy or simplify rule on v.
   - A context of type Negation whose referent is another context of type Negation is called a *double negation.* If u is a double negation around that includes the graph v, then let w be the graph obtained by replacing u with a scoping context around v:

   ```
   [Negation: [Negation: v]] => [SC: v].
   ```

   A double negation or a scoping context around a conceptual graph may be drawn or erased at any time. If v is a conceptual graph, the following three forms are equivalent:

   ```
   ~[ ~[ v]], [v], v.
   ```

2. *Specialization rules.*
   - If C is positive, then let w be the result of performing any specialization rule in C.
   - If C is negative, then let w be the result of performing any generalization rule in C.
3. *Generalization rules.*
   - If C is positive, then let w be the result of performing any generalization rule in C.
   - If C is negative, then let w be the result of performing any specialization rule in C.

In summary, negation reverses the effect of generalization and specialization, but it has no effect on the equivalence rules. Corresponding operations can be performed on formulas in predicate calculus. For frames and templates, the treatment of negation varies from one implementation to another; some systems have no negations, and others have many special cases that must be treated individually. But for any knowledge representation that supports negation, the same principle holds: negation reverses generalization and specialization.

3 Notation-Independent Rules of Inference

The canonical formation rules, which can be formulated in equivalent versions for conceptual graphs and predicate calculus, extract the logical essence from the details of syntax. As a result, the rules of inference can be stated in a notation-independent way. In fact, they are so completely independent of notation that they apply equally well to any knowledge representation for which it is possible to define rules of generalization, specialization, and equivalence. That includes frames, templates, discourse representation structures, feature structures, description logics, expert system rules, SQL queries, and any semantic representation for which the following three kinds of rules can be formulated:

- *Equivalence rules.* The equivalence rules may change the appearance of a knowledge representation, but they do not change its logical status. If a graph or formula u is transformed to another graph or formula v by any equivalence rule, then u implies v, and v implies u.
- *Specialization rules.* The specialization rules transform a graph or formula u to a graph or formla v that is logically more specialized: v implies u.
- *Generalization rules.* The generalization rules transform a graph or formula u to a graph or formula v that is logically more generalized: u implies v.

The notation-independent rules of inference were formulated by the logician Charles Sanders Peirce. Peirce [10] had originally invented the algebraic notation for predicate calculus with notation-dependent rules for *modus ponens* and instantiation of universally quantified variables. But he continued to search for a simpler and more general representation, which expressed the logical operations diagrammatically, in what he called a more *iconic* form. In 1897, Peirce invented *existential graphs* and introduced rules of inference that depend only on the operations of copying, erasing, and combining graphs. These five rules are so general that they apply to any version of logic for which the corresponding operations can be defined:

1. *Erasure.* In a positive context, any graph or formula u may be replaced by a generalization of u; in particular, u may be erased (i.e. it may replaced by a blank, which is the universal generalization).
2. *Insertion.* In a negative context, any graph or formula u may be replaced by a specialization of u; in particular, any graph may be inserted (i.e. it may replace the blank).
3. *Iteration.* If a graph or formula u occurs in a context C, another copy of u may be drawn in the same context C or in any context nested in C.
4. *Deiteration.* Any graph or formula u that could have been derived by iteration may be erased.
5. *Equivalence.* Any equivalence rule (copy, simplify, or double negation) may be performed on any graph, subgraph, formula, or subformula in any context.

Each of these rules preserves truth: if the starting graph or formula u happens to be true, the resulting formula v must also be true. Peirce's only axiom is the blank *sheet of assertion.* A blank sheet, which says nothing, cannot be false. Any statement that is derivable from the blank by these rules is a *theorem*, which must always be true.

When applied to entire graphs or formulas, these rules support propositional logic; but when they are applied to subgraphs and coreference links, they support full first-order logic. Peirce's rules take their simplest form when they are applied to his original existential graphs or to conceptual graphs, which are a typed version of existential graphs. When they are applied to the predicate calculus notation, Peirce's rules must accommodate various special cases that depend on the properties of each of the logical operators. That accommodation transforms Peirce's five rules to the rules of *natural deduction*, which were defined by Gerhard Gentzen over thirty years later. For Peirce's original statement of the rules, see [11]. For further examples and discussion of their application to other logics, see [13], [14].

4 Generalization Hierarchies

The rules of inference of logic define a generalization hierarchy over the terms of any logic-based language. Fig. 4 shows a hierarchy in conceptual graphs, but an equivalent hierarchy could be represented in any knowledge representation language. For each dark arrow in Fig. 4, the graph above is a generalization, and the graph below is a specialization. The top graph says that an animate being is the agent (Agnt) of some act that has an entity as the theme (Thme) of the act. Below it are two specializations: a graph for a robot washing a truck, and a graph for an animal chasing an entity. Both of these graphs were derived from the top graph by repeated applications of the rule for restricting type labels to subtypes. The graph for an animal chasing an entity has three specialization: a human chasing a human, a cat chasing a mouse, and the dog Macula chasing a Chevrolet. These three graphs were also derived by repeated application of the rule of restriction. The derivation from [Animal] to [Dog: Macula] required both a restriction by type from Animal to Dog and a restriction by referent from the blank to the name Macula.

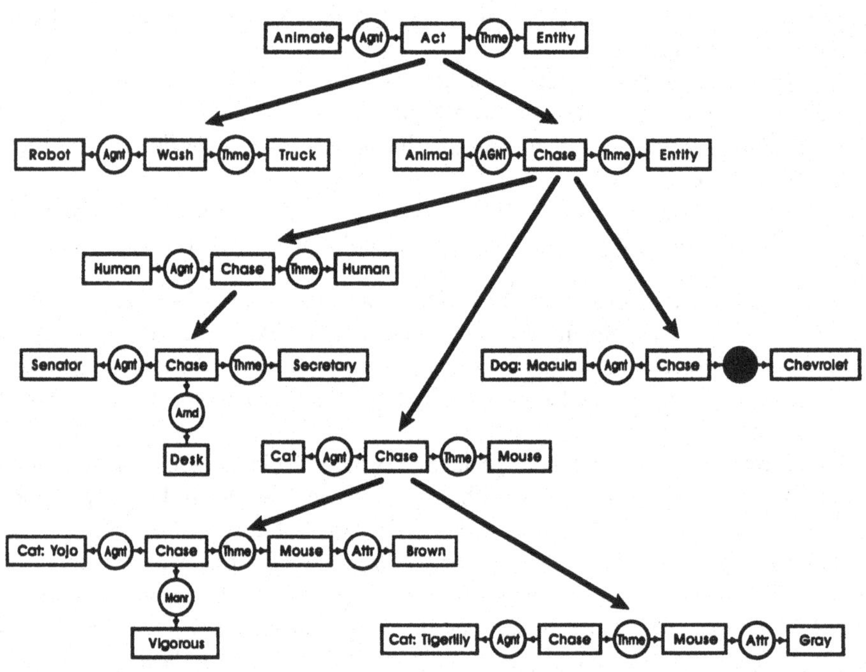

Fig. 4. A generalization hierarchy

Besides restriction, a join was used to specialize the graph for a human chasing a human to the graph for a senator chasing a secretary around a desk. The join was performed by merging the concept [Chase] in the upper graph with the concept [Chase] in the following graph:

```
[Chase] → (Arnd) → [Desk]
```

Since the resulting graph has three relations attached to the concept [Chase], it is not possible to represent the graph on a single line in a linear notation. Instead, a hyphen may be placed after the concept [Chase] to show that the attached relations are continued on subsequent lines:

```
[Chase]-
    (Agnt) → [Senator]
    (Thme) → [Secretary]
    (Arnd) → [Desk]
```

For the continued relations, it is not necessary to show both arcs, since the direction of one arrow implies the direction of the other one.

The two graphs at the bottom of Fig. 4 were derived by both restriction and join. The graph on the left says that the cat Yojo is vigorously chasing a brown mouse. It was derived by restricting [Cat] to [Cat: 'Yojo'] and by joining the following two graphs:

```
[Mouse] → (Attr) → [Brown]

[Chase] → (Manr) → [Vigorous]
```

The relation (Manr) represents manner, and the relation (Attr) represents attribute. The bottom right graph of Fig. 4 says that the cat Tigerlily is chasing a gray mouse. It was derived from the graph above it by one restriction and one join. All the derivations in Fig. 4 can be reversed by applying the generalization rules from the bottom up instead of the specialization rules from the top down: every restriction can be reversed by unrestriction, and every join can be reversed by detach.

The generalization hierarchy, which is drawn as a tree in Fig. 4, is an excerpt from a lattice that defines all the possible generalizations and specializations that are possible with the rules of inference. Ellis, Levinson, and Robinson ([6]) implemented such lattices with high-speed search mechanisms for storing and retrieving graphs. They extended their techniques to systems that can access millions of graphs in time proportional to the logarithm of the size of the hierarchy. Their techniques, which were designed for conceptual graphs, can be applied to any notation, including frames and templates.

5 Frames and Templates

Predicate calculus and conceptual graphs are domain-independent notations that can be applied to any subject whatever. In that respect, they resemble natural languages, which can express anything that anyone can express in any artificial language plus a great deal more. The templates for information extraction and the frames for expert systems are usually highly specialized to a particular application.

One expert system for diagnosing cancer patients represented knowledge in a frame with the following format:

```
(defineType MedPatient
  (supertype Person)
  . . .
  (motherMelanoma (type Boolean)
          (question ('Has the patient's mother had melanoma?')) ))
```

This frame says that a medical patient, MedPatient, has a supertype Person. Then it lists several attributes, including one named motherMelanoma, which has two *facets*: one facet declares that the values of the attribute must be of type Boolean; and the other specifies a character string called a question. Whenever the system needs the current value of the motherMelanoma attribute, it prints the character string on the display screen, and a person answers yes or no. Then the system converts the answer to a Boolean value (T or F), which becomes the value of the attribute.

Such frames are simple, but they omit important details. The words *mother* and *melanoma* appear in a character string that is printed as a question for some person at a computer display. Although the person may know the meaning of those words, the system cannot relate them to the attribute motherMelanoma, which by itself has no more meaning than the character string "MM". Whether or not the system can generate correct answers using values of that attribute depends on how the associated programs happen to process the character strings.

To express those details, Fig. 5 shows a conceptual graph for the sentence *The patient's mother suffered from melanoma.*

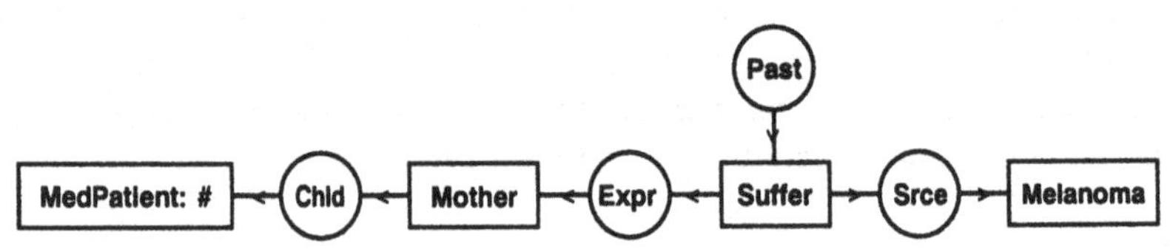

Fig. 5. CG for the English sentence

The concept [MedPatient: #] for the medical patient is linked via the child relation (Chld) to the concept [Mother]. The experiencer (Expr) and source (Srce) relations link the concept [Suffer] to the concepts [Mother] and [Melanoma]. The type hierarchy would show that a medical patient is a type of person; a mother is a woman, which is also a person; and melanoma is a type of cancer, which is also a disease:

```
MedPatient < Person
Mother < Woman < Person
Melanoma < Cancer < Disease
```

The type MedPatient could be introduced by the following definition:

```
type MedPatient(*x) is

    [Person: ?x] ← (Ptnt) ← [TreatMed] → (Agnt) → [Physician].
```

In this graph, the verb *treat* is represented by the type TreatMed to distinguish it from other word senses, such as giving the patient some candy. The definition may be read *The type MedPatient is defined as a person x who is treated by a physician.*

Fig. 6 defines MotherMelanoma as a dyadic relation that links a person x to a Boolean value y, where y is the mode of a proposition that x is the child of a mother who suffered from Melanoma.

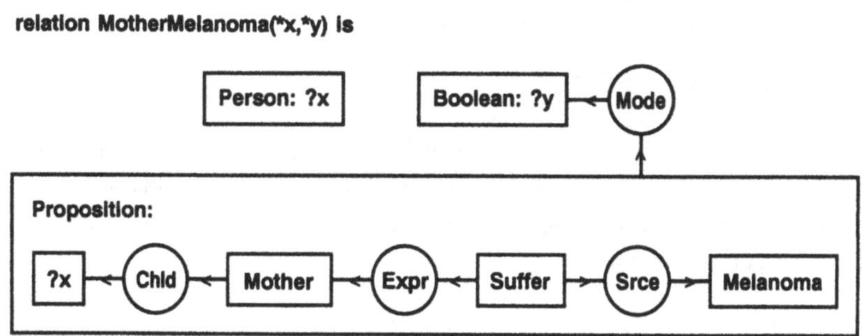

Fig. 6. Definition of the MotherMelanoma relation

The amount of detail required for semantics shows why most expert systems do not have a natural language interface. A system that translated *The patient's mother had melanoma* to Fig. 5 would be more complex than a typical expert system shell. Even then, it would still have to perform further inferences before it could deduce T or F for the motherMelanoma attribute. It is easier to print out a character string and let the user select yes or no from a menu. Yet that solution might make it harder to modify, extend, and link the system to other programs designed for other purposes. Consider some possible extensions:

- If the expert system were later linked to a database so that it could check the patient's records directly, the attributes stored in the database would probably not match the ones needed by the expert system. Instead of storing a motherMelanoma attribute for each patient, the database would be more likely to list the person's mother. Before the system could determine the value of that attribute, someone would have to write a database query or view with the more detailed concepts of Mother, Disease, and Melanoma.

- Besides the prompts, many expert systems include additional character strings for explanations. Many of them are stored as canned phrases that are typed whenever a particular rule is executed. But better explanations would require some tailoring of the strings to insert context-dependent values. As the system becomes more complex, the help, prompts, and explanations could take more space than the rules, and they would have to be revised or rewritten whenever the rules are changed.
- Writing the help, prompt, and explanation messages and keeping them consistent with every modification to the rules is difficult enough with one language, but for a system used in different countries, they would all have to be written and revised for every language.

These issues, which were illustrated in terms of frames, apply equally well to the frame-like IE templates. The definitional mechanisms enable the specialized frames or templates to be defined in terms of the more general representations that support the full detail of the statements in natural language.

6 Lambda Expressions

Besides the basic operators and quantifiers, a system of logic requires some method for defining new types and relations. The traditional method, illustrated in Section 5, is to use a variable, called a *formal parameter*, that appears in on both sides of the definition:

```
type MedPatient(*x) is
   [Person: ?x] ← (Ptnt) ← [TreatMed] → (Agnt) → [Physician].
```

In this example, the left side of the keyword is specifies the name MedPatient, and the right side is an expression that defines it. The symbol x, which links the two sides, is the formal parameter. Such definitions are convenient for defining named types and relations, but the connection of the definition to the name is an unnecessary complication. It creates difficulties for the operations of logic and computation, which may generate intermediate expressions that have no names.

As a systematic method for defining and evaluating functions and relations, the logician Alonzo Church ([2]) invented the *lambda calculus*. In Church's notation, the name can be written by itself on one side of an equation; on the other side, the Greek letter λ is used to mark the formal parameter. That technique, which Church defined for predicate calculus, applies equally well to conceptual graphs:

```
MedPatient =
     [Person: λ ]<-(Ptnt)<-[TreatMed]->(Agnt)->[Physician].
```

With this notation, the name is completely separated from the defining expression, which can be used in any position where the name is used. In particular, a lambda expression can replace the type label of a concept like [MedPatient] or the type constraint on a variable in typed predicate calculus.

To support the lambda notation, Church defined rules of *lambda conversion* for expanding and contracting the expressions. One of the central results of the lambda calculus is the *Church-Rosser theorem*, which says that a nest of multiple lambda expressions may be expanded or contracted in any order and the results will always be equivalent. In effect, the lambda calculus treats functions and relations as *first-class data types*, which can be manipulated and processed like any other kind of data. The equivalent of Church's rules can be stated for conceptual graphs and many other knowledge representations:

- *Type expansion.* Let g be a conceptual graph containing a concept c that has a defined type t and an existential referent (i.e. a blank or $\exists$ as its quantifier). Then the operation of *type expansion* performs the following transformations on g:
  1. The definition of t must be a monadic lambda expression whose body is a conceptual graph b and whose formal parameter p is a concept of b. Let the signature of t be the sequence (s), where s is the type of p.
  2. Remove the type t from the concept c of g, and replace it with s.
  3. Remove the λ marker from the concept p, and replace it with the designator of c.
  4. At this point, the concepts c and p should be identical. Combine the graphs g and b by joining p to c.
- *Relational expansion.* Let g be a conceptual graph containing an n-adic relation r that has a defined type t. Then the operation of *relational expansion* performs the following transformations on g:
  1. The definition of t must be an n-adic lambda expression whose body is a conceptual graph b and whose formal parameters $\langle p_1, ..., p_n \rangle$ are concepts of b. Let the signature of t be the sequence $(s_1,...,s_n)$, where each s_i is the type of p_i.
  2. Remove the relation r from g, and detach each arc i of r from the concept c_i of g.
  3. Remove the λ marker from each parameter p_i, and replace it with the designator of c_i.
  4. For each i from 1 to n, restrict the types of c_i and p_i to their maximal common subtypes. Then combine the graphs g and b by joining each p_i to c_i .

The corresponding rules of *lambda contraction* are the inverses of the rules of lambda expansion: if any conceptual graph g could have been derived by lambda expansion from a CG u, then u may be *contracted* to form u. The expansion rules and theg contraction rules are equivalence rules, which change the appearance of a graph or formula, but they do not change its truth or falsity. Those rules can be used as equivalence operations in the rules of inference stated in Section 3.

7 The IE Paradigm

As many people have observed, the pressures of extracting information at high speed from large volumes of text have led to a new paradigm for computational linguistics. Appelt et al. ([1]) summarized the IE paradigm in three bullet points:

- "Only a fraction of the text is relevant; in the case of the MUC-4 terrorist reports, probably only about 10% is relevant."
- "Information is mapped into a predefined, relatively simple, rigid target representation; this condition holds whenever entry of information into a database is the task."
- "The subtle nuances of meaning and the writer's goals in writing the text are of no interest."

They contrast the IE paradigm with the more traditional task of text understanding:

- "The aim is to make sense of the entire text."
- "The target representation must accommodate the full complexities of language."
- "One wants to recognize the nuances of meaning and the writer's goals."

At a high level of abstraction, this characterization by the logicians at SRI International would apply equally well to all the successful competitors in the MUC and Tipster evaluations. Despite the differences in their approaches to full-text understanding, they converged on a common approach to the IE task. As a result, some observers have come to the conclusion that IE is emerging as a new subfield in computational linguistics.

The central point of this paper is that the convergence of different approaches on a common paradigm is not an accident. At both ends of the research spectrum, the logicians and the Schankians believe that the IE paradigm is a special case of their own approach, despite their sharp disagreements about the best way to approach the task of full-text understanding. To a certain extent, both sides are right, because both the logic-based approach and the Schankian approach are based on the same set of underlying primitives. The canonical formation rules of generalization, specialization, and equivalence can be used to characterize all three approaches to language processing that were discussed in Section 1:

- *Chomskyan.* The starting symbol S for a context-free grammar is a universal generalization: every sentence that is derivable from S by a context-free grammar is a specialization of S, and the parse tree for a sentence is a record of the sequence of specialization rules used to derive it from S. Chomsky's original goal for transformational grammar was to define the equivalence rules that preserve meaning while changing the shape or appearance of a sentence. The evolution of Chomsky's theories through the stages of government and binding (GB) theory to his more recent minimalism has been a search for the fundamental equivalence rules of Universal Grammar.

– *Montagovian.* Instead of focusing on syntax, Montague treated natural language as a disguised version of predicate calculus. His categorial grammars for deriving a sentence are specialization rules associated with lambda-expressions for deriving natural language sentences. Hobbs ([9]) explicitly characterized the semantic interpretation of a sentence as abduction: the search for a specialized formula in logic that implies the more generalized subformulas from which it was derived.
– *Schankian.* Although Roger Schank has denounced logic and logicians as irrelevant, every one of his knowledge representations can be defined as a particular subset of logic with an idiosyncratic notation. Most of them, in fact, represent the existential-conjunctive (EC) subset of logic, whose only operators are the existential quantifier and conjunction. Those two operators, which happen to be the most frequently used operators in formulas derived from natural language text, are also the two principal operators in discourse representation theory, conceptual graphs, and Peirce's existential graphs. The major difference is that Schank has either ignored the other operators or treated them in an ad hoc way, while the logicians have generalized their representations to accommodate all the operators in a systematic framework.

In summary, the canonical formation rules reveal a level of processing that underlies all these approaches. The IE templates represent the special case of EC logic that is common to all of them. The detailed parsing used in text understanding and the sketchy parsing used in IE are both applications of specialization rules; the major difference is that IE focuses only on that part of the available information that is necessary to answer the immediate goal. The subset of information represented in the IE templates can be derived by lambda abstractions from the full information, as discussed in Sections 5 and 6. This view does not solve all the problems of the competing paradigms, but it shows how they are related and how innovations in one approach can be translated to equivalent techniques in the others.

References

1. D. E. Appelt, J. R. Hobbs, J. Bear, D. Israel, and M. Tyson. Fastus: A finite-state processor for information-extraction from real-world text. In *Proceedigs of IJCAI 93*, 1993.
2. A. Church. *The Calculi of Lambda Conversion.* Princeton University Press, Princeton, NJ, 1941.
3. J. Cowie and W. Lehnert. Information extraction. In *Communications of the ACM*, volume 39, pages 80–91, 1996.
4. G. F. DeJong. Prediction and substantiation. In *Cognitive Science*, volume 3, pages 251–273, 1979.
5. G. F. DeJong. An overview of the frump system. In W. G. Lehnert & M. H. Ringle, editor, *Strategies for Natual Language Processing*, pages 149–176. Kluwer Academic Publishers, Erlbaum, Hillsdale, NJ, 1982.
6. G. Ellis, R. A. Levinson, and P. J. Robinson. Managing complex objects in peirce. In *International J. of Human-Computer Studies*, volume 41, pages 109–148, 1994.

7. L. Hirschman and M. Vilain. Extracting information from the muc. In *ACL Tutorial*, volume 41, pages 109–148, 1995.
8. J. R. Hobbs, D. Appelt, J. Bear, D. Israel, M. Kameyama, M. Stickel, and M. Tyson. Fastus: A cascaded finite-state transducer for extracting information from natural-language text. In E. Roche & Y.Schabes, editor, *Finite-State Language Processing*, pages 383–406. MIT Press, Cambridge, MA, 1997.
9. J. R. Hobbs, M. Stickel, D. Appelt, and P. Martin. Interpretation as abduction. In *Artificial Intelligence*, volume 63, 1-2, pages 69–142, 1993.
10. C. S. Peirce. On the algebra of logic. In *American Journal of Mathematics*, volume 7, pages 180–202, 1885.
11. Don D. Roberts. *The Existential Graphs of Charles S. Peirce*. Mouton, The Hague, 1973.
12. J. F. Sowa. *Conceptual Structures: Information Processing in Mind and Machine*. Addison-Wesley, Reading, MA, 1984.
13. J. F. Sowa. The infinite variety of logics. In O. Herzog & A. Günter, editor, *KI-98: Advances in Artificial Intelligence, LNAI 1504*, pages 31–53. Springer-Verlag, Berlin, 1998.
14. J. F. Sowa. *Knowledge Representation: Logical, Computational, and Philosophical Foundations*. PWS, Pacific Grove, CA, 1999.

Inferential Information Extraction

Marc Vilain

The MITRE Corporation,
Bedford, Mass. 01730, USA
mbv@mitre.org

Abstract. This paper is concerned with an outlook on information extraction (IE) that is steeped to a large extent in the traditional semantic notion of inferential reasoning. We make the case for a continued presence of inferential methods in IE, despite the ongoing trend towards simpler extraction processing models. We demonstrate the role of this kind of inference in the *Alembic* message understanding system, and also discuss the upstream syntactic processing that enables this. We present the finite-state parsing models that until recently have served this role, and cover at some length the issues of semantic interpretation that they require. As a pointer towards work to come, we also mention briefly our work in progress on parsing via grammatical relations, an approach that we hope will add great generality to our extraction framework.

1 From Message Understanding to Information Extraction

Even the casual observer of our field must have noted its transformation over the course of the past ten years. Indeed, the very name of the endeavor has changed. We entered the decade speaking of message understanding, with all the lofty connotations that it entailed: cognitive modeling, linguistic inspiration, commonsense reasoning, and artificial intelligence. We leave the decade speaking of information extraction, a term that bespeaks a growing engineering focus, as well as more realistic and more quantifiable goals. And indeed, the force that has most propelled the transformation of this particular branch of computational linguistics is the same that has affected many other aspects of our field: a healthy concern with measuring the performance of our models, and by corollary the progress of the community as a whole.

The same casual observer will also have noted not just a change of nomenclature and a change of evaluational method, but also many changes in the repertory of techniques arrayed against the problem. We can judge these changes by simply considering the participants in the MUC community evaluations, a sample that is admittedly biased but influential. The participants in the first few MUC evaluations for the most part inherited the architectures of the previous decade's natural language database interfaces, namely the triumvirate of parser, semantic interpreter, and pragmatics/discourse processor. However, in the face of this preponderance of "traditional" systems, a small number of participants brought to these early MUC evaluations systems that were based on much simpler methods.

Pazienza (Ed.): Information Extraction, LNAI 1714, pp. 95–119, 1999.

As goes the cliché, the rest is history. In the third MUC, one of these simpler systems brought home the highest score. This was the work of Lehnert and her colleagues [1], who replaced the traditional parsing, interpretation, and discourse modules with (respectively) a simple phrase finder, event pattern matcher, and template merging procedure. By the fourth MUC, one of the established "traditional" groups (SRI International) had abandoned their original system and recast the approach of Lehnert's group in terms of cascades of finite-state transducers [2]. By the seventh MUC evaluation (and the final one under this name - for the time being), architectures based on some variant of finite-state machines had completely come to dominate the participating systems.

Our casual obsever may well ask: has the information extraction community fallen prey as a group to technological fashion? Though cynics may speak in these terms, the truth is that these newer approaches provide a host of advantages. Finite-state interpreters tend to be fast. The simplicity of the methods make them easy to develop and - more importantly - make it easy to adapt them to new problem definitions. This latter point can not be sufficiently emphasized: the first few of the MUC evaluations afforded developpers a period of quite literally years in which to port their systems to the common evaluational domain. In contrast, the final two evaluations in the series allowed only four weeks of system development, a lag time that is much more commensurate with realistic expectations. Finally, simple methods tend almost universally to be better suited to automatic or semi-automatic adaptation by means of machine learning. In the MUC evaluations (and the related MET evaluations), we have seen this in systems fielded by such diverse groups as the University of Massachusetts [3], New York University [4], the University of Edinburgh [5], BBN [6], the University of New Mexico [7], SRA [8], our own group at MITRE [9], and others.

2 Is Semantics Irrelevant?

The lesson to be drawn from this abbreviated history of the Message Understanding Conferences would thus appear to be that great progress can be made through simplifications to syntax. And indeed, if syntax is simplified in a suitable way, then semantic processing can be reduced to simple pattern matching over the output of the syntactic processor. In information extraction, semantic processing arguably amounts to detecting and merging individuals or events that are of relevance to the extraction task. If syntax is simplified enough, then syntactic "parses" can be cast in terms of these relevant classes of events and individuals, much as in the semantic grammars of 20 years ago (*e.g.*, [10]). Semantic processing then becomes itself a parsing problem, in this case, parsing the output stream of the syntactic processor.

Indeed, to pick just one example, one of the more successful system architectures to have come out of this trend towards simpler syntax is that of FASTUS [2], in which the entire extraction task is performed by successive stages of a finite-state transducer cascade. Specifically, FASTUS first parses a text into names, small non-recursive nominal chunks (noun groups) and small verbal chunks (verb groups); technically speaking, the text's original sequence of characters has been replaced by a sequence written in the alphabet of chunks. These are then further parsed into partial event descriptions (partial templates, a.k.a. partial frames), thus producing a sequence written in the alphabet of templates, and so on.

Notably absent in this process is any notion of logical form, of propositional representation, or of any of the other trappings of formal semantics. Our casual observer may legitimately ask: Has traditional semantics become irrelevant?

In fact, traditional semantics has not so much become irrelevant, as has become simplified and streamlined in much the same way as has syntax. Semantic individuals have been replaced by instances of event templates, and propositional facts have been replaced by the slots of template frames. So the question is not so much whether traditional semantic representations have become irrelevant, so much as whether there is still relevance to the kinds of processing enabled by traditional semantics, in particular inference and equality reasoning.

If we mention these two classes of semantic reasoning, it is because they have long been a part of the semantic processing in our own message understanding system, *Alembic.*[1] Alembic is unusual among recent message understanding systems in that we have attempted with its architecture not to throw out the semantics baby along with the syntax bathwater. In Alembic, semantic processing occurs at a distinct semantic level, where the analysis focuses on the facts in a text, as distinct from the strings of the text. And though we have been actively investigating current notions of simplified syntax through our own approach to phrase parsing, Alembic has always relied strongly on the inferential processes of its semantic underpinnings.

This synthesis between non-traditional syntax and traditional semantics is enabled by the idiosyncratic brand of semantics that Alembic has adopted.We will give many details below, but the aspect of the approach of most relevance here, is that Alembic's semantic framework supports incremental degrees of syntactic analysis. To be specific, the semantic interpretation of a syntactic analysis is given in terms of propositional facts; this is much like a flattened version of the unscoped interpretations in such work as the SRI core language engine. Syntactic analyses inform the semantic representation of texts by producing various degrees of these propositional facts.

Shallower analyses produce fewer facts, deeper ones produce more. ¿From the perspective of semantics, parses need therefore neither be complete nor comprehensive.

2.1 A Road Map of this Paper

This is most readily understood by tracing the actual course of syntactic processing in Alembic and by noting the corresponding interpretations. As this is something of an involved story, roughly the first third of this paper focuses on

[1] An alembic is an archaic distillation apparatus, the mainstay of the alchemical laboratories of old.

the issues of parsing and interpretation. We cover, in particular, our approach to phrase parsing based on rule sequences and our semantic interpretation framework that relies on tractable propositional inference. The middle third is concerned with the approach to task-level extraction that we investigated for some years; it too was built on these same syntactic and semantic mechanisms.

This much, at least is historical material. In the second half of this paper, we turn to our current extraction research, focusing in particular on a new approach to syntax based on core phrases (chunks) and on grammatical relations. This new approach produces a level of analysis that we believe can be more readily attained than in standard linguistic parsing, that is directly interpretable into semantic representations, and that provides a task-independent foundation for task-level extraction. This is very recent work, and though we are buoyed by our results to date, these results are primarily concerned with the coverage and learnability of this approach, not its specific application to extraction. The paper thus ends on somewhat of a speculative note, poised between the familiar techniques of our earlier work and the untapped potential of our new approach.

3 A Stratified Approach to Syntax

We noted above that the approach taken to syntactic processing in Alembic is stratified. Rather than treating the syntactic analysis of a text as a single monolithic task (as in traditional natural language parsing), parsing proceeds as a sequence of specialized processes. Each is responsible for a fraction of the overall analysis, and the fractional output that each produces receives its own level of semantic interpretation. In particular, Alembic currently recognizes the following initial steps of syntactic analysis:

- Preliminaries: numerals and other numeric forms, such as expressions of money, measurements, and the ilk.
- Titles: various fixed albeit productive forms of identification for individuals. These include honorifics (*Mr.*), appointed and elected titles (*Israeli prime minister-elect*), and job descriptions (*noted photographer*).
- Names: these correspond to the named entity level of MUC, and identify the names of people, organizations, locations, and dates or times.
- SLAP: short for simple local appositional parsing. This level combines several of the preceding ones to provide an analysis of stereotypical noun-noun appositions found in journalistic text, *e.g.*, *John J. Dooner Jr., age 45* or *Mr. Daedalus, president and chief executive officer of Cambridge-based Dreadco*).

These first four levels of processing are to be understood as parsing subgrammars, principally those for names and for the appositional references so ubiquitous in journalistic text. From a strictly theoretical standpoint, these subgrammars may appear of little interest, as the languages they generate are typically subsumed by those generated by a standard grammar of noun phrases. From a practical perspective, however, designating these levels independently and parsing them with specialists removes a major degree of ambiguity from the general parsing process. Indeed, a common experience in writing a standard phrase structure grammar for journalistic text is that the details of these journalistic sub-grammars are legion, and the proliferation of derivational rules required to cover them rapidly leads to an explosive growth of the parsing search space. For this reason, a number of message understanding efforts in the early 90's implemented finite-state pre-processors to parse these sub-grammars ahead of the primary phase of syntactic analysis [11]. The initial levels of syntactic analysis in Alembic are in this spirit: they produce a broad range of the tokens on which the primary syntactic analysis operates.

Beyond these pre-parsing stages come the primary stages of syntactic analysis. We have explored several approaches towards this: combinatory categorial grammar (CCG) [12], task-specific finite-state parsing, and our current approach based on core phrases and grammatical relations. Of the CCG endeavor, we will have little to say, other than to note that we chose it not simply out of inexperience with the challenge of parsing real-world texts, but out of an appreciation for its ready mapping from syntax to semantics. Although the CCG parser has long since been retired, its legacy remains in the form of its associated semantic representations. These have continued to serve as the basis of semantic interpretation for the various approaches to parsing that we have since investigated.

3.1 Parsing with Phrase Rule Sequences

Another point of commonality between Alembic's more recent approaches to syntax, is that to varrying degrees they rely on a finite-state phrase parser based on rule sequences [9]. The pre-parsing stages are entirely performed using the rule sequence parser; the same is true for the task-specific phrase parsing. Even our recent grammatical relations approach relies on the rule sequence parser to produce a finite-state-like chunking of noun groups, verb groups, and so forth.

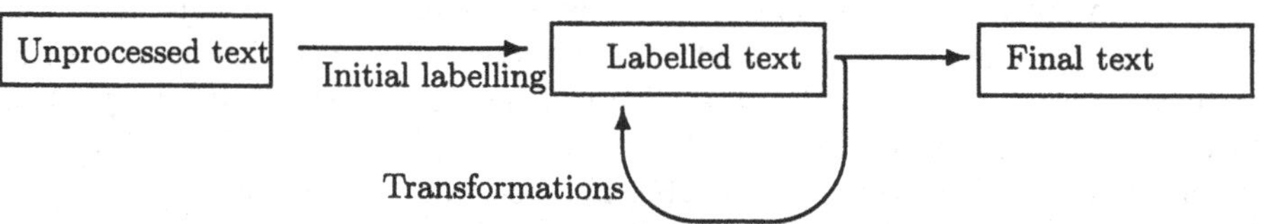

Fig. 1. Architecture of a Rule Sequence Processor

This rule-sequence phrase parser (or phraser, for short)is unusual in that it is amenable to both machine learning and hand-tailored engineering. As a rule sequence processor, it is based on the approach popularized by Eric Brill in his widely-distributed part-of-speech tagger [13,14]. As with other rule sequence processors, our phrase rule parser operates in several steps (see Fig. 1). Given a string, a rule sequence processor begins by assigning an initial labelling to the string. This initial labelling is then incrementally modified by applying a sequence of transformation rules; each rule in the sequence attempts to improve the labelling of the string by patching any residual errors left in place by the preceding rules or by the initial labelling.

In the Alembic phraser, the initial labelling process is responsible for seeding a string with likely candidate phrases of various kinds. This seeding process is driven by word lists, part-of-speech information, and pre-taggings provided by any pre-parsers that may have previously run. To see this, consider the following example, drawn from the MUC-6 corpus:

> *McCann made official what had been widely anticipated: Mr. James, 57 years old, is stepping down as chief executive officer on July 1 and will retire as chairman at the end of the year.*

Say, for the sake of argument, that we are at the beginning of the name-tagging stage proper. By this point of processing, several pre-parsers have been run, yielding phrasal analyses for numbers, titles, and dates. In addition, the initial labelling computed for the purposes of name tagging identifies runs of proper nouns, meaning in our case runs of lexemes tagged with the NNP part of speech (Alembic runs a version of the Brill part-of-speech tagger ahead of all parsing stages). This yields the following labelling of the MUC-6 example, where SGML elements designate the phrases that have been parsed by the phraser.

> *<none>McCann</none> made official what had been widely anticipated: <ttl>Mr.</ttl> <none>James</none>, <num>57</num> years old, is stepping down as <ttl>chief executive officer</ttl> on <date>July 1</date> and will retire as <ttl>chairman</ttl> at the end of the year.*

The *<ttl>*, *<date>*, and *<num>* elements are produced by pre-parsing, and the phrases identified by *<none>* are the initial labelling of the name-tagging stage. Once this initial phrasing has taken place, the phraser proceeds with phrase identification proper. This is driven by a sequence of phrase-finding rules. Each rule in the sequence is applied in turn against all of the phrases in all the sentences under analysis. If the antecedents of the rule are satisfied by a phrase, then the action indicated by the rule is executed immediately. The action can either change the label of the satisfying phrase, grow its boundaries, or create new phrases. After the ith rule is applied in this way against every phrase in all the sentences, the $i+1$st rule is applied in the same way, until all rules have been applied. After all of the rules have been applied, the phraser is done.

It is important to note that the search strategy in the phraser differs significantly from that in standard parsers. In standard parsing, one searches for any and all rules whose antecedents might apply given the state of the parser's chart: all these rules become candidates for application, and indeed they all are applied (modulo higher-order search control). In our phraser, only the current rule in a rule sequence is tested: the rule is applied wherever this test succeeds, and the rule is never revisited at any subsequent stage of processing. After the final rule of a sequence is run, no further processing occurs.

The language of the phraser rules is as simple as their control strategy. Rules can test lexemes to the left and right of the phrase, or they can look at the lexemes in the phrase. Tests in turn can be part-of-speech queries, literal lexeme matches, tests for the presence of neighboring phrases, etc. There are several reasons for keeping this rule language simple. In the case of hand-crafted rules, it facilitates the process of designing a rule sequence. In the case of machine-learned rules, it restricts the size of the search space on each epoch of the learning regimen, thus making it tractable. In either case, the overall processing power derives as much from the fact that the rules are sequenced, and feed each other in turn, as it does from the expressiveness of the rule language.

To make this clearer, consider a simple named entity rule that is applied to identifying persons.

```
(def-phraser-rule
  CONDITIONS (phrase phrase-label NONE)
             (left-1 phrase-label TTL)
  ACTIONS    (set-label PERSON))
```

This rule changes the label of a phrase from *none* to *person* if the phrase is bordered one term to its left by a *ttl* phrase. On the sample sentence, this rule causes *<ttl>Mr.</ttl> <none>James</none>* to become relabelled as *<ttl>Mr.</ttl> <person>James</person>*

Once rules such as this have run, the labelings they instantiate become available as input to subsequent rules in the sequence, or to downstream stages of phrase parsing. As with other sequence-based processors, phraser rules tend to over-generalize early in the rule sequence and thus make errors that are eventually patched applies later rules in the sequence. This is particularly obvious in the case of machine-learned rules, where often the learning procedure makes sweeping generalizations with rules that appear early in a sequence, and then refines these generalizations with subsequent rules in the sequence.

4 Semantic Representation in Alembic

We have alluded several times to the centrality of Alembic's semantic representation. It has three roles.

- As a representational substrate, it records propositions encoding the semantics of parsed phrases;
- As an equational system, it allows initially distinct semantic individuals to be equated to each other, and allows propositions about these individuals to be merged through congruence closure.
- As a limited inference system, it allows domain-specific and general constraints to be instantiated through carefully controlled forward-chaining.

This representational architecture draws its inspiration from McAllester's RUP [15], a truth maintenance system that has received widespread use in the qualitative reasoning community. Our purpose here is, of course, not qualitative reasoning so much as semantic interpretation, and our approach differs significantly from McAllester's in the actual details - see [16,17].

4.1 Phrase Interpretation

Facts enter the propositional database as the result of phrase interpretation. The phrase interpreter is itself controlled by mapping functions in the Montague mold, meaning in this case, having one mapping per phrase type. Base-level phrases, *i.e.* phrases with no embedded phrases, are mapped to unary interpretations. The *<person>* phrase in

Mr. <person>James</person>, 57 years old

for example is mapped to the following propositional fact. Note the *pers-01* term in this proposition: it designates the semantic individual denoted by the phrase, and is generated in the process of interpretation.

```
person(pers-01)                  ; "Mr. James"
```

Complex phrases, those with embedded phrases, are typically interpreted as conjuncts of simpler interpretations. Consider the phrase "Mr. James, 57 years old" which is parsed by the phraser as follows. Note in particular that the overall person-age apposition is itself parsed as a person phrase.

<person><person>Mr. James</person>,
<age><num>57</num> years old</age></person>

The treatment of age appositions is compositional, as is the case for the interpretation of all but a few complex phrases. Once again, the embedded base-level phrase ends up interpreted as a unary person fact. The semantic account of the overall apposition ends up as a `has-age` relation modifying `pers-01`, the semantic individual for the embedded person phrase. This proposition designates the semantic relationship between a person and that person's age. More precisely, the following facts are added to the inferential database.

```
person(pers-01)                  ; "Mr. James"
age(age-02)                      ; "57 years old"
has-age((pers-01 age-02) ha-03) ; "Mr. james, 57 years old"
```

What appears to be a spare argument to the has-age predicate above is the event individual for the predicate. Such arguments denote events themselves (in this case the event of being a particular number of years old), as opposed to the individuals participating in the events (the individual and his or her age). This treatment is similar to the partial Davidsonian analysis of events due to Hobbs [18]. Note that event individuals are by definition only associated with relations, not unary predicates.

As a point of clarification, note that the inference system does not encode facts at the predicate calculus level so much as at the interpretation level made popular in such systems as the SRI core language engine [19,20]. In other words, the representation is actually a structured attribute-value graph such as the following, which encodes the age apposition above.

```
[[head person]
[proxy pers-01]
[modifiers ([[head has-age]
            [proxy ha-03]
            [arguments (pers-01 [[head age]
                                 [proxy age-02]])]])]]
```

The first two fields correspond to the matrix phrase: the head field is a semantic sort, and the proxy field holds the designator for the semantic individual denoted by the phrase. The interpretation encoding the overall apposition ends up in the modifiers slot, an approach adopted from the standard linguistic account of phrase modification. Inference in Alembic is actually performed directly on interpretation structures, and there is no need for a separate translation from interpretations to more traditional-looking propositions. The propositional notation is more perspicuous to the reader, and we have adopted it here.

4.2 Interpreting Complex Phrases: Some Additional Details

In the preceding section, we noted briefly an example of person-age apposition, and glossed over the details of how this syntactic construct was actually parsed and interpreted. These details are worth pursuing, since they shed further light on Alembic's idiosyncratic approach. Indeed, consider another simple example, drawn from elsewhere in the same sample MUC-6 article: "*Walter Rawleigh Jr., retired chairman of Mobil Corp.*" Syntactically, this apposition is treated by the so-called SLAP phase of our stratified pre-parsing. The role of this phase is to capture and normalize the commonplace journalistic combinations of person names, organizations, and titles. In the English journalistic style, these manifest themselves primarily as NP-NP appositions. To wit:

<person>
<person>Walter Rawleigh Jr.</person>
<ttl>
<ttl>retired
<ttl>chairman</ttl>
<ttl> of
<org>Mobil Corp.>
</ttl>
</person>

These embeddings are produced by the SLAP analysis, and indicate modifier and argument-mapping relationships in much the same way as would a more traditional grammar of the noun phrase. In effect, the SLAP processing phase implements a rudimentary $\overline{X}$ analysis for named entities and related constructs.[2] In this way, named entity phrases denoting people, organizations, and jobs are grown into larger phrases of the same type, but with embedded modifiers and more-complex denotations. Semantically, these larger phrases are translated to propositional form by appropriately mapping the grammatical relationships of modification (such as apposition or function application). The function application of a job title phrase to an organization via of-PP attachment is mapped to a `job` proposition, name-job appositions map to `has-job` propositions, and so forth. Interpreting the sample above, we obtain the following.

```
organization(org-04)               ; "Mobil Corp."
title(ttl-05)                      ; "chairman"
retired-ttl(ttl-05)                ; "retired"
job((ttl-05 org-04) job-06)        ; "retired chairman of Mobil"
                                   ;  NB: job = title + org
person(p-07)                       ; "Walter Rawleigh Jr."
holds-job((p-07 job-06) h-08)      ; person-job apposition
```

What makes this tenable as a domain-independent analysis is two things: the ubiquitous nature of this journalistic style on the one hand, and the relatively restricted repertoire of semantic relations to which the SLAP analysis is mapped. Indeed, part of the object here is to normalize the diversity of syntactic forms in which these constructs appear, *e.g.* possessive pre-determiners (*"Mobil's retired chairman"*), prenominal modifiers (*"retired Mobil Corp. chairman"*), PP attachement (*retired chairman of Mobil Corp.*), and so on. Despite the variance of syntactic form, all three of these receive the same underlying semantic representation. This is one of the major advantages of having an explicit semantic level, and is one of the reasons that we did not jettison Alembic's semantic models at the time that we retired the categorial grammar parser.

4.3 Equality Reasoning

Another strength that Alembic derives from this representational framework is due to its equality mechanism. This sub-component allows one to make two semantic individuals co-designating, *i.e.*, to equate them. Facts that formerly held of only one individual are then copied to its co-designating siblings. This in turn enables inference that may have been previously inhibited because the necessary antecedents were distributed over (what were then) distinct individuals.

This equality machinery is exploited at many levels in processing semantic and domain constraints. One of the clearest such uses is in enforcing the semantics of coreference, either definite reference or appositional coreference. Take for

[2] There is some irony to this, since a hallmark of $\overline{X}$ syntax is its treatment of large scale attachments: prepositional phrases, relative clasuses, *etc.* In our current framework, these large-scale attachments are handled by grammatical relations, and it is only the minutiae that are treated with an $\overline{X}$ approach.

example the following phrase from the same sample MUC-6 message, which we show here as parsed by the phraser.

<org>
<org>Creative Artists Agency</org>,
<orgnp>the big <loc>Hollywood</loc> talent agency</orgnp>
</org>

In propositional terms, the embedded organization is interpreted as

```
organization(org-09)              ; "Creative Artists Agency"
```

The appositive noun phrase is interpreted as

```
organization(org-10)              ; "the ... agency"
geo-region(geo-11)                ; "Hollywood"
has-loc((org-10 geo-11) hl-12)    ; locational pre-modifier
```

Pressing on, the phraser parses the overall org-orgnp apposition as an overarching org. To interpret the apposition, the interpreter also adds the following proposition to the database.

```
eq((org-09, org-10) eq-13)
```

This ultimately causes *org-09* and *org-06* to become co-designating through the equality system, and the following fact appears in the inferential database.

```
has-loc((org-09, geo-07) hl-14)   ; i.e., Creative Artists
                                  ; is located in Hollywood
```

This propagation of facts from one individual to its co-designating siblings is the heart of our coreference mechanism. Its repercussions are particularly critical to the subsequent stage of extraction. By propagating facts in this way, we can dramatically simplify the

process of collating information into extraction records (templates, to use the MUC term). This is so because all the information relevant to, say, an individual company will have been attached to that company by equality reasoning.

4.4 Inference

The final role of the Alembic representation component is to derive new facts through the application of limited forward inference. By limited inference, we mean unit clause resolution, an inference strategy inherited from McAllester's approach, but also noted in some form in the work of Frisch and Patel-Schneider. In the general case, unit clause resolution is incomplete as a decision procedure, even restricted to the propositional calculus without quantifiers. However, there is a class of axioms for which the strategy yields a complete and tractable inference procedure. This is the so-called DATALOG class, and tractability is guaranteed just in case the axioms meet a syntactic well-formedness criterion (namely that their variables can be sorted into proper dependency trees). One of the more curious aspects of this approach is that there is good reason to believe that for the specific case of natural language inference, this criterion is met in a widespread way (see again [16]).

These details are interesting in their own right, but our purpose here is primarily concerned with how inference supports information extraction in Alembic. We will thus have little more to say about Alembic's tractable deduction machinery, other than in the context of extraction per se.

5 Task-Specific Extraction

With the syntactic and representational comments in the preceding sections, we have covered the domain-independent foundation upon which Alembic performs task-specific extraction. To recapitulate the main points so far:

- On the syntactic side, Alembic operates by stratified parsing. Cumulative levels of analysis produce an incrementally detailed syntactic analysis of a text.
- On the interpretation side, the cumulative layers of parsing produce cumulative semantic interpretations in a framework that (for our purposes) can be viewed as propositional. In particular, each subsequent level of parsing produces a subsequently deeper semantics.
- On the inferential side, equality reasoning collapses separate semantic individuals into single entities and merges facts that would otherwise be distributed across a text.

We can now turn our attention to the way in which Alembic performs task-specific extraction. This involves both syntactic and semantic correlates. Syntax, as always, groups the participants of events and maps them to their corresponding grammatical roles. Semantics, in the form of interpretation and inference, maps events to task-specific entities, provides domain constraints, and models discourse by merging entities and events through equality reasoning.

5.1 Task-Specific Extraction: Syntax

Historically, Alembic has approached the syntactic aspect of this task through domain-specific phrase parsing rules. In other words, just as in CIRCUS [1], FASTUS [2], and similar systems, we have approached the problem with a finite-state-like level in our parsing cascade. In our case, this amounted to a task-specific level in our stratified parsing scheme, implemented (as with the pre-parsers) through the Alembic phrse rule parser. For example, in the management transition task made popular by MUC-6, we had a phrase-parsing rule sequence that identified relevant clauses, *e.g.* "Smith resigned", "Jones will step down as CEO", "Williams was promoted to chief partner", and so forth.

This is, however, not an especially satisfactory approach in the long-term, as it requires composing a large number of domain-specific pattern-parsing rules, rules which have little chance of finding applicability to new domains (most of the domain-independent analysis having already been performed by pre-parsing). What is more, many of these rules end up being simply syntactic variations one of the other, *e.g.*, a rule for the "step down" pattern in the active voice, one for relative clauses, one for reduced relatives, and so forth. One approach towards reducing this latter rule-writing burden is through automated pattern expansion, an approach taken by Appelt *et al* [21] as well as by Grishman and his colleagues [4]. Adapting the extraction system to a new task still requires writing task-specific parsing patterns, but these are specified in an abstract syntactic form, which then gets expanded into specific rule patterns that cover the range of syntactic variations(active voice, relative clause, etc).

Our recent work takes an alternative approach to decreasing the burden of domain engineering, through grammatical relations parsing. This is the subject of the final section of this paper, and deferring that discussion until then, we will assume for the remainder of this section that Alembic models the syntactic aspect of a domain through some kind of task-specific phrase parsing. For expository purposes, we will assume that Alembic generates obvious-sounding phrases that span the relevant events of the MUC-6 management transition domain, for instance:

<org>McCann</org> made official what had been widely anticipated:
<stepdown>
Mr. <person>James</person>, 57 years old, is stepping down
as <ttl>chief executiveofficer</ttl> on <date>July 1</date>.
</stepdown>
<succeed-passive>
...He will be succeeded by Mr. <person>Dooner</person>, 45.
</succeed-passive>

5.2 Task-Specific Extraction: Semantics

Task-specific phrase types are interpreted and reasoned with in much the same way as domain-independent ones. So for example, the *stepdown* and *succeed* or *succeed-passive* phrase types map to propositions ranging over task-specific relations, *e.g. job-in*, *job-out*, *suceed*, and so on. These facts enter into referential and inferential reasoning in the same way as facts corresponding to phrases that were derived by domain-independent

parsing.

A simple example of this can be seen in our treatment of journalistic SLAP appositions. Recall or analysis of the person-job apposition *"Walter Rawleigh Jr., retired chairman of Mobil Corp."*.

```
organization(org-04)            ; "Mobil Corp."
title(ttl-05)                   ; "chairman"
```

```
retired-ttl(ttl-05)                ; "retired"
job((ttl-05 org-04) job-06)        ; "retired chairman of Mobil"
                                   ;  NB: job = title + org
person(p-07)                       ; "Walter Rawleigh Jr."
holds-job((p-07 job-06) h-08)      ; person-job apposition
```

This much, at least, represents the domain-independent semantics of this sentence fragment. But task-specific extraction is performed on task-specific semantics, and these facts need to be mapped to the relevant predicates for the task, in this case a `job-out` fact. The job of enforcing these kinds of domain-specific constraints falls to Alembic's inference mechanism, and the particular inference rule that maps these propositions to a `job-out` fact is as follows.

```
job-out(?p ?t ?o) <- holds-job((?p ?j) -)
                     + job((?t ?o) ?j)
                     + retired-ttl(?t)
```

The antecedents of the rule (or premises) are to the right of the back-arrow, and the consequent (or conclusion) is to the left. Variables are indicated by names that start with a question mark or by the "don't care" indicator, a hyphen. In this particular instance, the rule matches the `holds-job` proposition, and binds the `?j` variable in its argument list to what is expected to be an instance of a `job`. This variable appears again as the event instance of the `job` predicate, which in the process of matching further binds the `?t` variable in its argument list, this time to what is expected to be a title. The rule adds a `job-out` fact just in case `retired-ttl` is also found to be true of `?t`. In this case, the rule yields `job-out((pers-07 ttl-05 org-04) jo-15)`. This fact is all that is required for downstream stages of processing to subsequently issue the appropriate template output for this management transition task.

5.3 Task-Specific Extraction: Discourse Inference

It is not always, however, that task-specific facts can be inferred in this simple compositional way from what amounts to little more than local appositional analysis. The interesting cases of domain inference encode discourse considerations. In the MUC-6 management transition task, for example, succession events are not always fully fleshed out, but depend for their complete interpretation on information provided earlier in the discourse. In the sample message that we have been scutinizing here, this kind of contextualized interpretation is required to combine the information contained in these two key sentences.

Yesterday, McCann made official what had been widely anticipated: Mr. James, 57 years old, is stepping down as chief executive officer on July 1. [...] He will be succeeded by Mr. Dooner, 45.

In particular, the `job-out` interpretation for *James* must somehow incorporate the fact that he is leaving *McCann*. Further, the `job-in` interpretation for *Dooner* must obliquely note from the facts about *James* that the former is entering the same job at the same company that the latter is leaving.

Discourse-based reasoning such as this is a particularly elegant example of what Alembic does with inference. To describe this, we need to introduce three notions. First, Alembic distinguishes between rules that fall under traditional control of inference and those that fall under sequenced control. The former are available at all points during the inference process, as in standard forward-chaining regimens. Sequenced rules operate as a Brill rule sequence, i.e., discourse inference starts by evaluating the first rule in the sequence, instantiating its consequent wherever its antecedents match, going on to the second rule, and proceeding in this way until the end of the sequence is reached. After each rule has been run at its place in the sequence, it is never reconsidered.

The second important notion that we need to introduce is that of a second-order test for boundedness of variables, meaning in this case the determination of whether a predicate instantiated during rule matching leaves one or more variables unbound. For example, the sentence announcing *James*' resignation in our example produces the following interpretation.

```
person(pers-01)                       ; Mr. James
title(ttl-16)                         ; CEO
job-out((pers-01 ttl-16 org-x) jo-17) ; org-x is not bound
```

The `job-out` fact added by semantic interpretation leaves a variable unbound - indeed, `job-out` is a three-place predicate, connecting a person, title, and an organization. In the present case the variable normally bound to an organization (`org-x`) is left unassigned, since no mention of is made in the immediate clause of the organization from which *James* is resigning. This can be detected in an inference rule by invoking the `unbound?` predicate, as in:

```
job-out(?p ?t ?o) + unbound?(?o) ...
```

The discourse inference to be made here is of course that the missing organization is *McCann*, saliently mentioned earlier in the sentence, but not in the present clause. This we arrive at through a simple table-based context model, the third notion that we noted above. In particular, the predicate `in-ctxt(x, y, T)` is true just in case the fact `T(y)` resulted from the semantic interpretation of the "most salient phrase in the context" of the phrase producing the interpretation with proxy x. For our purposes, this model of contextual saliency is extraordinarily simple-minded: it simply evaluates y to be the most chronologically recent relevant mention that precedes the mention of `x`. But even this simple-minded scheme allows us to complete the `job-out` fact above by instantiating its missing organization argument. The relevant rule is

```
job-out((- - ?org) ?j) <- job-out((- - ?o) ?j)
                          + unbound?(?o)
                          + in-ctxt(?j ?org ORGANIZATION)
```

In the present case, the first antecedent of the rule matches the `job-out` interpretation of the sentence fragment, the second antecedent determines that the organization element is missing, and the third antecedent finds a potentially suitable organization through the context model. The consequent of the rule instantiates this new organization as the third argument of the original `job-out` fact (this happens as a result of the two `job-out` patterns sharing a proxy variable – `j`).

This rule may appear to be hopelessly second-order because of the mention of a predicate name (`ORGANIZATION`) in the `in-ctxt` term. But in fact, this type argument is a constant – we do not allow quantification over such terms – and so the rule overall can be thought of as a shortcut for a class of first-order two-place predicates like `organization-in-ctxt`. Finally, note that the rule interpreter escapes to a specialized table-lookup mechanism to evaluate such predicates, as the alternative is to have large numbers of these facts clutter up the propositional database.

Discourse-processing rules such as this one belong to a discourse-related rule sequence that is run after Alembic is done with parsing, interpretation, and any standard inference that should follow from these compositional processes. The fact that discourse inference is sequence-based allows for a degree of controlled non-monotonic reasoning. Indeed, we have just seen a case where a rule adds a fact to the database precisely because its antecedents failed to match such a fact (or more precisely, failed to instantiate a variable). This is exactly the kind of inference that was sought in early work on non-monotonic reasoning, especially non-monotonic truth maintenance systems [22]. Both controlling and (especially) formalizing such systems was fraught with complexity, however, since inference had to be understood in terms of a quiescent and static model, namely the state of affairs that would be arrived at once all of non-monotonic inference had come to completion. The flies in the ointment were so-called odd-length cycles, caused among others by such rules as the preceding one, whose non-monotonic conclusion removes the very antecedent required for the rule to run. In our case, these formal and implementational headaches are neatly side-stepped by formulating the non-monotonic inference in terms of a rule sequence. This can be formally understood in terms of the sequence of models that the sequence engenders, as opposed to a single model that must be analyzed via heroic acts of fixed-point semantics!

5.4 Task-Specific Extraction: Merging Events

Returning to the key passage from our sample article, we note that there is one more salient discourse inference that we must cover here, namely the oblique interpretation of *Dooner* as succeeding *James* in the same organization and position. The relevant sentence (*"He will be succeeded by Mr. Dooner, 45."*) interprets as follows.

```
person(pers-18)                    ; "Mr. Dooner"
succeed((pers-18 pers-y) s-19)  ; pers-y is not bound
```

As in the previous example, the pers-y term is unbound, in this case because it represents an anaphoric pronoun. In order to reason from this succession fact and produce the intended discourse analysis, we need to refer back to the job-out facts about *James*. As before, we rely on the context table mechanism to locate the relevant information. In particular, we can use the following rule.

```
job-in((?p ?t ?o)) <- succeed((?p -) ?s)
                      + in-ctxt(?s ?jo JOB-OUT)
                      + job-out((- ?t ?o) ?jo)
```

In plain English, this rule keys off of a suceeed fact, locates the most chronologically recent contextual job-out proposition, destructures its arguments, and uses them to assert the occurence of a job-in fact. When applied in the context of the present example, this rule appropriately adds *Dooner* as entering the *CEO* position of *McCann*. As with job-out facts, this job-in proposition is mapped directly onto the task-specific template output (to use MUC parlance).

Note that this process of combining job-out and successor facts effectively achieves what is often accomplished in information extraction systems by template merging. However, since the merging takes place in the inferential database, all the machinery of semantic processing is made available to perform the necessary discourse inference. Additionally, propagation of facts by equality reasoning eliminates the need for the library of template merging rules that would otherwise be required.

5.5 Task-Specific Extraction: In Summary

In summary then, we have covered here the gammut of processing that Alembic applies to specific information extraction applications. We have dwelled at some length on issues of semantic interpretation and inference. Our hope is that by not skimping on these details we have made a case for the simplicity and compactness that an explicit semantic level can provide the information extraction endeavor.

Indeed, while our conceptualization of syntax has undergone many changes, our underlying semantic notions have remained steady, and have in fact adapted readily to our range of syntactic models. Of the various aspects of this semantic processing, that which we have found most compelling is the inferential approach to discourse enabled by the combination of equality reasoning, tractable inference, and non-monotonic rule sequences. This much we believe will remain a key feature of workaday applications of Alembic, both now and in the future.

What we are less sanguine about, however, is the top level of our stratified syntactic hierarchy, at least as we have described it so far. In our work to date (aside from the early CCG parser), this top level has been occupied by a task-specific layer of finite-state parsing. As noted above, this is not a particularly satisfying approach, since it requires a proliferation of task-specific patterns, with explicit variants for each verbal form, explicit variants for different lexical heads, and so forth.

6 Grammatical Relations as a Basis for Extraction

The approach we are coming to adopt to address this proliferation is based on a new model of parsing. Our approach is stated tersely by the formula

syntax = chunks + grammatical relations.

Chunks in this framework are small units of syntax: noun phrases without their modifiers, or verbs without their argument mappings. These modifiers and argument mappings are described separately by a graph of grammatical relations. It is our current working hypothesis that this approach to syntactic description can be both (1) effectively recovered by simple methods, and (2) readily translated to semantics. Our hope is that this approach will provide the degree of syntactic normalization that is currently missing in the task-specific level of our stratified syntactic processing.

What follows then is a preliminary report on our attempts to parse with grammatical relations. The report is preliminary for several reasons. First, the grammatical relations work *per se* is in its early stages, though significant details can be found in [23], from which the following notes are partially exerpted. Second, the grammatical relations that we do recover are only starting to be exploited by Alembic's semantic interpretations. There is thus much to be discovered about the effectiveness of this approach, and much to be reported on at some later point. The present discussion is thus primarily a pointer towards the future.

Let us begin by addressing the formula above.

6.1 Chunks

By chunks we mean the kind of non-recursive simplifications of the NP and VP that in the literature go by names such as core phrases, noun/verb groups [2] or base NPs [24]; the term "chunk" is due to Abney [25].

The common thread between these approaches and ours is to approximate full noun phrases or verb phrases by only parsing their non-recursive core, and thus not attaching modifiers or arguments. For English noun phrases, this amounts to roughly the span between the determiner and the head noun; for English verb phrases, the span runs roughly from the auxiliary to the head verb. We call such simplified syntactic categories *chunks* or *groups*, and consider in particular, noun, verb, adverb, adjective, and *IN* groups. The latter designate prepositions and subordinating conjunctions (the name *IN* comes from the Brown corpus tag for these parts of speech).

In Alembic, chunks are parsed by the rule-sequence phrase praser, as we noted earlier, during the final level of what we have called pre-parsing. For example, consider the simple sentence *"I saw the cat that ran."*, for which we have the following core phrase analysis:

$[I]_{ng}$ $[saw]_{vg}$ $[the\ cat]_{ng}$ $[that]_{ig}$ $[ran]_{vg}$.

where $[...]_{ng}$ indicates a noun group, $[...]_{vg}$ a verb group, and $[...]_{ig}$ an IN group.

Distinguishing chunks from traditional syntactic phrases (such as NPs) is of interest because it singles out what is usually thought of as easy to parse, and allows that piece of the parsing problem to be addressed by such comparatively simple means as we do here: with finite-state-like rule sequences. What is then left of the parsing problem is the difficult stuff: namely the attachment of prepositional phrases, relative clauses, and other constructs that serve in modification, adjunctive, or argument-passing roles.

6.2 Grammatical Relations

In the present work, we encode this hard stuff through a small repertoire of *grammatical relations.* These relations hold directly between constituent chunks, and as such define a graph, with chunks as nodes in the graph, and relations as labeled arcs. Our previous example, for instance, generates the following grammatical relations graph (head words underlined):

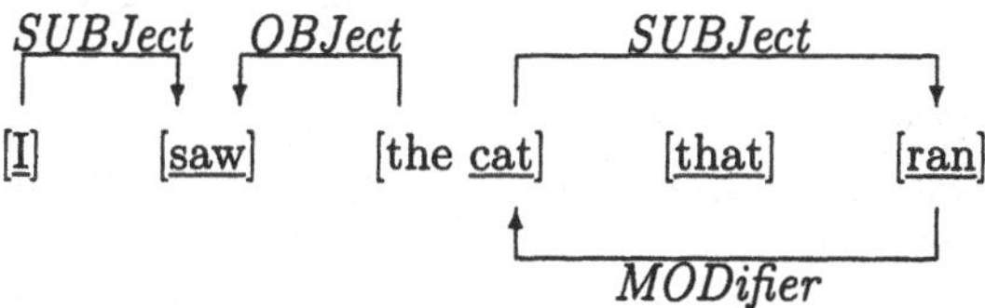

The purpose of this level of analysis is of course to produce semantic interpretations. In particular, SUBJ and OBJ relations map out the arguments of predicates, so in the case of this sample sentence, the semantic interpretation that is ultimately derived is as follows. Note that unlike with the examples we gave for the MUC-6 messages, these argument and modifier mappings are produced by following general rules of interpretation for the grammatical relations, not ad hoc rules of interpretation for task-specific phrase types.

```
see((i20 c21) s22)            ; "I saw the cat"
I(i20)                        ; "I"
cat(c21)                      ; "the cat"
run((c21) r23)                ; "the cat ran"
mod(r23 c21)                  ;  -- this modifies "the cat"
```

This is of course an illustrative example, not the actual input of any meaningful extraction task. Nevertheless, the example does point to the way our new syntactic approach is being integrated into the overall extraction processing in Alembic, namely through semantic interpretation.

Returning now to syntactic considerations, our grammatical relations effectively replace the recursive $\overline{X}$ analysis of traditional phrase structure grammar. In this respect, the approach bears resemblance to a dependency grammar, in that it has no notion of a spanning S node, or of intermediate constituents corresponding to argument and modifier attachments.

One major point of departure from dependency grammar, however, is that these grammatical relation graphs can generally not be reduced to labeled trees. This happens as a result of argument passing, as in

[Fred] [promised] [to help] [John]

where *[Fred]* is the subject of both *[promised]* and *[to help]*. This also happens as a result of argument-modifier cycles, as in

[I] [saw] [the cat] [that] [ran]

where the relationships between *[the cat]* and *[ran]* form a cycle: *[the cat]* has a subject relationship/dependency to *[ran]*, and *[ran]* has a modifier dependency to *[the cat]*, since *[ran]* helps indicate (modifies) which cat is seen.

There has been some work towards extracting grammatical relationships from dependency tree structures [26,27]. Our approach is closer to the more direct approaches taken under the SPARKLE umbrella [28,29]: namely, we derive grammatical relations from the chunk level of analysis, and altogether bypass spanning tree parses.[3]

A reason for skipping the tree stage is that extracting grammatical relations from a surface structure tree is often a nontrivial task by itself. For instance, the precise relationship holding between two constituents in a surface structure tree cannot be derived unambiguously from their relative attachments. Contrast, for example *"the attack on the military base"* with *"the attack on March 24"*. Both of these have the same underlying surface structure (a PP attached to an NP), but the former encodes the direct object of a verb nominalization, while the latter encodes a time modifier. Also, in a surface structure tree, long-distance dependencies between heads and arguments are not explicitly indicated by attachments between the appropriate parts of the text. For instance in *"Fred promised to help John"*, no direct attachment exists between *"Fred"* and *"help"*, despite the fact that the former is the subject of the latter.

For our purposes, we have delineated approximately a dozen head-to-argument relationships as well as a commensurate number of modification relationships. Among the head-to-argument relationships, we have the deep subject and object (SUBJ and OBJ respectively), and also include the surface subject and object of copulas (COP-SUBJ and the various COP-OBJ forms). In addition, we include a number of relationships (e.g., PP-SUBJ, PP-OBJ) for arguments that are mediated by prepositional phrases. An example is in

PP-OBJect *OBJect*

[the attack] [on] [the military base]

[3] We say this at the risk of gross oversimplification, as the SPARKLE architecture allows for deriavation of grammatical relations from both the level of chunks and that of derivation trees. Indeed, one of the heterogeneous SPARKLE projects includes one of the more established statistical parsers for English.

where *[the attack]*, a noun group with a verb nominalization, has its object *[the military base]* passed to it via the preposition in *[on]*. Among modifier relationships, we designate both generic modification and some specializations like locational and temporal modification. A complete definition of all the grammatical relations is beyond the scope of this paper, but we give a summary of usage in [23].

6.3 Parsing with Grammatical Relations

We have implemented a simple parsing method based on these notions. In brief, it takes the form of a rule-sequence processor that attempts to recover the grammatical relations in a text; the method is trainable using a variation of Brill's transformation-based error-driven learning [13].

As with the rule-sequence phrase parser, the basic schema for a grammatical relation rule is simple. We are given a chunk α, and chunks in the neighborhood of α, namely $\alpha - n \ldots \alpha - 1$ and $\alpha + 1 \ldots \alpha + n$, the left and right neighborhoods respectively. A rule then may test for certain conditions to hold of α and its neighbors, and if these tests succeed, the rule adds a grammatical relation between α and one of the neighboring α_i.

For example, the following rule introduces the deep subject relation between the surface subject and surface object of a copula verb.

Given a noun group α with
- to its immediate right a chunk $\alpha + 1$, whose head word is some form of the verb *"be"*
- to its immediate left a chunk $\alpha - 1$ that is not an IN group (preposition, *wh*-word, etc.) and
- the restriction that α's head-word is not an existential *"there"*

make α a SUBJ of $\alpha + 2$, the chunk that is two over to α's right.

For instance, in the sentence *[The cat] [was] [very happy]*. (head words are underlined) this rule makes *[The cat]* a SUBJect of *[very happy]*.

If this rule appears odd for its purpose (especially the second clause), it is because it was not crafted by human hands, but was drawn from the middle of a machine-learned rule sequence. The sequence in question was acquired by training on a small hand-annotated corpus of grade school reading comprehension stories (the so-called Remedia corpus, after the name of their publisher). The fact that we initially trained our learning procedure with these children's stories, as opposed to the more traditional newswire text, is something of a historical accident. It is interesting, however, that in almost all respects, these stories contain the same range of linguistically challenging phenomena that are found in texts intended to be read by adults, *e.g.*, control and raising verbs, a broad range of modifiers, verb nominalizations, and so on. The differences that exist between journalistic text and these reading comprehension stories have to do with the former's comparatively longer sentences, comparatively greater distances between the source and target of grammatical relations, and with their journalistic form (including all the productive SLAP appositions that we have discussed above).

6.4 Evaluating the Parser

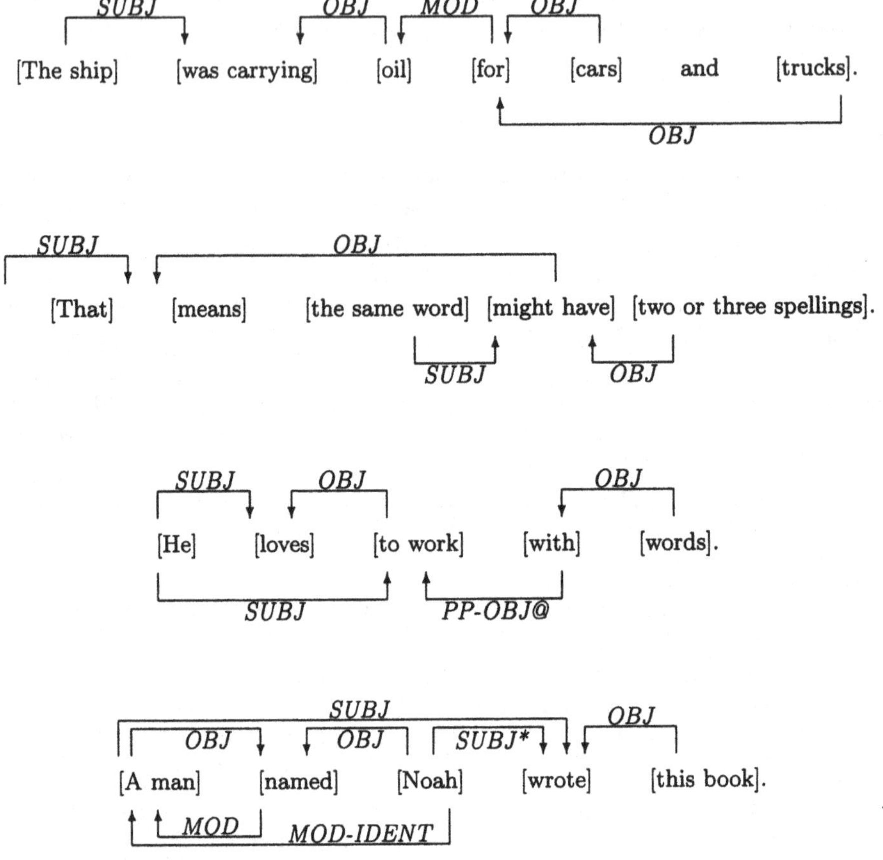

Fig. 2. Sample grammatical relation assignments produced by our parser. @ marks missed keys. * marks spurious responses.

We noted at the onset that this work on recovering grammatical relations is still in its early stages. Nevertheless, we are encouraged by our initial results. Even though our training corpora have been small, certainly by Penn Treebank standards, we are already beginning to observe interesting behavior on the part of the grammatical relations parser. Figure 2 shows some of the linguistic phenomena that the parser is correctly recovering.

In the first sentence, for example, the direct object of the verb is a coordinated form *"cars and trucks"*; the parser correctly distributes the deep object relation over these conjuncts. Note that co-ordination is a problematic phenomenon for dependency grammars, since it requires a level of constituency that is generally avoided by these approaches. The second sentence demonstrates verbal complements. In this case the clause *"the same word might have two or three spellings"* stands in the deep object relation to the matrix verb. The third sentence *"He loves to work with words"* has a verb phrase complement which in this case undergoes subject control from the matrix verb. Finally note the treatment of reduced relative clauses in the fourth sentence *"a man named Noah"*.

Errors in these samples are marked in the figure with "@" (false negatives) and "*" (false positives). There are, of course, relatively few of these, as we have specifically chosen sample sentences that show the parser recovering interesting phenomena. The overall performance of the parser, however, has been assessed by evaluation against a blind test corpus under a variety of conditions. Our best performance was obtained by ignoring subtle distinctions among modifiers. This yielded a grammatical relations recall of 67.7, with precision at 78.6 (f-score of 72.6). More details are in [23].

7 Parting Thoughts

Our intention in this paper was two-fold. First, we wanted to show how the Alembic message understanding system exploits an explicit semantic level to perform extraction. By doing so, we hope to have built a convincing case for the utility of such a level, old-fashioned as semantics may now sound in a community dominated by approaches based on finite-state machines. Our hope is that others may find these notions compelling enough to exploit them as well.

Our second aim was to point towards the future of our work, in this case our new research on grammatical relations parsing. We have much yet to accomplish in this area: retraining on newswire text (and the related corpus development), further integration of grammatical relations into the semantic processing model, and experimentation on various extraction tasks. It is in part because so much about Alembic's architecture is currently in flux that we have not belabored here the performance figures that are often associated with MUC participants.[4]

From a system development perspective, then, these are very interesting times for Alembic. From a broader programmatic perspective, these are interesting times as well. Our concern has always been with trainable and self-extensible systems. For this reason, many of our long-term concerns are thus centered on extending Alembic's coverage and flexibility through training. We envision more use of unsupervised learning, especially in the acquisition of named-entity patterns and verb subcategorization frames. We also, and most importantly, envision a mixed-initiative framework for the system, one in which end users can tailor the extraction capabilities of the system interactively, and without requiring detailed knowledge of the system's internals. In this way, we hope that times remain interesting for Alembic for many years ahead.

[4] Qualitatively speaking, our results in MUC-6, MET-1, and MUC-7 are as follows. English NE – middle of the pack (MUC-7) to good (MUC-6). Spanish NE – very good (MET). English TE – very good (MUC-6). English ST – middle of the pack (informal evaluation on the MUC-6 task).

References

1. W. Lehnert, C. Cardie, D. Fisher, E. Riloff, and R. Williams. University of Massachusetts: Description of the CIRCUS system as used for MUC-3. In Beth Sundheim, editor, *Proceedings of the Third Message Understanding Conference (MUC-3)*. Morgan Kaufmann Publishers, 1991.
2. D. Appelt, J. Hobbs, J. Bear, D. Israel, and M. Tyson. FASTUS: A finite-state processor for information extraction. In *13th Intl. Conf. On Artificial Intelligence (IJCAI-93)*, 1993.
3. E. Riloff. An empirical study of automated dictionary construction fo information extraction in three domains. *Aritificial Intelligence*, 85, 1996.
4. R. Yangarber and R. Grishman. Customization of information extraction systems. In *Proceedings of the International Workshop on Lexically-driven Information Extraction*, 1997.
5. A. Mikheev, M. Moens, and C. Grover. Named entity recognition without gazetteers. In *Proceedings of the Ninth Conference of the European Chapter of the ACL (EACL-99)*, Bergen, Norway, 1999.
6. D. Bikel, S. Miller, R. Schwartz, and R. Weischedel. Nymble: A high-performance learning name-finder. In *Proceedings of the Fifth Conference on Appled Natural Language Processing*, 1997.
7. J. Cowie. CRL/NMSU: Description of the CRL/NMSU system used for MUC-6. In *Proceedings of the Sixth Message Understanding Conference (MUC-6)*, 1995.
8. G. Krupka. SRA: Description of the SRA system as used for MUC-6. In *Proceedings of the 6th Message Understanding Conference (MUC-6)*, 1995.
9. M. Vilain and D. Day. Finite-state phrase parsing by rule sequences. In *Proceedings of the 16th Intl. Conference on Computational Lingusitics (COLING-96)*, 1996.
10. R. Burton and J. S. Brown. Semantic grammar: A technique for constructing natural language interfaces to instructional systems. BBN Report 3587, Bolt Beranek and Newman, 1977.
11. P. Jacobs, G. Krupka, and L. Rau. Lexico-semantic pattern matching as a companion to parsing. In *Proceedings of the 4th DARPA Speeach and Natural Language Workshop*, 1991.
12. R Pareschi and M Steedman. A lazy way to chart-parse with categorial grammars. In *Proceedings of the 25th Annual Meeting of the ACL (ACL-87)*, 1987.
13. E. Brill. *A Corpus-based Approach to Language Learning.* PhD thesis, U. Pennsylvania, 1993.
14. E. Brill. Some advances in rule-based part of speech tagging. In *Proc. of the 12th National Conf. on Artifical Intelligence (AAAI-94)*, 1994.
15. D. McAllester. Reasoning utility package user's manual. AI Memo 667, MIT AI Laboratory, 1982.
16. M. Vilain. Semantic inference in natural language: Validating a terminological approach. In *Proceedings of the 14th Intl. Conference on Artificial Intelligence (IJCAI-95)*, Montreal, 1995.
17. M. Vilain. Deduction as parsing: Tractable inference in the KL-ONE framework. In *Proceedings of the Ninth Natl. Conference on Artificial Intelligence (AAAI-91)*, Anaheim, CA, 1991.
18. J. Hobbs. Ontological promiscuity. In *Proceedings of the 23rd Meeting of the ACL (ACL-85)*, Chicago, Ill., 1985.
19. H. Alshawi and J. Van Eijck. Logical forms in the core language engine. In *Proceedings of the 27th Meeting of the ACL (ACL-89)*, Vancouver, B.C., 1989.

20. S. Bayer and M. Vilain. The relation-based knowledge representation of KING KONG. *SIGART Bulletin*, 2(3), 1991.
21. D. Appelt, J. Hobbs, J. Bear, D. Israel, M. Kameyama, A. Kehler, D. Martin, K. Myers, and M. Tyson. SRI international FASTUS system MUC-6 test results and analysis. In *Proceedings of the Sixth Message Understanding Conference (MUC-6)*, 1995.
22. J. Doyle. Truth maintenance systems for problem solving. AI-TR 419, MIT Artificial Intelligence Laboratory, 1978.
23. L. Ferro, M. Vilain, and A. Yeh. Learning transformation rules to find grammatical relations. In *Proceedings of the 1999 Workshop on Computational Natural Language Learning (CoNLL-99)*, 1999.
24. L. Ramshaw and M. Marcus. Text chunking using transformation-based learning. In *Proc. of the 3rd Workshop on Very Large Corpora*, pages 82–94, Cambridge, MA, USA, 1995.
25. S. Abney. Partial parsing via finite-state cascades. In *Proc. of ESSLI96 Workshop on Robust Parsing*, 1996.
26. N. Bröker. Separating surface order and syntactic relations in a dependency grammar. In *COLING-ACL'98*, pages 174–180, Montréal, Canada, 1998.
27. T. B.Y. Lai and C. Huang. Complements and adjuncts in dependency grammar parsing emulated by a constrained context-free grammar. In *COLING-ACL'98 Workshop: Processing of Dependency-based Grammars*, Montréal, Canada, 1998.
28. J. Carroll, T. Briscoe, N. Calzolari, S. Federici, S. Montemagni, V. Pirrelli, G. Grefenstette, A. Sanfilippo, G. Carroll, and M. Rooth. SPARKLE work package 1, specification of phrasal parsing, final report. Available at `http://www.ilc.pi.cnr.it/sparkle/sparkle.htm`, November 1997.
29. J. Carroll, T. Briscoe, and A. Sanfilippo. Parser evaluation: a survey and a new proposal. In *1st Intl. Conf. on Language Resources and Evaluation (LREC)*, pages 447–454, Granada, Spain, 1998.

Knowledge Extraction from Bilingual Corpora

Harold Somers

Department of Language Engineering,
UMIST, Manchester, England
harold@ccl.umist.ac.uk

Abstract. The use of corpora has become an important issue in IE. In this chapter we consider a specific type of corpus, the bilingual parallel corpus, and ways of automatically extracting information from such corpora. This information, "linguistic metaknowledge", is essential for techniques such as tokenization, POS-tagging, morphological analysis, used in IE. Where we wish to extract information from multilingual texts, we must rely on these linguistic resources being available in several languages. This chapter discusses locating and storing parallel texts, alignment at various levels (sentence, word, phrase), and extraction of bilingual vocabulary and terminology.

1 Introduction

The use of corpora has become an important issue in IE. In this chapter we will be considering a specific type of corpus, the bilingual parallel corpus.

By "parallel corpus", we mean a text which is available in two (or more) languages: it may be an original text and its translation, or it may be a text which has been written by a consortium of authors in a variety of languages, and then published in various language versions. A corpus of this type of text is sometimes called a "comparable corpus", though this term is also used (confusingly) for a corpus of similar but not necessarily equivalent texts. Another term sometimes found is "bitext", due to Brian Harris [27].

We will be considering parallel corpora not as source of primary information, as is usually the case in IE, but as valuable sources of a kind of metaknowledge, namely *linguistic knowledge.* IE uses techniques such as tokenization, POS-tagging, morphological analysis, all of which depend on linguistic resources, while associated techniques such as text mining rely on terminology. Where we wish to extract information from multilingual texts, we must rely on these linguistic resources being available in several languages. For example, in connection with the ECRAN project, co-ordinated by Thomson-CSF, France, it is stated:

> "It is broadly agreed that the most successful implementations of information extraction so far have been those based on lexicons, [...] but based on hand-built lexicons which have obvious problems for size extension (beyond, say, the 7-8000 word barrier) and for portability to new domains. The [...] core part of the proposal [... is] lexicon extraction, construction and development against corpora." (http://www.dcs.shef.ac.uk/

Pazienza (Ed.): Information Extraction, LNAI 1714, pp. 120–133, 1999.

research/ilash/Ecran/overview.html; see also Wilks's contribution in this volume).

Another example, the AVENTINUS project, co-ordinated by the Amt für Auslandsfragen, Germany, deals with information on multinational drug enforcement where texts to be searched may be in different languages, as are the requests.

This paper focuses on problems (and solutions) related to the extraction of linguistic meta-knowledge from parallel corpora. The following topics will be discussed:

- "First, catch your corpus": Fully annotated aligned multilingual parallel corpora are becoming more widely available, but often not in the language pair and for the domain that you may need. On the other hand, the World Wide Web is a huge (and always growing) source of such texts. We begin by considering some ways of automatically locating parallel texts, and some issues involved in retrieving and storing such data (character sets, encoding, markup, corpus interchange).
- Alignment: An important prerequisite for most linguistic knowledge extraction tasks with parallel corpora is that they be "aligned". This term is used to describe two separate but related processes: matching up of two texts at a structural level, usually paragraphs or sentences; and matching at the much finer lexical level. We prefer to use the term "alignment" only for the first of these tasks, which nevertheless has many difficulties, among which are "noisy" text pairs (where segments in one text are missing in the other, or segment order is different), non-parallelism of structural units (e.g. no 1:1 correspondence of "sentences" between Chinese and English). We will discuss and illustrate several techniques which have been proposed for alignment of both clean and noisy texts.
- Extraction of bilingual vocabulary and terminology: Statistical techniques based on the premise that words and their translations will be similarly distributed throughout parallel texts are discussed. Issues include initial segmentation into words where writing systems do not conventionally separate them (e.g. Chinese, Japanese); interference of homographs and their corollary, inflected forms; identification of collocations; extraction of likely terms.

2 "First, Catch Your Corpus"

The first requirement for knowledge extraction from bilingual corpora is, rather obviously, a parallel corpus. Fully annotated aligned multilingual parallel corpora in a number of languages are becoming increasingly widely available through various co-ordinated international efforts. A visit to any of a number of websites devoted to corpora in general and bilingual corpora in particular reveals a long list of such collections. The W3C website at Essex University (clwww.essex.ac.uk/w3c/general.html) is a good starting point. Nevertheless, even though the number of collections is ever increasing, the number of different languages featured is still rather small. Also, some of the collections are relatively unfocused in terms of subject matter. In either case there may be a problem of coverage for a particular need. In this case, you might need to attempt to locate and analyse your corpus from scratch. So we begin by considering some ways of automatically locating parallel texts, and some issues involved in retrieving and storing such data.

2.1 Locating Parallel Corpora Automatically

Although English is overwhelmingly the *lingua franca* of the World Wide Web, a great number of web sites have parallel material in several languages. These evidently provide an instant source of parallel texts, if they can be located and successfully aligned. Interesting work on automatically identifying and locating parallel corpora has been initiated by Resnik [40,41], and is also being conducted by the present author.

The idea is first of all to find likely candidate pairs of texts using such "tricks" as searching for sites which seem to have parallel "anchors", often accompanied by images of flags, or pairs of filenames which differ only in the identification of a language, e.g. with alternative directories in the paths, or suffixes such as ".en" and ".fr".

These candidates are then evaluated by comparing, in a very simplistic manner, their content: since they are usually HTML documents, it is quite easy to align the HTML mark-up (heading and subheading identifiers, for example), and to compare the amount of text between each anchor. In this way, we get a rough map of the structures of the two documents. These can then be compared using a variety of more or less sophisticated techniques which may or may not include the kinds of linguistic methods used in the alignment of known parallel texts – see next section.

These techniques can also be linked to language identification if the languages of interest are sufficiently similar to risk confusion [26]. For example, the above-mentioned techniques could identify as plausible pairs two texts which were in fact similarly structured texts in the same language!

2.2 Storage and Encoding

Having located a suitable parallel corpus, there remain a number of aspects to consider before the process of linguistic knowledge extraction can begin. One, which should not be ignored, is the issue of determining the legal position with respect to the text: even though the WWW is a kind of public domain, much of the text found on it is nevertheless subject to copyright and ownership. It is thus important to obtain the owners' agreement before using the material, especially if, as we will suggest below, you intend to make the data available through various data sharing initiatives. Some suggestions on these legal issues are offered in [48].

Another issue, obvious if you are interested in a language pair which use a different script, is the question of character sets. Although for some languages there are uniquely recognised standards for web pages, for others there are conflicting standards, or no standards at all. Furthermore, although we have just been considering finding parallel text on the WWW, there are of course other sources of such material which are still susceptible to the kind of treatment we are discussing here. Even for languages that use the Latin alphabet, this is also an issue inasmuch as many languages use accented characters, which may be encoded differently. We can give no easy answers here, except to alert the reader to the potential pitfalls in this area.

Another issue that has been widely addressed is the question of "encoding". This term refers to annotations which are added to the text in order to facilitate data manipulation and analysis. The type of "mark-up" that can be added to the text ranges from identification information such as its source, subject matter, language, date of capture, and so on, to more linguistic mark-up as the result of analysis: part-of-speech tags, document structure codes and so on. There have been various standardisation efforts in this area, most notably the Text Encoding Initiative (TEI), whose guidelines and recommendations [42] seem to have been widely accepted. Standardisation facilitates the exchange of data, and equally, there have been numerous movements towards sharing and exchanging corpus material.

3 Alignment

In order to extract information from our parallel text, it is first necessary to align the two texts at some global level, typically paragraph or sentence. By "align" is meant the association of chunks of text in the one document with their translation or equivalent text in the other document. Some approaches to alignment involve the use of some sort of traditional analysis of the texts (e.g. parsing, tagging, or the use of bilingual lexica), while others take an entirely automatic approach. For our purposes – i.e. extraction of linguistic knowledge – the former would seem to involve a kind of vicious circle, since they make use of precisely the kind of information we are trying to extract. There is a huge and continually growing body of literature on this subject. The paragraphs that follow are not intended as an exhaustive review.

Gale and Church [22] and Brown et al. [2] both developed alignment programs based on the simple assumption that there is a significant correlation in the relative length of sentences which are translations of each other. The former measured length in characters, the latter in words. Simard et al. [43] suggested that such alignments could be improved upon if apparent cognates in the two texts were used as crutches. Gale and Church [23] took the output of their alignment program and used it to identify correspondences at the word level. Much of the early success of all these approaches was no doubt due to the fact that the universally used Canadian Hansard corpus was very "well-behaved" in that most of the sentences and paragraphs lined up nicely, and also syntactically and lexically French and English are quite similar. McEnery and Oakes [37] illustrate widely varying success rates for different language pairs and domains.

Inspired by [43], Church [4] addressed the problem of "noisy" texts by trying to align on the basis of similar short stretches of characters ("cognates"). This type of "approximate string matching" is familiar in IR [28] as a crude form of lemmatization. Other researchers using cognates include [30] and [38], though obviously this technique only readily applies to languages using the same writing system.

Church looked at texts which had been scanned in from hard copy, and so contained misalignment problems caused by different pagination, e.g. a footnote suddenly appearing in the middle of a paragraph, or figure headings out of sequence. Similarly, Chen [3] overcame the noise problem by aligning sentences on the basis of word alignments. Dagan et al. [11] found that a combination of sentence and word alignment gave good results on small and noisy corpora.

Although Fung and Church [15] initially reported good results with their "K-vec" algorithm for alignment of noisy French–English texts, Jones and Somers [32] reported less impressive results with this algorithm with English, Japanese and German texts. Fung and McKeown [16] also reported the poor performance of the K-vec algorithm with Japanese–English and Chinese–English parallel corpora, and proposed an interesting alternative, based on comparing "recency vectors". Somers [47] reported mixed results with a similar algorithm.

Most of the approaches have in common a technique which involves identification of anchor points and verification of the comparability of the textual material between the anchors. These anchors can, in the simplest case, be structural, as in early work by Gale and Church [22] where sentence boundaries are taken to make an initial segmentation. Then, certain types of alignment across sentence boundaries are permitted and quantified (e.g. where two sentences in one text are merged in the translation, or vice versa), with all possible alignments being compared using dynamic programming techniques.

Alternatively, and quite commonly, translation word-pairs are taken as the anchor points. This alignment at the word level is often an end-goal in itself, as exemplified by the pioneering work of Kay and Röscheisen [34]. Their algorithm performs the two functions of sentence alignment and word alignment simultaneously, the one feeding off and reinforcing the other. As Church says of this apparent vicious circle,

> The idea is that you are trying to maximize both the lexical and alignment probabilities. From either one, you can estimate the other. So you start with a simple approximation of one and estimate the other. Then you use the other to get a better estimate of the one and so on (personal communication, cited in [47, p.118]).

Apart from automatic estimation of translation pairs, a number of sentence alignment algorithms rely on machine-readable dictionaries as a method for finding lexical anchor points. This technique of course relies on the availability of a suitable dictionary, not to mention the need for efficient lemmatization in the case of highly inflected languages. Again, this seems like a vicious circle if the aim of the alignment is to extract vocabulary; but as we will see below, aligned parallel corpora can be used for the extraction not of everyday vocabulary, but of domain-specific lexical pairings, notably novel terminology and, especially where different writing systems are involved, transliterations of proper names.

4 Extraction of Bilingual Vocabulary and Terminology

Algorithms for extracting bilingual vocabulary from aligned parallel corpora exploit – or depend on – the following characteristics of translated texts [20, p.2]:

- Words have one sense per corpus.
- Words have a single translation per corpus.
- There are no missing translations in the target document.
- The frequencies of words and their translations are comparable.
- The positions of words and their translations are comparable.

The algorithms that we will be discussing take advantage of the above facts, and their principle weaknesses are the extent to which the above do *not* hold. We will return to this point later.

4.1 Identifying Likely Word-Pairs

One of the earliest attempts to extract bilingual vocabulary from a parallel corpus was [34]. As mentioned above, their method was a hybrid of sentence- and word-alignment. Their technique is to find word pairs which are most probably alignable on the basis of similar distribution. This distribution is defined in terms of text sectors, and Dice's coefficient is used to quantify the probability. Dice's coefficient (1) is a simple calculation which compares c, the number of times the two candidate words occur in the same sector with a and b, the number of times the source or target words occur independently.

$$\text{Dice} = \frac{2c}{a+b} \tag{1}$$

The algorithm is iterative in that the sentences containing high-scoring word pairs are established as anchors which allow the text to be split up into smaller segments, affording more and more results.

Another distribution-based algorithm is K-vec [15]. In this case, the parallel texts are split into K equal-sized segments and the distributions of each word are recorded in binary vectors $1..K$. The binary vectors for two candidate words w_s and w_t, are then compared, the similarity of any two distributions being quantified using two measures, Mutual Information (MI) and a t-score, as in (2–3).

$$MI(w_s, w_t) = \log_2 \frac{P(w_s, w_t)}{P(w_s)P(w_t)} \tag{2}$$

$$t(w_s, w_t) = \frac{P(w_s, w_t) - P(w_s)P(w_t)}{\sqrt{\frac{P(w_s, w_t)}{K}}} \tag{3}$$

The probabilities in (2–3) are defined (4–6) in terms of a contingency matrix, where a is the total number of segments where both words co-occur, b and c the number of sectors where one or the other occurs, and d the number of sectors where neither occurs. Obviously $a+b+c+d=K$.

$$P(W_s) = \frac{a+b}{K} \tag{4}$$

$$P(W_t) = \frac{a+c}{K} \tag{5}$$

$$P(W_s, W_t) = \frac{a}{K} \tag{6}$$

As mentioned above, K-vec achieved mixed results, and so a number of variations have been tried. [16] proposed a weighted MI, calculated as in (7).

$$wMI = \frac{a}{K} \log_2 \frac{aK}{(a+b)(a+c)} \tag{7}$$

[21] noted that in addition to the Dice coefficient, other similarity measures widely used in IR could also be applied in this case, including the Jaccard coefficient (8) and the Cosine coefficient (9). Gao tested the various measures with his parallel English–Chinese text, and found the Jaccard the best measure.

$$\text{Jaccard} = \frac{c}{a+b-c} \tag{8}$$

$$\text{Cosine} = \sqrt{\frac{c}{ab}} \tag{9}$$

Another variant of the K-vec algorithm is reported in [32]. Believing one of the drawbacks of the original K-vec to be the rigidity of the equal-sized segments, which both introduces spurious matches and misses matches when words happen to fall near the sector boundaries, they proposed allowing the segments to grow in size around a pre-determined point. Using K-vec to determine initial anchor points, their algorithm allows words either side of the anchor point to be "sucked" into the "bags" centred on these points. At some point, a candidate translation emerges as the word which, significantly, has been sucked into all the bags, and which, typically, does not occur outside these regions.

Recognising some flaws in the performance of K-vec, [16] developed DK-vec: like K-vec, it tries to recognise translation pairs by considering their distribution. This time, the distribution is expressed as "recency vectors", i.e. sequences of integers representing the gap, in characters, between each instance of a word. The strings of integers are then compared using the Dynamic Time Warping algorithm, although simpler distance measures such as Minimal Edit Distance or Levenshtein distance are used by [6] and [47] respectively in replications of Fung and McKeown's work with different language pairs.

4.2 Extracting Terminology: Identifying Multiword Equivalents

One major drawback to all the techniques described in the previous section is the necessary assumption that word equivalents are on a 1:1 basis. Apart from the fact that this is generally not always true in languages (even making the prior assumption that we know what a word is!), it is especially unhelpful if our aim is to identify bilingual terminology. It is in this endeavour that parallel corpus work comes to the fore: often, the goal of extracting parallel vocabulary is undermined somewhat by the existence of machine-readable bilingual dictionaries. Specialist terminology, however, is almost always absent from such resources, and bilingual parallel corpora become the primary – perhaps only – source of such material.

Searching for multiword terms in a parallel corpus introduces a further aspect of word distribution which can be addressed by statistical means: considering the corpora independently, we can search for likely terms by looking for "collocations", i.e. sequences of words which co-occur frequently and – if we are lucky – tend not to occur on their own.

There is a considerable literature on collocations e.g. [5,45], though we should perhaps distinguish "loose collocations" – sets of words which typically co-occur in a text and can be used, for example, for indexing or retrieval purposes in IR, or to disambiguate polysemous words – and "contiguous collocations" which might be candidates for terminology. We will concentrate on the latter type. Readers will be familiar with the range of measures for (monolingual) collocations. The z-score (10) is perhaps the most familiar: it quantifies the collocational force of one word w_i with respect to another w_j as follows.

$$z = \frac{O - E}{\sigma} \tag{10}$$

where O is the observed frequency of w_i co-occurring with w_j (in close proximity, or contiguous with it, as the case may be), E the expected frequency of w_i, and σ is the standard deviation of occurrence of w_i in the whole text. The calculation of the standard deviation is as in (11),

$$\sigma = \sqrt{N(p(1-p))} \tag{11}$$

where p is the probability of occurrence of w_i, and N is the total number of tokens in the text.

Other measures used are MI and t-score as already seen above in K-vec (2–3). Further alternatives have been proposed. Based on contingency tables as described above, Gale and Church [24] introduced the Φ^2 coefficient (12), Dunning [14] proposed the loglike coefficient G^2 (13), while Daille used two measures closely related to MI, the cubic association ratio (14) [7] and the association ratio IM (15) in [9]. Kitamura and Matsumoto [33] propose (16) a modification of Dice's coefficient weighted to take into account the coocurrence frequency.

$$\Phi^2 = \frac{(ad - bc)^2}{(a+b)(a+c)(b+c)(b+d)} \tag{12}$$

$$
\begin{aligned}
G^2 = & f(a) + f(b) + f(c) + f(d) \\
& -f(a+b) - f(a+c) - f(b+d) \\
& -f(c+d) + f(a+b+c+d) \\
\text{where} f(x) = & x \log x
\end{aligned} \tag{13}
$$

$$
MI^3 = \log_2 \frac{a^3}{(a+b)(a+c)} \tag{14}
$$

$$
IM = \log_2 \frac{a}{(a+b)(a+c)} \tag{15}
$$

$$
sim(w_i, w_j) = \log_2 c \times \frac{2c}{a+b} \tag{16}
$$

All of these measures have drawbacks however, and there are a number of studies which compare them and try to mitigate their weaknesses. It should also be noted that not all collocations are terms. A number of studies take advantage of what is known about the structure of terms to help try to extract terminology automatically. For example, [12,8] look for appropriate sequences of POS tags as well as recurring word sequences, recognising that terms (in French) are often of the form *N de N.* [31] similarly incorporate knowledge about typical term structure into their algorithm.

Once candidate terms have been determined monolingually, we can turn our attention to identifying their translation equivalents in the parallel corpus.

Gaussier and Langé [25] describe two methods for assessing the translations of terms found monolingually. The first method compares a number of measures like MI, Φ^2 and so on, that we have already seen. The second method relies more on the previously calculated scores for single-word alignment. Following up on that work, McEnery et al. [36] incorporated the use of cognates (see above) to improve their results. Smadja et al. [46] describe a program named *Champollion* which takes a parallel corpus which has been sentence-aligned, uses Xtract [45] to identify possible collocations, and then uses a method very similar to the contingency tables seen in K-vec, above, to evaluate the probability that collocations thus identified are translations of each other. They used Dice's coefficient and MI to quantify the matches, and experimented with data from the Canadian Hansard corpus. Dagan and Church [10] proposed a semi-automatic tool, *termight* for constructing bilingual glossaries. Like *Champollion*, the task is divided into two parts: identifying monolingual term lists, and then finding their translations. The first step is closely modelled on the approach of [31], combining frequent coocurrence with appropriate syntactic pattern as a criterion. Importantly, the human terminologist has a major role in the process, so much of the effort in *termight* is focussed on presenting the results in a user-friendly manner. The second step relies on the fact that the bilingual corpora have been aligned both at sentence and at word level. Even though this alignment might be flawed, it means that for every word sequence identified as a possible term monolingually, there is a corresponding sequence of aligned words in the parallel corpus. Again the human terminologist has a role to play here. One advantage of this method is that it deals well with the typical word-order scrambling effect found especially with language pairs like English and French (e.g. *optional parameters box* corresponds to *zone paramètres optionnels*, which Dagan and Church use to test their program.

An exception to the generalisation stated above is Kupiec [35] who describes an iterative algorithm based on the EM algorithm [13].

4.3 How Good Are these Algorithms?

The success rates of the algorithms described here varies tremendously. Somers [47] has identified some of the factors impinging on one particular algorithm, DK-vec, including obvious factors such as genre, language-pair, amount and homogeneity of data. As mentioned above, most of the algorithms make certain assumptions about the nature of parallel corpora, and it is useful to revisit those assumptions here to see what their effect is.

Words Have One Sense per Corpus

This is the basic assumption underlying the "sublanguage" approach to natural language processing. It is often true, especially for words which have terminological status; but homonymy is not avoidable, even in narrow domains.

Words Have a Single Translation per Corpus

This is a much less safe assumption, which is particularly undermined by the fact that inflectional morphology and compounding methods differ from language to language. The assumption of 1:1 word correspondence is of course naive, bearing in mind polysemy and homonymy, and the converse problem of translation divergence (e.g. German has two competing terms for 'computer', *Rechner* and *Computer*). The assumption is undermined further by the fact that local syntactic conditions might result in inflectional morphology in one language but not the other: in particular, the distribution of singular and plural can differ widely between otherwise closely related languages, without even considering grammatical case and gender. Where possible, this can be overcome by subjecting the corpora to a process of lemmatization. Another problem is that multi-word compounds in one language may correspond to what are typographically single words in another. This problem has been discussed for German [29], and for Swedish [1]. And for languages such as Chinese, Japanese and Korean, the problem is further compounded by the fact that their writing systems do not mark word-boundaries explicitly, so a prior step in any word-alignment task is always word segmentation, which may introduce a certain amount of error, cf. [21,49,44].

There Are no Missing Translations in the Target Document

This is a somewhat safer assumption, but not entirely so. It is not unusual to find that some portion of the source text has been omitted in the target text, either through carelessness, or because it does not apply to the target-language readership. Interestingly, one off-shoot of work on alignment has been the development of tools to help translators check for missing text in translations [39].

The Frequencies of Words and Their Translations Are Comparable

The main problem with this assumption is again the fact that a single word in one language can have a variety of translations in the other just because of grammatical inflection. Somers [47, p.130] gives the example of the word *all* occurring 40 times in a certain English corpus, while in the corresponding Spanish corpus we get *todas* 25 times, *todo* 19, *todo* 5, and *toda* once. Another source of discrepancy is the use of capitalisation, especially comparing, say, English with German (where all nouns are capitalised irrespective of their position in the sentence), or Japanese (which does not distinguish upper and lower case).

The Positions of Words and Their Translations Are Comparable

This seems to be the most fundamental of assumptions in alignment. The extent to which it is true depends on the granularity of the alignment. Clearly, at sentence level it is hardly true at all: word-order is a fundamental difference between many languages, not just the obvious case of, say, adjectives preceding or following the noun, but also the relative order of main and subordinate clauses (*A because B* vs. *B and so A*, for example). But as the size of the text element being considered grows, this effect becomes minimised. For some language pairs, there remains a certain amount of "scrambling". For example, [21] reports that minor omissions and changes in the order of presentation of material was a major feature of his English–Chinese parallel corpus, taken from a Taiwanese current affairs magazine.

We might end by noting the pioneering work by Fung and associates [17,18,19,20] on bilingual lexicon extraction from *non*-parallel corpora. Here the attention turns to corpora which are not translations of each other, but are "comparable" corpora, i.e. collections of texts of the same genre, covering the same domain, and so on. Clearly, the assumptions we have just discussed are not applicable to non-parallel comparable corpora. Individual word distributions and frequencies, and the possibilities of lexical alignment are obviously not available in this scenario. But the corpus linguist *can* look for other useful patterns, notable comparable contexts and usage. Fung's algorithms owe a lot to IR techniques, in particular measures of distribution (term frequency), and similarity of context (IDF). This seems to be a promising new departure, and one, appropriately, where the techniques of corpus linguistics and IR can come together.

References

1. Ahrenberg, L., Andersson, M., Merkel, M. 1998: A Simple Hybrid Aligner for Generating Lexical Correspondences in Parallel Texts. *COLING-ACL '98: 36th Annual Meeting of the Association for Computational Linguistics and 17th International Conference on Computational Linguistics*, Montreal, Quebec, pp. 29–35.
2. Brown, P.F., Lai, J.C., Mercer, R.L. 1991: Aligning Sentences in Parallel Corpora. *29th Annual Meeting of the Association for Computational Linguistics*, Berkeley, California, pp. 169–176.

3. Chen, S.F. 1993: Aligning Sentences in Bilingual Corpora using Lexical Information. *31st Annual Meeting of the Association for Computational Linguistics*, Columbus, Ohio, pp. 9–16.
4. Church, K.W. 1993: Char_align: A Program for Aligning Parallel Texts at the Character Level. *31st Annual Meeting of the Association for Computational Linguistics*, Columbus, Ohio, pp. 1–8.
5. Church, K., Hanks, P. 1989: Word Association Norms, Mutual Information, and Lexicography. *27th Annual Meeting of the Association for Computational Linguistics*, Vancouver, British Columbia, pp. 76–83.
6. Dagan, I. 1996: *Bilingual Word Alignment and Lexicon Construction.* Tutorial handout, COLING-96: The 16th International Conference on Computational Linguistics, Copenhagen.
7. Daille, B. 1995: *Combined approach for terminology extraction: lexical statistics and linguistic filtering*, UCREL Technical Papers, No. 15, Department of Linguistics, Lancaster University. [cited in [36].
8. Daille, B. 1995: Repérage et extraction de terminologie par une approche mixte statistique et linguistique. *Traitements Probabilistes et Corpus, t.a.l.* **36**.1–2, 101–118.
9. Daille, B. 1996: Study and Implementation of Combined Techniques for Automatic Extraction of Terminology. In J. Klavans and P. Resnik (eds) *The Balancing Act: Combining Symbolic and Statistical Approaches to Language*, MIT Press, Cambridge, Mass., pp.49–66.
10. Dagan, I., Church, K. 1997: *Termight*: Coordinating Humans and Machines in Bilingual Terminology Acquisition. *Machine Translation* **12**, pp. 89–107.
11. Dagan, I., Church, K.W., Gale, W.A. 1993: Robust Bilingual Word Alignment for Machine Aided Translation. *Workshop on Very Large Corpora: Academic and Industrial Perspectives*, Columbus, Ohio, pp. 1–8.
12. Daille, B., Gaussier, É., Langé, J.-M. 1994: Towards Automatic Extraction of Monolingual and Bilingual Terminology. *COLING 94: The 15th International Conference on Computational Linguistics*, Kyoto, Japan, pp. 515–521.
13. Dempster, A.P., Laird, N.M., Rubin, D.B. 1977: Maximum Likelihood from Incomplete Data via the EM Algorithm. *Journal of the Royal Statistical Society B*, **39**, pp. 1–38.
14. Dunning, T. 1993: Accurate Methods for the Statistics of Surprise and Coincidence. *Computational Linguistics* **19**, pp. 61–76.
15. Fung, P., Church, K.W. 1994: K-vec: A New Approach for Aligning Parallel Texts. *COLING 94: The 15th International Conference on Computational Linguistics*, Kyoto, Japan, pp. 1096–1102.
16. Fung, P., McKeown, K. 1997: A Technical Word- and Term-Translation Aid using Noisy Parallel Corpora across Language Groups. *Machine Translation* **12**, 53–87.
17. Fung, P., McKeown, K. 1997: Finding Terminology Translations from Non-parallel Corpora. *Proceedings of the Fifth Workshop on Very Large Corpora*, Beijing and Hong Kong, pp. 192–202.
18. Fung, P. 1995: Compiling Bilingual Lexicon Entries from a Non-Parallel English-Chinese Corpus. *Proceedings of the Third Workshop on Very Large Corpora*, Cambridge, Mass., pp. 173–183.
19. Fung, P. 1998: A Statistical View on Bilingual Lexicon Extraction: From Parallel Corpora to Non-parallel Corpora. In D. Farwell, L. Gerber and E. Hovy (eds) *Machine Translation and the Information Soup*, Springer, Berlin, pp. 1–17.

20. Fung, P., Yee, L.Y. 1998: An IR Approach for Translating New Words from Nonparallel, Comparable Texts. *COLING-ACL '98: 36th Annual Meeting of the Association for Computational Linguistics and 17th International Conference on Computational Linguistics*, Montreal, Quebec, pp. 414–420.
21. Gao, Z-M. 1997: *Automatic Extraction of Translation Equivalents from a Parallel Chinese-English Corpus*, PhD thesis, UMIST, Manchester, England.
22. Gale, W.A., Church, K.W. 1991: A Program for Aligning Sentences in Bilingual Corpora. *29th Annual Meeting of the Association for Computational Linguistics*, Berkeley, Calif., 177–184.
23. Gale, W.A., Church, K.W. 1991: Identifying Word Correspondences in Parallel Text. *Workshop on Speech and Natural Language Processing*, Asilomar, California.
24. Gale, W.A., Church, K.W. 1991: Concordances for Parallel Texts. *Seventh Annual Conference of the UW Centre for New OED and text Research Using Corpora*, Oxford, pp. 40–62.
25. Gaussier, É., Langé, J.-M. 1997: Some Methods for the Extraction of Bilingual Terminology. In D. Jones and H. Somers (eds) *New Methods in Language Processing*, UCL Press, London, pp. 145–153.
26. Grefenstette, G. 1995: Comparing two Language Identification Schemes. *JADT 1995: III Giornate internazionali di Analisi Statistica dei Dati Testuali*, Rome, Vol. I, pp. 263–268.
27. Harris, B. 1988: Bi-text, a New Concept in Translation Theory. *Language Monthly* **54**, 8–10.
28. Hall, P.A.V., Dowling, G.R. 1980: Approximate String Matching. *Computing Surveys* **12**, 381-402.
29. Jones, D., Alexa, M. 1997: Towards automatically aligning German Compounds with English Word Groups. In D. Jones and H. Somers (eds) *New Methods in Language Processing*, UCL Press, London, pp. 199–206.
30. Johansson, S., Ebeling, J., Hofland, K. 1993: Coding and aligning the English–Norwegian Parallel Corpus. In K. Ajimer, B. Altenberg and M. Johansson (eds) *Languages in Contrast: A Symposium on Text-Based Cross-Linguistic Studies*, Lund University Press, Lund, pp. 87–112.
31. Justeson, J.S., Katz, S.M. 1995: Technical Terminology: some Linguistic Properties and an Algorithm for Identification in Text. *Natural Language Engineering* **1**, pp. 9–27.
32. Jones, D.B., Somers, H. 1995: Bilingual Vocabulary Estimation from Noisy Parallel Corpora using Variable Bag Estimation. *JADT 1995: III Giornate internazionali di Analisi Statistica dei Dati Testuali*, Rome, Vol. I, pp. 255–262.
33. Kitamura, M., Matsumoto, Y. 1996: Automatic Extraction of Word Sequence Correspondences in Parallel Corpora. *Proceedings of the Fourth Workshop on Very Large Corpora*, Copenhagen, Denmark, pp. 79–87.
34. Kay, M. and Röscheisen, M. 1993: Text Translation Alignment. *Computational Linguistics* **19**, 121-142.
35. Kupiec, J. 1993: An Algorithm for Finding Noun Phrase Correspondences in Bilingual Corpora. *31st Annual Meeting of the Association for Computational Linguistics*, Columbus, Ohio, pp. 17–22.
36. McEnery, T., Langé, J.-M., Oakes, M., Véronis, J. 1997: The Exploitation of Multilingual Corpora for Term Extraction. In R. Garside, G. Leech and A. McEnery (eds), *Corpus Annotation: Linguistic Information from Computer Text Corpora*, Addison Wesley Longman, London, pp. 220–230.

37. McEnery, T., Oakes, M. 1996: Sentence and word alignment in the CRATER Project. In J. Thomas and M. Short (eds), *Using Corpora for Language Research*, Longman, London, pp. 211–231.
38. Melamed, I.D. 1996: A Geometrical Approach to Mapping Bitext Correspondence. *Proceedings of the Conference on Empirical Methods in Natural Language Processing*, Philadelphia, Pa., pp. 1–12.
39. Melamed, I.D. 1996: Automatic Detection of Omissions in Translation. *COLING-96: The 16th International Conference on Computational Linguistics*, Copenhagen, Denmark, pp. 764–769.
40. Resnik, P. 1998: Parallel Strands: A Preliminary Investigation into Mining the Web for Bilingual Text. In D. Farwell, L. Gerber and E. Hovy (eds) *Machine Translation and the Information Soup*, Springer, Berlin, pp. 72–82.
41. Resnik, P. 1999: Mining the Web for Bilingual Text. *37th Annual Meeting of the Association for Computational Linguistics*, University of Maryland.
42. Sperberg-McQueen, C., Burnard, L. 1994: *Guidelines for Electronic Text Encoding and Interchange: TEI-P3* ACH-ACL-ALLC Text Coding Initiative, Chicago and Oxford.
43. Simard, M., Foster, G., Isabelle, P. 1992: Using Cognates to Align Sentences in Bilingual Corpora. *Quatrième colloque international sur les aspects théoriques et méthodologiques de la traduction automatique, Fourth International Conference on Theoretical and Methodological Issues in Machine Translation: Méthodes empiristes versus méthodes rationalistes en TA, Empiricist vs. Rationalist Methods in MT (TMI-92)*, Montréal, Canada, 67–82.
44. Shin, J.H., Han, Y.S., Choi, K-S. 1996: Bilingual Knowledge Acquisition from Korean-English Parallel Corpus Using Alignment Method (Korean-English Alignment at Word and Phrase Level). *COLING-96: The 16th International Conference on Computational Linguistics*, Copenhagen, Denmark, pp. 230–235.
45. Smadja, F. 1993: Retrieving Collocations from Text: Xtract. *Computational Linguistics* **19**, 121–142.
46. Smadja, F., McKeown, K.R., Hatzivassiloglou, V. 1996: Translating Collocations for Bilingual Lexicons: A Statistical Approach, *Computational Linguistics* **22**, 1–38.
47. Somers, H. 1998: Further Experiments in Bilingual Text Alignment. *International Journal of Corpus Linguistics* **3**, 115–150.
48. Thompson, H. in press: Corpus Creation for Data-Intensive Linguistics. To appear in R. Dale, H. Moisl and H. Somers (eds) *A Handbook of Natural Language Processing*, Marcel Dekker, New York.
49. Wu, D., Xia, X. 1994: Learning an English-Chinese Lexicon from a Parallel Corpus. *Technology Partnerships for Crossing the Language Barrier: Proceedings of the First Conference of the Association for Machine Translation in the Americas*, Columbia, Maryland, pp. 206–213.

Engineering of IE Systems: An Object-Oriented Approach

Roberto Basili, Massimo Di Nanni, and Maria Teresa Pazienza

University of Rome Tor Vergata,
Department of Computer Science, Systems and Production,
00133 Roma (Italy),
{basili,dinanni,pazienza}@info.uniroma2.it

Abstract. In order to design complex, effective and adaptable NLP systems a methodology able to satisfy two traditionally conflicting requirements in software engineering, i.e (linguistic) expressiveness and robustness, is necessary. By combining NLP methodologies and Language Engineering (LE) methods with Software Engineering (SE) criteria, we propose a software infrastructure able to optimize the design and development of complex IE applications. The basic idea is to embed within the software infrastructure itself a suitable linguistic description and make available at a computational level relevant portions of the linguistic abstraction required by a variety of applications.

1 Introduction

The interest in robust systems to automatically process unstructured data sets (like document bases or multimedia sources) is continuously growing. This is mainly due to several factors: the evolution and diffusion of freely available information sources, the changed ratio between electronically available unstructured information sources with respect to more structured data (e.g. databases), the awareness of the maturity of information technology that allows the development of systems able to achieve a considerable improvement in tasks like Information Retrieval (IR), Information Extraction (IE), Data Mining (DM), Machine Translation (MT), Knowledge Management (KM), etc. The most important source of information is currently represented by Internet and WWW with more than 40M sites [21]. Most of the WWW pages mainly contain textual information, so that it is not possible to ignore the central role assumed by Natural Language Processing (NLP) methods.
Information Extraction can be seen as the process by which an automatic system is able to process textual data sets in a linguistically motivated way and derive a structured representation of (part of) their content. It is to be seen as a process through which a structure is derived from unstructured and noisy texts. This represents its distinguishing features with respect to IR (where the source and output information has the same format, i.e. texts) and Data Mining (where source information is characterized by a more precise set of structures). It is not accidental the fact that IE has been pervasively influenced by linguistic

Pazienza (Ed.): Information Extraction, LNAI 1714, pp. 134–164, 1999.

models and methods ([16]), and has assumed a central role in determining NLP successful contributions as well its limitations.

The research in NLP area started almost forty years ago in academic community where it was confined for a long time. First experiences in developing NLP system concerned testing and validation of language theories and algorithms. According to these objectives NLP systems were designed and implemented to support the research activity and the main features of such kind of systems were linguistic expressiveness, coverage and linguistic accuracy. A minor role was assumed by time efficiency and software quality that are indeed crucial in software engineering practice. Maintenance has been also a neglected property for a long time. Only recently the switch to Language Engineering studies has stressed the role of testing, robustness, reusability and design optimization in this area.

Recently the industrial community has become more aware of the role assumed by NLP systems in information and knowledge management. In this perspective efficiency and *large-scale*-ness in systems for IE or DM becomes even more attractive as the potential user community is faced with the well-known problem of "Information Overflow". These strong requirements push both the academic and industrial institutions towards NLP techniques and tools that can be efficiently used within larger and more complex application systems. Robustness starts to be considered a crucial property for a linguistic processor required to manage heterogeneous input (e.g. sometimes ungrammatical), and asked to avoid the, so called, silence problem. Of course time efficiency and linguistic performances are very important. Even more important are software quality indexes like modularity, reusability and maintenance as integration of a linguistic processing core within larger software systems is a basic need.

It is thus often the case that a satisfactory design of a NLP systems must consider conflicting needs expressed by the involved entities: academic and industrial communities. It is of course true that linguistic expressiveness and theoretical elegance is still a strong motivation for NLP (and IE) research, but often other inspiring criteria (traditionally considered at a lower level of importance) cannot be neglected. They play a primary role as design principles. The integration of newer techniques, original linguistic architectures or even basic algorithms within any application system constitutes a primary motivation even at research time. The standardization of linguistic formalisms, of basic resources and knowledge bases as well as the assessment of the required computational infrastructures (i.e. from interfaces among basic linguistic processors to data models) is an inherent crucial core of this process. Any successful research needs large resources to be tested. These do not simply reduce to benchmarks data sets but often refers to larger systems where operational (i.e. external) testing is made possible (e.g. text retrieval for word sense disambiguation algorithms). Dually, advanced industrial systems need to be open to improvements coming from the research. Integration of more advanced components or more granular (e.g. more deeply lexicalised) resources is to be supported, avoiding complex redesigning processes.

By joining NLP studies with Language Engineering (LE) and Software Engineering (SE) methodologies, we can derive feasible and more effective design strategies. An OO approach has been adopted in order to enable the use of "objects" as a representation/communication medium for linguistic knowledge among processes. As it will be shown in the paper, the OO approach has revealed to be an appropriate solution for improving the NLP system design, development and testing phases. In fact whenever a linguistic concept is expressed through the definition of abstract data types and classes (with associated operations) the prototype definitions support any kind of user (i.e. consumer of such information). This realizes the suitable abstraction level. Moreover, the OO approach enables also a distributed client-server communication environment, where different cooperating processors ensure the scalability of the target application systems.

2 Designing NLP Applications

As a result of the above mentioned software requirements that characterize more and more as design principles for linguistic processing systems, recent trends have shown that a so-called *software infrastructure* for NLP is needed. In [9] a software infrastructure is defined as "(a set of) *common models for the representation storage and exchange of data in and between processing modules in NLP systems, along with graphical interface tools for the management of data and processing and visualization of data*". Although other close definitions are given by other authors ([19],[22]) all of them aim to define computational frameworks suitable to support and easy the design and implementation of complex NL-based applications. This section is devoted to discuss the basic problems and the research trends in this relatively young area.
The first subsection presents the aspects and information requirements that must be taken into account during the design phase: how to represent and relate each other the documents and the linguistic information that enter in their processing, how to describe linguistic resources as well as functional units, i.e. linguistic processors (i.e. basic NLP modules) and application components. The above issues are characterizing features for the most important frameworks proposed in literature that will be briefly analysed and compared in section 2.2.

2.1 Methodological and Software Design Issues in NLP Processes

Complex NLP tasks are characterized by a set of requirements that are methodologically very important whatever the target application of the entire linguistic process is. Any systematic methodology, although taking into account the entire set of requirements, should thus be independent from any specific application task .

A central concern here relates to the representational issue, i.e. the definition of a framework for linguistic knowledge representation. Such representation has to satisfy different needs as they derive from the adopted linguistic theory/model as well as from the different potential applications relying on the same NLP process. In fact texts provide a variety of information ranging from its structure to basic semantic properties (e.g. word senses and events). Any NLP-based task deals with a non trivial subset of them and often different applications rely on different views of the same source. Word senses may be used as indexes in an information retrieval scenario while playing the role of constraints in the slot filling process in IE. As a result texts provide different kinds of "information" that can be used in a variety of different ways in different application scenarios. Information that has a linguistic origin, i.e. is embodied in some textual component or refers to a given linguistic level, comes in a variety of forms:

- information on text structures: different text forms, e.g. e-mail messages, news, web documents, scientific papers, show a specific format that is carrier for specific meanings;
- linguistic knowledge: different kind of resources are used in different modalities in distinct processing phases, each of them embodies part of the knowledge related to the information of the source text;
- information local to the source text: linguistic units (e.g. lemmas) fully express their contribution in textual contexts. This level of description is required thus to explicit requirements and contributions of several basic linguistic processes. In morpho-syntactic analysis lemma information is a contribution of lemmatization phases as well as a requirement for noun phrase chunking or parsing;
- information global to large sets of texts (global information): forms of corpus-driven lexical acquisition usually rely on linguistic information expressing a synthesis over large samples of language use. This is the basis for deriving linguistic regularities (e.g. disambiguation rules) in a corpus. The evaluation of statistics scores on documents collections makes use of such kind of information as a basic requirement;
- domain information also can play a role in guiding some linguistic processes. This information not only refers to lexical knowledge specific to the target sublanguage, but is also related to application processes modeled in a linguistic fashion. A typical example of this knowledge are the template filling rules in an IE scenario, where lexicalised (i.e. strictly linguistic) rules have a role in the specific kind of application as well as in the underlying knowledge domain.

The ability to homogeneously treat all these kind of information is mandatory for NLP systems development.

Most of the current NLP design platforms adopt comprehensive data layer formalisms for the treatment of linguistic information. This means that the intervening linguistic features are described using a neutral formalism. Typical examples are attribute-value pairs or direct acyclic graphs (DAGs). These unifying formalisms, in general, allow to express every kind of language-related information posing no constraints on the underlying theory. As a positive consequence,

the corresponding homogeneous and general treatment makes possible the integration of processes heterogeneous from the computational and theoretical point of view. This positive aspect has a counterpart in the inherent complexity of using a general formalism for different specific tasks (with no opportunity offered for local optimization). Moreover, it is not trivial to adopt the same formalism also for information related to linguistic knowledge as this last usually exhibits a very different behavior.
An alternative approach foresees the definition of a linguistic layer formalism where each different linguistic entity is fully described by joining data and their corresponding behavioral aspects. In this case the linguistic information is described at a conceptual level, as the information comes with procedures that force a specific semantics. In this case the formalism must be strong enough to capture and describe data and functionalities. As a result a linguistic entity is completely characterized by its representation and can be easily exchanged among components of a larger NLP-based system.
Another inherent requirement of NLP system is the mechanism used to link linguistic information to its source textual component, e.g. a sequence of tokens expressing a complex proper noun in a text. It is worth noticing that the choice of a binding strategy is basically independent from the adopted linguistic formalism. The only required specification is how the underlying linguistic information is (explicitly or implicitly) linked to the corresponding portion of text.

In the next subsection four different software architectures (or better infrastructures) that have been recently presented to support the design of large scale NLP applications: distinctive features of these frameworks are differences in the formalization and support they give to the requirement issues suggested above. They represent concrete solutions to the relatively recent field of software engineering of large scale NLP systems. They will be presented in a chronological order that is representative of the growth of the interest for these themes in a wider scientific community.

2.2 Existing NLP Frameworks and Their Design Perspectives

The NLP frameworks that will be here discussed analyzed are basically devoted to fill the above mentioned gap between requirements of the research community and industrial needs. All of them propose themselves as architectures or software frameworks for supporting research activities and/or development of large scale industrial tools.

ALEP -Advanced Language Engineering Platform- [19] can be considered the first integrated environment for NLP design. In this framework all the linguistic information, processing modules and resources are homogeneously described using ALEP User Language (AUL). AUL is an high level specification language based on an DAG formalism, and is independent from any adopted implementation language. It is also important to emphasis the availability of an inheritance operator in order to explicitly implement hierarchical relations between different linguistic entities (e.g. grammatical hierarchies of syntactic types or Ontologies of concepts)

ALEP supports modular platforms and architectures and offers possibilities to manage different kinds of (public and private) linguistic resources and processing tools according to users requirements/constraints. Conversely, the conceptual separation between the user language and the implementation is a basic limitation in the optimization of complex processes. Quantitative approaches (e.g. statistical NLP methods) are weakly supported.

In [9] the GATE infrastructure (General Architecture for Text Engineering) is described. A basic assumption in GATE is that a set of basic tasks are needed in a NLP system, whatever is the specific target application; Examples of these are at least document management, annotation of textual and linguistic information, and visualization/browsing of the processing results, integration of different resources in a processing flow. To fulfill these assumptions an integrated environment composed of three different modules is defined:

- the GATE Document Manager (GDM) to manage documents with related linguistic information (added during linguistic analysis),
- a set of CREOLE (Collection of Reusable Object for Language Engineering) objects,
- a set of GDM compatible linguistic processors and, finally,
- a Graphical User Interface (GUI) to define complex NLP systems as combination of different modules.

GATE supports integration of different linguistic processing modules by defining

- a unified formalism for linguistic knowledge representation
  and
- an appropriate set of CREOLE modules.

Textual information is represented by using the notion of textual annotation firstly introduced in the TIPSTER project [1], a mechanism to associate data to spans of text. Each annotation is characterized by: a unique identifier, a type, a set of spans and a sequence of attribute-value pairs. Annotations ensure an homogeneous formalism to describe any kind of textual information. In fact to specify CREOLE processing module interfaces is only needed to define requirements and contributions in term of involved annotation and attributes. However, only in the last GATE version (ver. 1.5) it was explicitly mentioned a mechanism to represent Lexical Resources specifying access and query methods. In previous versions the linguistic knowledge bases required by linguistic modules was hidden within CREOLE objects lacking of common access interfaces.

A different approach inspired the design of the Corelli Document Processing Architecture [22]. The main purpose was to define an environment to support distributed NLP application design and implementation. The software-level engineering requirements for properties like robustness, portability, scalability or inter-language communication facilities was realized by using an Object-Oriented approach to design the overall architecture; the CORBA [17] services architecture is used to support distributed processing. A Tipster based mechanism is used to represent linguistic information, the Document Services component of the CORBA architecture is devoted to documents and textual annotations management. In the Corelli architecture the Lexical Resources play the role of Distributed Information Servers, managing also concurrency, privileges and access rights. Each CORBA system component must be described by using a programming language independent formalism denoted as IDL (Interface Definition Language). It forces an explicit definition for each component involved in an NLP system (e.g. linguistic information object, computational module, lexical resource, etc.) specifying, at design time, all the functionality they carry out.

In [15] is described an experiment that pertains to an extensive usage of SGML language to represent any kind of linguistic information related to a text. Text Encoding Initiative (TEI) directives are adopted to represent linguistic properties using SGML elements. The LT-NSL, a general purpose system for SGML input stream processing, is contextually used to perform linguistic functionalities. It represents one more environment to support data layer formalisms for textual information adopting TEI standard to achieve a linguistic layer description. In LT-NSL, structured processes are realized via pipelines of basic linguistic processors that communicate through Normalized-SGML documents where processing results are incrementally added. Nevertheless, representing complex linguistic information (e.g. graph structures), usually carried out via competing/concurrent mark-ups, is very hard to implement and reuse.

In Table 1 the relevant characteristics of previously described platforms have been summarized and organized to show different behaviors in respect with linguistic knowledge representation formalisms, allowed resources, functional description of processing and inter-process communication modalities.

It clearly emerges that no formal description of linguistic information is supported by any mentioned frameworks. All frameworks adopt an attribute-value data layer formalism (e.g. AUL, TIPSTER, SGML) to represent linguistic data, neutral with respect to the linguistic theory and the application purposes. This choice is of course more general in supporting NLP system design. As counterpart, it forces the designer of the NLP applications to fill the gap existing between the data and the linguistic layer. Moreover, apart from the Corelli architecture, in all mentioned platforms, all the information is managed in the same way: for example no different modalities are used to represent/define Lexical Information/Resource access methods. Application requirements violating this constraint highly reduce the applicability of the overall framework.

Table 1. NLP architecture design instruments

Architecture	Linguistic Data layer	information Linguistic layer	Language resources	Process description	Inter-process communication
ALEP	AUL	Undefined	AUL	AUL	unspecified
LT NSL	SGML	Undefined (TEI)	Unspecified	Unspecified	Unix pipe
GATE	Text annotation	Undefined (TIPSTER)	Unspecified (CREOLE based)	CREOLE	centralized GDM
Corelli	Text annotation	Undefined (TIPSTER)	Unspecified (IDL based)	IDL interface	centralized DMS (client server Corba)

3 Data vs. Conceptual Layer Representation for Linguistic Information

The focus on the Linguistic Layer of description has several positive implications on the design and the implementation of a NLP system. They are mostly related to the problems related to the Data Layer oriented approach.

Firstly, representing basic linguistic information as well as complex language-related information (e.g. syntactic or semantic graph structures or highly connected lexical networks) is very hard when small constituents or blocks like textual annotations or SGML elements are used. A data oriented formalism has to define simple constituents (annotations) or (SGML) elements, that can be combined in larger and more significant structures: this is unavoidable when general linguistic knowledge has to be represented. The problem is that complex information forces a representation made of longer compositions of small elements. Especially highly connected data structures require cryptic data layer representations, each conceptual relation across linguistic entities requiring a linkage between the corresponding data instances.

Secondly, the management of linguistic information under a Data Layer oriented approach is very complex. Linguistically significant functionalities require usually convoluted software modules that operate upon low level data. For example, traversing a conceptual relation between linguistic entities requires (to the developer) knowledge about the data formalism related to linguistic information. Moreover, in order to accomplish such process several low level operations are needed: getting the handler of the underlying entities from the source data representation and also retrieving the entities, usually accomplished by means of several operational steps. This kind data layer oriented software needs, usually, repetitive and annoying computations, reduces the readability of NLP module code, without adding significant improvement (i.e. basic optimization).

A Linguistic Layer perspective for representing textual information offers several advantages:

- all the information is immediately available to the developer and mapping between the data and the linguistic layer is ensured by the framework itself. Data interpretation is hidden in the linguistic objects and specific linguistic oriented functionalities are coded once independently from their complex compositions. In this way the developer is relieved from the annoying activities related to data management and can better concentrate on the use of linguistic information
- the abstraction of the specific data layer representation for linguistic entities allows different data formalisms for the same linguistic layer description. Different NLP applications may require slightly different data formalisms. When a linguistic entity is fully described in term of its features and behavior, it is not important for the developer to know exactly how the linguistic functionalities are implemented. Moreover alternative (equivalent) realizations for the same linguistic specification could be really interchangeable even within the same application.
- all the operations defined upon a linguistic entity are linguistically motivated. It makes no further sense to define data dependent functionalities related to linguistic entities. For example, if a *token* linguistic object is available, a potential operator may be designed that returns a syllabic decomposition of the word. Under a data oriented layer (e.g. annotation based) the same functionality would require primitive annotations (i.e. unique identifier or attributes for representing syllables) and operations to get or set annotation fields. The burden is not only related to more structured and costly data but also to a larger number of required low level operations.

The above aspects suggest to define a formalism in which "active" linguistic information can be expressed. Within this formalism the NLP system designer is able to homogeneously describe linguistic entities, computational modules and lexical resources. Basic repositories of linguistic information ranging from lexical resources, like dictionaries, to the actual textual information (e.g. a terminological concept occurring in a given text), can be made available to the developers, thus reducing design to an application-driven composition of existing and rich entities.

The above advantages are derived from the adoption of an Object Oriented paradigm in the design and implementation of a generic linguistic component in a wider NLP-driven system. OO interfaces guarantee a linguistic layer description for each involved entity, specifying properties, methods and mutual relationships. Objects are abstraction from the data layer and the intrinsic information hiding, provided by linguistic objects, makes fully transparent to the (different) developer(s) the implementation details required to manage the data layer representation mechanism. Alternative data formalisms are also allowed by defining alternative implementations for the linguistic layer interfaces. The last, but not least, aspect worth to be stressed is related to *scalability* and *portability*:

standard communication protocols, like CORBA [17], make available functionalities for distributed client-server communication, pushing for scalable NLP systems whose design is independent from the "internal" linguistic specifications. In figure 1 the communication among producers (i.e. servers) and consumers (i.e. clients) of linguistic information under a CORBA-based architecture is reported.

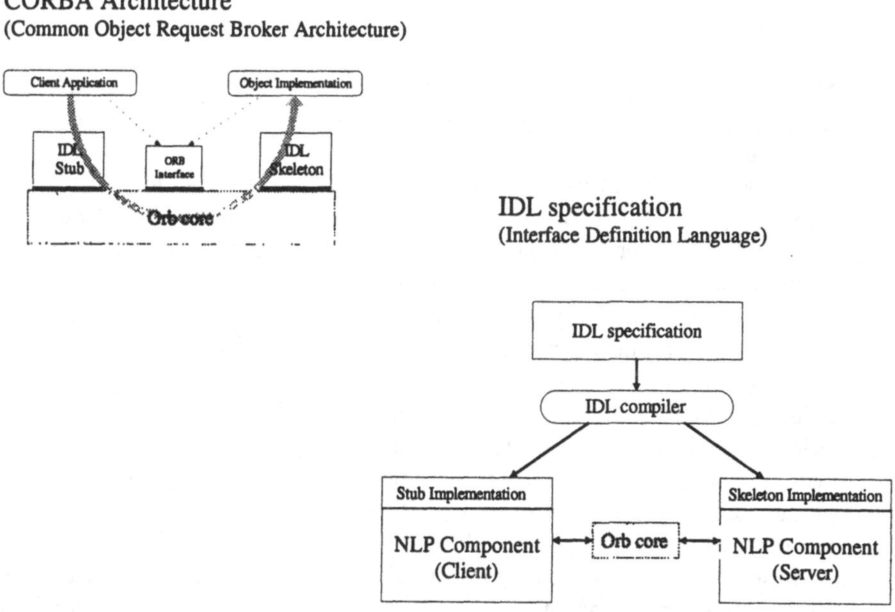

Fig. 1. Communication among NLP modules via CORBA

Orb supports the required exchange of information by means of IDL (i.e. Interface Definition Language) oriented interfaces. The higher is the level of abstraction embodied by linguistic objects to be exchanged the more effective will be the potentials for reuse and redesign (within alternative NLP architectures).

4 An High Level Classification for Linguistic Information

As the basic requirement of an OO framework for engineering Information Extraction systems is to define a Linguistic Layer and make available a repository of linguistic and reusable entities described within such a layer, a detailed analysis of basic types, properties and requirements for linguistic information is needed. The design activity starts thus with an high level classification of the linguistic information involved in an NLP application, willing to clarify the variety and nature of the different information associated with textual data and the related different roles played within a generic target system. Basically, this information may be partitioned into four different classes:

- *Structural Information* (S) - used to describe textual structure decomposition and some corresponding properties. It is information usually related with document structure and text segmentation. Two different types of segmentation can be defined:
  - information deriving from formatted text analysis (e.g. mark-up functions as those employed by HTML) where specific tags are used to explicitly denote titles, sections and paragraphs.
  - information that is determined during the overall linguistic processing, as for example, the identification of sentences or sub-sentences within paragraphs.

  It is important to note that some linguistic process, e.g. lemmatization, proper noun recognition or syntactic analysis, are basically sentence-based in nature. Several other linguistic capabilities has a larger scope, e.g. anaphora resolution or summarization that involve larger textual components. An explicit representation of the text structure naturally brings to a linguistically motivated binding between text sub-components and the corresponding linguistic processes.
- *Textual Information* (T) - textual information includes the variety of information related to a given text (i.e. the one is recognized and explicitly stored in connection to the text during a linguistic process). According to the role the information plays within the overall NLP system, two subclasses of textual information can be identified:(T_e), (T_c). We denote with (T_l) (where l stands for *local*) the information directly connected to a piece of text. It strictly relates to a span of text and it will be useful during future analysis of the same span of text. This is typically the information, like lemma, or syntactic relationship, that comes from a text within the context of a given sentence or document. It has no sense outside such a context. This information is in some sense *actual* (or *in vivo*).

  On the contrary cumulative linguistic information, expressing synthetic information throughout the wider context of sets of documents, or entire corpora, will be denoted with (T_c) (where c stands for *corpus*). A typical example of this kind of linguistic information is the one derived from processes of statistical estimation from training corpora, basically used within statistical (or hybrid quantitative-qualitative) linguistic inferences. The basic difference between (T_l) and (T_c) concerns access methods: specifically, the management of T_c information should guarantee efficient access methods to retrieve the form of T_c synthetic information while linking to the source text(s) are left out. Management of (T_l) information is generally easier according to the reduced locality of the access. Basically most of the before mentioned methods (see Section 2.2) are focusing only on the T_l information.
- *Linguistic Knowledge Information* (K) - Information of this type is usually stored in knowledge bases or linguistic resources. Knowledge Information

supplies *a priori* (i.e. independent from a given text) knowledge on lexicals, grammars or other basic components useful to support linguistic processing. Lexical knowledge bases, dictionaries of Proper Nouns are typical examples of this kind of knowledge. Knowledge information is generally highly structured and interconnected via a variety of linguistically rich relationships (e.g. syntactic dependencies vs. semantic or ontological relations). It is worth noting that representing Knowledge Information via the same formalism adopted for other linguistic information is very important. Small grain but linguistically crucial interaction between the linguistic resource and the different linguistic processing modules is allowed even if implementation details on both sides are unknown: this make the information transparent to the developer and preserve the linguistic consistency of the potential reuse of resources and functions.

- *Application Information* (A) - Several information, extracted during linguistic analysis, are linguistic in nature (e.g. event structures represented in templates) but are strictly related to the final application (e.g. IE and not IR). For example a set of filled templates represent relevant information about the document content and are strictly related to the language, as they derive from the detection of events, in an IE system. Anyhow, this information is not so general, as different applications may not require at all such class of information. They must thus be separated by the textual (T) information: (A) information lifetime exceeds linguistic processing boundary. Furthermore, application information A is usually stored separately from the document and managed differently from other linguistic information, by other application modules.

5 NLP Computational Modules Classification

The above mentioned linguistic entities play a major role in an object oriented design of a NLP system. As our aim is to define a set of general objects that are *active* in their contexts and *reusable* within different application scenarios, a categorization of the different computational components of a target NLP system is also required. Computational linguistic task can be grouped according to the classes of source and output information that they manage. Three main groups were identified: *Linguistic Processing Modules*, *Application Modules* and *Lexical Acquisition Modules.* Next sections briefly describe each of these categories by specifying their source and output data and stressing on their different roles within a NLP system.

5.1 Linguistic Processing Modules - LM

The class of *Linguistic Processing Modules* (LM) includes all the computational modules used to carry out linguistic activities during text processing. The Data Flow Diagram (DFD) depicted in Figure 2 explicitly shows the requirements and contributions of a generic LM module.

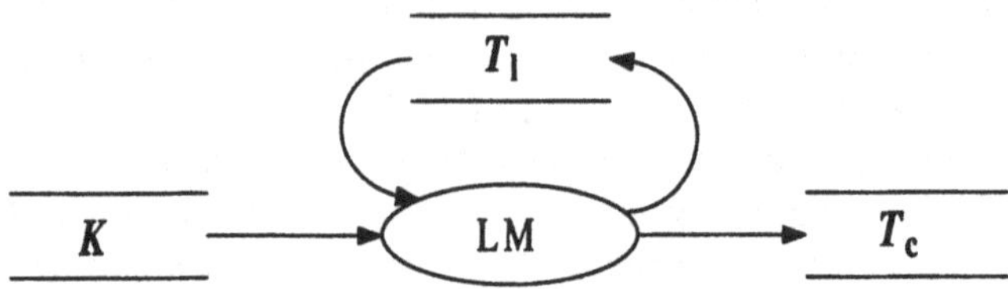

Fig. 2. Linguistic Processing Modules

Generally a LM updates information strictly related to text (i.e. T_l) by accessing to previously defined knowledge. The results of processing may be used for further text processing or as an information on linguistic corpus structure. For example, a Lemmatizer requires tokenization information that suggests text segmentation (i.e. significant linguistic string units) and produces, for each token, the corresponding lemmatization information (including lemma and morphological derivation information typical of each token found in the document, with alternatives if ambiguous). A parser is also a LM, as it builds over lemmatization (of possibly part-of-speech information) the grammatical structure legally assignable to the incoming data (i.e. sentences or smaller fragments). In this processes (K) information is important in supporting linguistic inferences (e.g. syntactic analysis or disambiguation). It is worth noticing that a LM module usually is responsible of the mapping between language general (e.g. sense enumeration for a given lemma) and text specific information (e.g. sense disambiguated lemmas within their contexts/sentences). The potential information available in resources is here specialized to the incoming texts, providing in vivo textual information of the type T_l. Here general information used to describe language properties is specialized in terms of specific text instantiation (including actual textual objects and their "*local*" features).

5.2 Lexical Acquisition Module - LAM

There is a growing evidence that robust language processing in large scale applications is crucially dependent on *adaptivity* to the domain sublanguage and to the evolving nature of language itself. Very often NLP system are more or less strictly coupled with inductive components able to learn from static (i.e. corpora of domain texts) or more dynamic linguistic evidences (e.g. success/failure in the task according to a feedback from the user). These inductive components are responsible for extracting (linguistic) regularities from sample data or from the current performance feedback and devoted to create domain and task specific resources. Lexical Acquisition systems (e.g. [23], [12], [6]) are typical examples of these kind of computational components, although large scale integration of a dedicated lexical acquisition system within an application has not yet been fully demonstrated. Figure 3 outlines a typical Data Flow Diagram for a Lexical Acquisition Module.

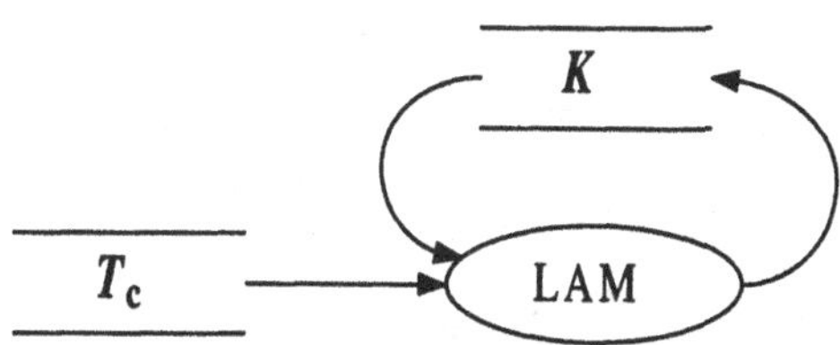

Fig. 3. Lexical Acquisition Module

Corpus based approaches to LAM make use of (T_c) information in order to produce corpus-dependent (or to extend/specialize pre-existing (K)) information. A good example is the Lexical Tuning architecture proposed in [5]. The cycle depicted in this DFD highlights the capability of iterating the different acquisition steps resulting in a form of incremental learning.

5.3 Application Module - AM

Application Modules are characterized by the purpose of extracting (A) information. This is central in the target application, basically supported by the earlier NLP engine. Figure 4 shows the DFD of a generic AM in terms of requirements and contributions.

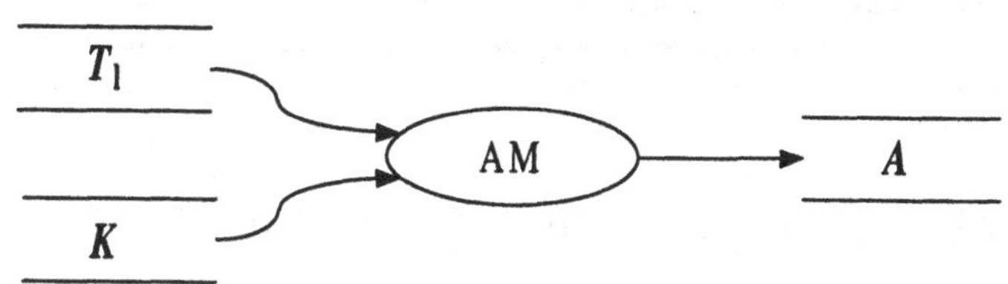

Fig. 4. Application Module

One or more specific AMs generally are terminal nodes in cascades of NLP processes. It is important to separate them from LM as, factorizing application specific tasks from linguistic functionalities, crucially improve infra-module cohesion and inter-module independence. These two are basic requirements for engineering of large scale software system either in terms of design cost and flexibility as well as in terms of higher reusability of existing resources and tools.

A high level functional description of a general purpose NLP system can be obtained as a mere combination of the different DFD already presented, as shown in Figure 5.

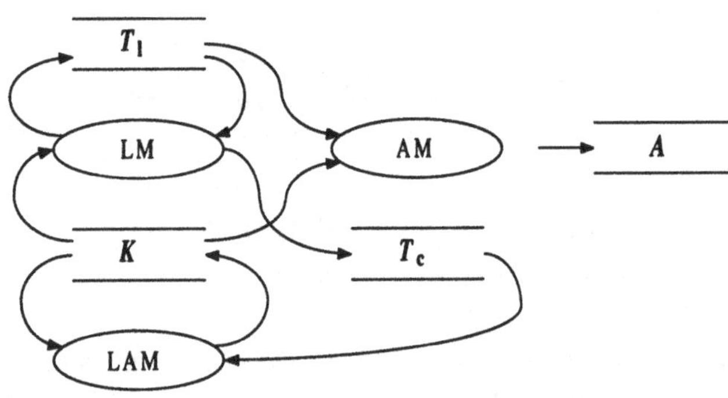

Fig. 5. A generic NLP system

The functional description of a specific NLP system is obtained by simply projecting this DFD. For example a lexical acquisition system is derived by ignoring (deleting) the AM process and (A) information. A static application system would be obtained by excluding LAM components and consequently the related (T_c) information. It is worth noticing that although the inner complexity of the different components cannot be entirely neglected (as a crucial factor for NLP system design), Figure 5 represents an ideal system, that is linguistically effective with respect to a given task (i.e. it is crucially tight to the linguistic processes) and also dynamically adaptable, as it includes (at least one) LAM functionalities.

6 OO Model for Linguistic Information

Linguistic functionalities and entities that enter in a complex process, pose strict constraints to the design activity. Development, testing and porting of different component need specific interfaces to be available. For example, a LAM process that can be useful to a linguistic process for improving (via adaptivity) a given task is often integrated in a later phase of the system development. In order to limit the effort required for re engineering of the system, it should be designed with preci9se and high-level interfaces to the rest of the system. In Fig 6 a class diagram that implements the conceptual interface of a generic LAM module is reported. The availability of a precise interface both to the requirements of the

LAM (i.e. K and T_c linguistic information) and to the consumers (e.g. later linguistic processors of type LM) minimize the re engineering effort. Moreover such an high-level interface is also independent from the implementation details, hidden by other OO techniques (e.g. the use of the `Factory` design patterns). As a result the software engineer can concentrate only on conceptual levels of descriptions (i.e. methods of linguistic representation and algorithmic inferences) rather than on lower level (and less important) aspects like formats for the exchange of data i.e. wrapping modules.

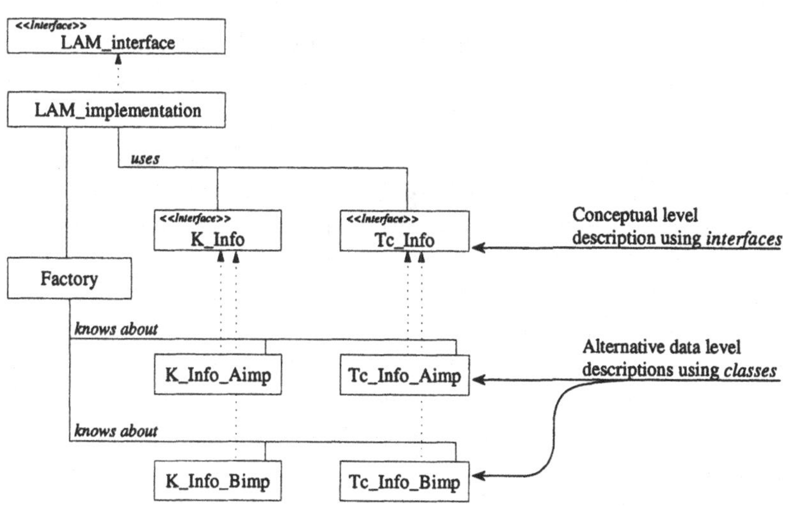

Fig. 6. Design of a LAM module under an OO perspective: a class diagram

Once the variety of linguistic entities and functions entering the main process of a language sensitive application has been clarified, a suitable OO modeling can be defined. In order to demonstrate feasibility of an OO approach to NLP system design, it is important to clearly determine how different types of linguistic information can be coherently represented. UML compliant Class Diagrams will be hereafter used to specify the OO representation for (S), (T_l), (A) and (K) entities. This results into a full definition for the corresponding information classes. The Class Diagram reported in Figure 7 shows a set of interfaces used to describe text structures (class S).

Specifically the concept of structured test is represented by the `Formatted Text` interface, it can be specialized in two different way: the `Complex Formatted Text` interface is used to represent a text fragment that can be further decomposed into several `Formatted Text` components, referred by specific labels. The `Text Segment` interface is hence used to describe a `Formatted Text` for which no further decomposition using explicit text format markers exists. The same class diagram also shows the `Linguistic Information` interface. It represents

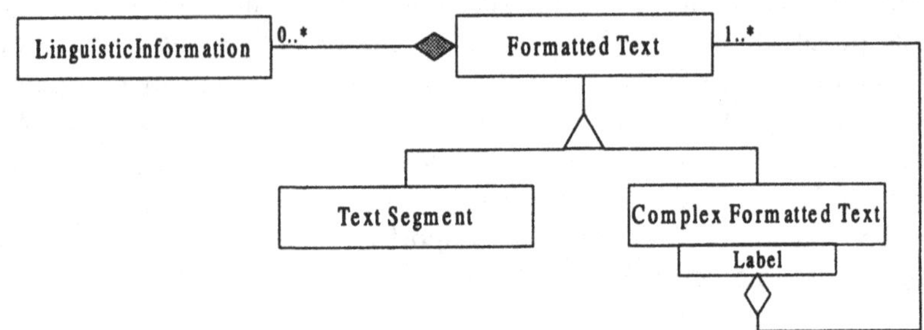

Fig. 7. Class Diagram for Structural Information

any kind of linguistic entities that are to be joined to text segment (i.e. lemmas in the title). The specialization of `Linguistic Information` is described by the class diagram shown in Figure 8, concerns the text constituent representations.

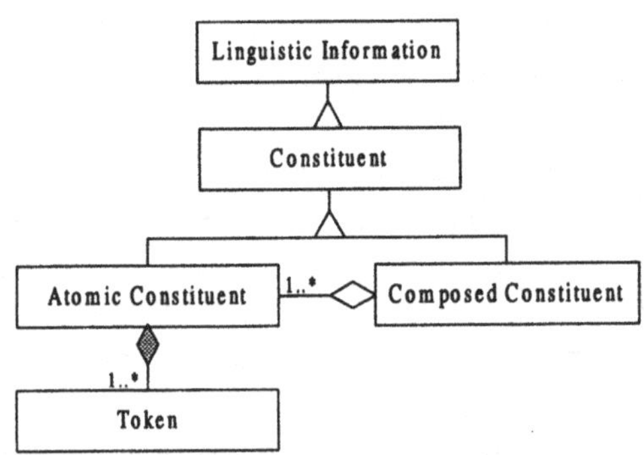

Fig. 8. Class Diagram for Phrasal Constituents

The `Constituent` interface can be specialized into `Composed Constituent` or `Atomic Constituent` depending on the possibility (or not) of considering its components as independent from the entire constituent structure.

The object diagram reported in Figure 9 shows the OO representation for the constituent *European Commission Officer*. It highlights a sub constituent (*European Commission*) which can be referred as an independent linguistic relevant component and used for further linguistic inference.

Another example of specific (i.e. a specialization of) Linguistic Information is represented by *events*, which are typical (A) information in IE tasks [10,18]. They can be described using a linguistic layer formalism by defining an `Event`

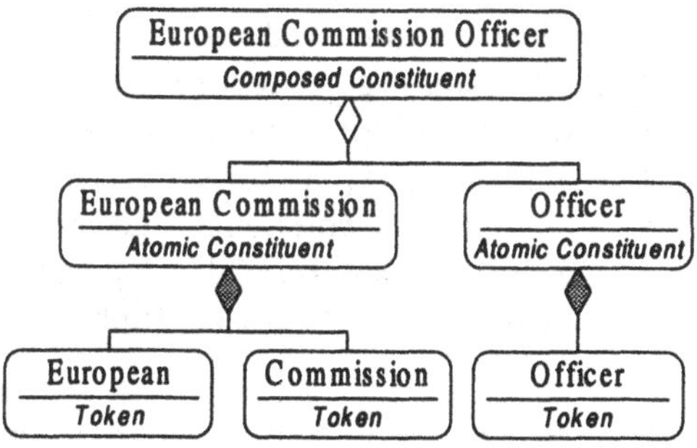

Fig. 9. Object Diagram for Constituents

`Information` interface, shown in Figure 10. Here an homonymous interface is made available and supports a transparent access to information about event categories (e.g. "*joint ventures*") and participants (e.g. "*companies*").

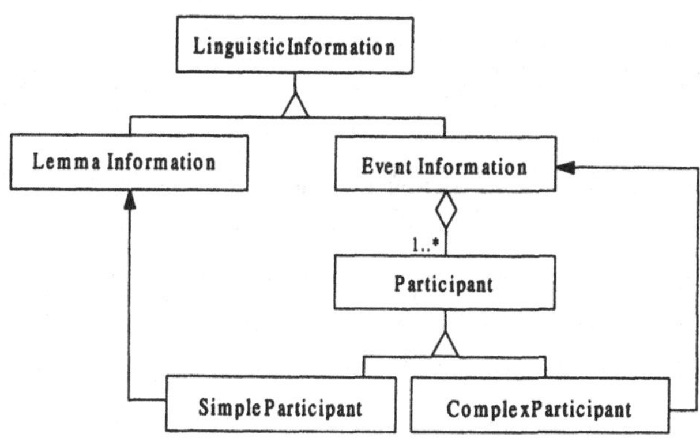

Fig. 10. Class Diagram for Events representation

It is worth noticing that complex events (i.e. events whose participants may be realized by another event, e.g. *causative events*) can be represent by introducing two `Participant` specializations:

- `Simple Participant`, used to represent a participant entity and link it to the specific text constituent
- `Complex Participant`, used to link an event to another related event realized by its own `Event Information` object.

All the above definitions enter, as a unifying framework, in the design of the variety of linguistic (i.e. lexical, grammatical and textual) information circulating within a complex NLP system. Fig. 11 reports an overview of the previous definitions. It does not represent a comprehensive view with respect to the different theories and architectures proposed in literature but constitutes a systematic starting point for a lexical information workbench that is (1) open to further extension and (2) enough general (in its current development) to *cover* wide sets of phenomena (as those met in complex linguistic applications, e.g. IE).

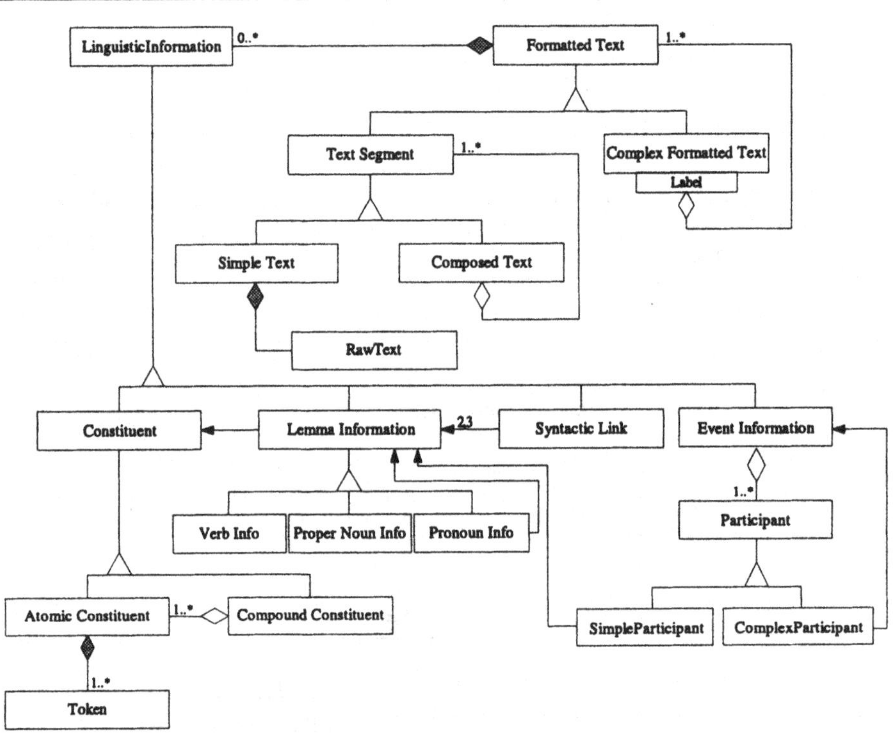

Fig. 11. A comprehensive view on the `LinguisticInformation` class

As we mentioned in previous section an homogeneous representation of linguistic objects and linguistic resources is a key aspects for augmenting the flexibility and linguistic significance of the design activity. We thus need here to show how (K) information can be described under the same OO paradigm . Figure 12 shows a class diagram that represents a conceptual model for the WordNet lexical knowledge base [7]. Wordnet is a psycho linguistically motivated semantic network of English words. Synonymy sets (named *Synsets*) are the basic units of knowledge, and are constituted of sets of words: under a specific projection of their meanings these words can be regarded as synonyms. As an example, two senses of the word *stock* are: (1) a supply of something available for future use and (2) the handle of a handgun. They are represented in Wordnet respectively by the following synsets: (1) "*store, stock, fund*" and (2) "*stock, gunstock*". Here words like *fund* or *store* "select" meaning (1) for *stock*, while *gunstock* characterizes the second one. Note that Wordnet represents the different meanings of *stock* in 17 different synsets. In Wordnet a variety of lexical relations between synsets are represented: hypnoid/hyperonimy as well as meronimy or antonymy. Hyperonims of the two senses for stock are for example: h(1) "*accumulation*" and h(2) "*handle, grip, handgrip, hold*". A meronimy relation links the synset "*artillery, heavy weapon, gun, ordnance*" with the sense (2) "*store, stock, fund*".

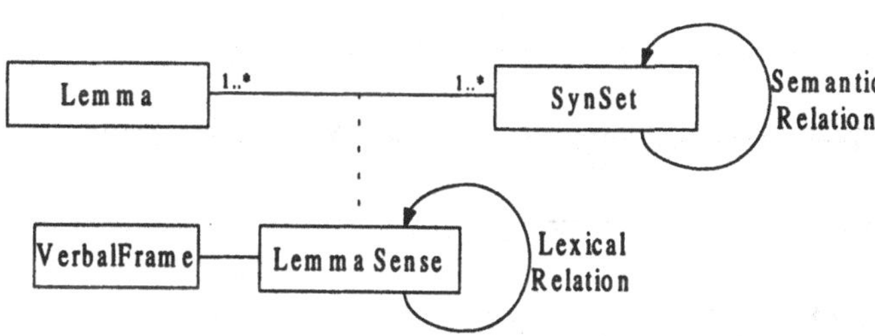

Fig. 12. Conceptual perspective Class Diagram for WordNet Lexical Resource

The `SynSet` interface in Figure 12 is used to represent the synset properties and relations. `SynSet` is connected to the `Lemma` interface by a reflexive association which information is described by the `Lemma Sense` association interface. Semantic and lexical relations between respectively `SynSets` and `LemmaSenses` are also shown. The corresponding implementation perspective class diagram is then reported in Figure 13.

"`Factory` design patterns" ([11]) are here used to guarantee a real implementation independence between the linguistic level description (achieved by using interfaces) and the corresponding data level description (obtained defining classes that implement these interfaces). Alternative data level implementations are only known by the `Factory` that is responsible of the linguistic-data layer binding. Representing in this way a lexical resource (like Wordnet) allows direct access by means of linguistically meaningful primitives to the information available for lemmas, i.e. sense and relations. This makes the design of complex linguistic inference needed by an application fully independent from implementation details. A flexible design is thus encouraging experimentation of different inference models as well as fast prototyping and final engineering.

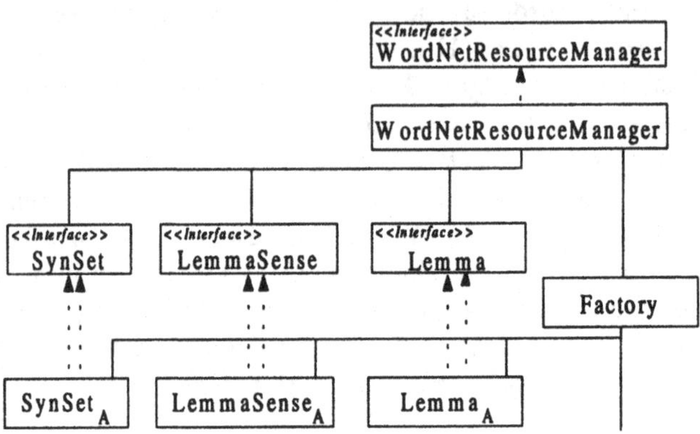

Fig. 13. Implementation perspective Class Diagram for WordNet Lexical Resource

7 Using the OO Approach

Examples reported in the previous section have shown how the OO approach can be used to describe linguistic information at a conceptual level. It is still important to describe which are the implications of the above presented conceptual modeling on the computational (i.e. implementation) aspects. The aim is to support a full definition and implementation of the target NLP-based system by extensive application of OO modeling techniques. In the next subsections, an OO design strategy will be introduced as guideline to a linguistically motivated and coherent description of linguistic information, resources, computational modules and the application front-end. Experiments carried out following this approach will be described in the remaining subsections. In particular (section 16) the design of the TREVI system ([14,4]) will be discussed. TREVI is a distributed OO system for document categorization and enrichment driven by user profiles. TREVI represents a concrete (and large-scale) application of a design strategy following the above principles and will be here used as an evaluation framework and to discuss benefits and limitations within a real design process.

7.1 A Design Strategy Focused on Linguistic Information

The main objective of a design strategy is to support the definition of a software infrastructure to build up general NLP systems. The design of an NLP based application is made of at least the following phases:

1. to select/define a suitable language model able to describe and manipulate the linguistic information useful to the target application

2. to realize the NLP components that are consistent with the selected language model
3. to integrate the different required NLP modules within the final application

Activity 1 requires the definition of a suitable set of linguistic information necessary to the final application (e.g. *events* in IE systems) and required by the temporary linguistic processes (e.g. verb subcategorization information used by the parser or by the event recognizer, but not realized finally as not meaningful to the application task). In this phase the linguistic entities described in section 6 result in a general repository that can be used as basic linguistic models for characterizing the required linguistic inferences as well as source information on requirements and contributions of the different linguistic modules. Note that reuse of the above entities ensure also the transparent linking to linguistic resources implied by the `Lemma` and `LemmaSenses` interfaces. In this phase a relevant role is also assumed by domain information, that should be taken into account for specific adaptation tasks, or for the integration of resources available to the final user. Again OO modeling ensure a modular approach to the integration problem. The existing interfaces for linguistic object may play here the role of models for a consistent mapping: user resources can be considered as a K form of information and undergo to a similar integration process.

Activity 2 is devoted to the definition of the different computational modules that cooperate to the activity foreseen by the adopted linguistic model. Here the design of the different required processes makes a direct access to the linguistic entities functionalities (embedded in their interfaces). The development is thus independent from implementation details and can concentrate on the linguistically meaningful aspects (e.g. disambiguation and/or decomposition methods). Furthermore testing of alternative solutions and models is also supported. It is worth noticing that each required linguistic module results in a computational object that can be instantiated whenever necessary (in a given time point during the overall computational process) and that can be directly integrated (i.e. invoked) by the target application.

Activity 3 refers to the integration of the different linguistic modules within the overall application. This integration reduces to the design of suitable invocation phases that, relying on the explicit interfaces made available at the previous step, make available to the application the set of required linguistic information for the application dependent final computation.

Note that the extreme relevance of the above methodology for engineering of general NLP systems, and in particular IE ones, relies on the availability of a set of alternative OO models corresponding to different languages or linguistic theories. This makes available a large repository of pre-designed and interrelated object representations for linguistic information (i.e. structural, textual (T_l, T_c), general-purpose (K) and application dependent (A)). Simple units of textual information are general enough to be widely reused within different applications (e.g., token or lemmas). More complex units, like *Events* described by larger text fragments, have also significant implications in different applications. IE is not the only application where events play a role. Event based indexing can also be seen as a significant basis for a retrieval model in IR. For these reasons, current work concentrate on the definition of a wider repository of linguistic entities reflecting most of the constraints and principles of linguistic theory. Conflicting theory would require different objects. Criteria to integrate different (and possibly conflicting) object models constitute a significant research activity. Linking of the objects to specific kinds of textual information and consistent composition of them throughout a linguistic process requires further work. The medium-term perspective of this work is to fully support the design of a given application in terms of a structured composition of existing OO representations of the relevant textual information.

7.2 A Lexical Acquisition Process: Extraction of Terminological Knowledge

The lexical information that trigger linguistic induction in lexical acquisition systems varies from simple word/tokens to syntactically annotated or semantically typed collocations (e.g. *powerful* vs. *strong tea* ([20])), syntactic disambiguation rules (e.g. [13], [8]) or sense disambiguation rules are usually derived. Such information is lexical as it encodes constraints (of different types) at the word level, to be thus inherited by morphologic variants of a given lemma.

This strongly lexicalised knowledge, as it is extracted from corpus data, requires lexical entries to be known in advance in some morphologic database. It has been repeatedly noted that lemmas in a corpus depends on the underlying sublanguage and their nature and shape is not as general as it is usually encoded in morphologic dictionaries. As an example, the noun *studio* in a corpus of environment related texts written in Italian language is found within the following collocates

... *studi di base ..., (*basic studies)*
... *studi di impatto ambientale ...,(*studies on the environmental impact)*
... *studi di fattibilita' ..., (*feasibility studies),*
... *studi di riferimento..., (*reference studies)*

It is very common in a corpus (not balanced, thus focused to a limited domain) to find a set of specifications of nouns that:

- are not always compositional (e.g. *studio di base*);
- describe complex concepts (e.g. *studi di fattibilita'*) in the underlying technical domain, so they are relevant for text understanding and classification/extraction
- select specific and independent senses of the related term: *studi di base* refers to *study* as an *abstraction*, while *studi di fattibilita'* is a specific engineering *activity*;
- for the related nominal compounds show independent lexical properties as they enter in specific lexical semantic as well domain specific relations.

A method for automatic extraction of terminological information from corpora of texts has been proposed in ([2,3]). Figure 14 shows the functional architecture of the system. The entire process is based on a preliminary preprocessing of tokenization, basic morphological analysis and POS tagging. Noun Phrase Identification is carried out for the detection of potential term structures. It is guided by a special purpose grammar, aiming to capture legal instances of nouns and nominal compounds. Then statistical and semantic filters are used to filter out accidental co-occurrences (i.e. nominal structures that are not in relation with any specific domain concept) and select the target terms set. The recognized structures generate terms as the set of their grammatically legal realizations: this is the role of the grammatical filtering phase run over the source corpus contexts. Finally a structured terminological database is produced (Terminology production phase).

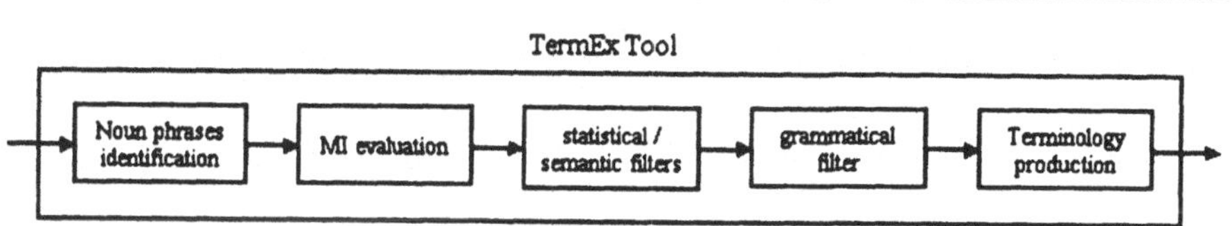

Fig. 14. TermEx: Functional architecture of the system for terminology extraction

The system supports manual inspection to validate the derived entries. It is also possible to directly reuse the structured terminological database during a second form of (advanced) morphological analysis: the lexical information derived during the first corpus processing step is ready to be integrated within the morphological processing chain: this improves the next acquisition phases (e.g. subcategorization frame learning) from the same corpus. This is not the only use of the derived terminology as other computational modules (consumers) different from the morphological analyser rely on this information: for example an indexing device can profitably use this information (i.e. from simple keywords to term-based retrieval)analogously an IE system could be interested in selected "terms" belonging to predefined classes to be interested in templates. The derived terminology can also be made available to different final users of the system: from humans that are not expert of the domain, to automatic (agent-like) systems aiming to improve their retrieval capabilities throughout text repositories (e.g. the Web itself).

Terminological information is thus a perfect example of linguistic information that enters in very different (linguistic and non-linguistic) processes: it is the result of a linguistic induction, it is crucial in some linguistic process (i.e. morphological recognition) and it is also crucial for application purposes like search in textual databases. We thus expect that a suitable modeling, according to the principles sketched in previous section, produces its best results: it could allow a suitable level of conceptualization, push for information hiding and make easier the design and integration of the final application(s).

Figure 15 shows the UML class diagram for conceptual modeling of the `Term` objects. A term is a linguistic entity headed by a given `Lemma`, that represents its linguistic head. A specific class `Complex Term` represents complex terminological entries, that have an head (inherited from the `Lemma` class) and a set of additional lemmas, acting as specifier or modifiers.

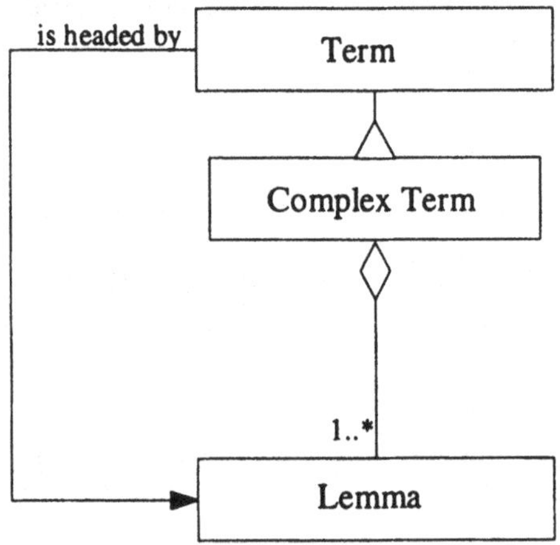

Fig. 15. Class diagram for the class `Lemma`

The above structure has been adopted as a representation in our acquisition system and reused within the following modules:

- `TermEx`, the module for induction of terminological information (according to the model described in [2])
- the lemmatization module used throughout a number of linguistic processes: Ariosto ([6]), a system for corpus-driven lexical acquisition, TREVI (see next chapter) a NLP processing system for text categorization and enrichment
- a graphical user interface for navigation and browsing, devoted to support final users in accessing domain-specific dictionaries.

Note that the adopted representation supports also a transparent linking to existing lexical resources. As mentioned in section 6 in our framework, Wordnet has been modeled under an OO paradigm as well. The `Lemma` class appearing in both representations represents exactly the same objects. In this way, mapping the induced terminological entries to the Wordnet hierarchy requires only to focus on the linguistic problems raised by polisemy aspects of words. Implementation details for representing lemmas are here hidden in a similar way by the use of different "`Factory` design patterns" (see section 6). In this way integration is guarantee by a careful design of the Conceptual Layer (class Lemma). This results in a higher improvement of the quality and and in a lower complexity for the design task: the only problems that have to be solved are inherent to the linguistic nature of the problem (i.e. polisemy) and no care is to be put on other details. We will show how this positive side-effect is preserved not only in a typical LAM process (like terminology induction) but also within a target NLP application, as discussed in the next section.

7.3 An Application: Large-Scale Document Categorization

The design activity of a real NLP application system constitute a further evaluation test bed for the proposed design framework. In this section an application of document categorization developed following principles described in this paper will be described.

One of the foremost needs expressed by small and large enterprises over the last few years is the capability to suitably exploit textual data available to users since the beginning of information networks. The experiment described in this subsection is focused on the definition of a distributed system for document categorization and enrichment of thematic texts cataloguers driven by user profiles. The first prototype of the system has been fully designed and partially integrated within the TREVI (Text Retrieval and Enrichment for Vital Information) project (EP23311) (see [14]) In TREVI a stream of incoming documents is processed in a distributed environment. A client server approach is adopted where each system component co-operate to the information flow to provide several classes of final users with those documents matching their needs (expressed via general profiles), enriched with structural information and possibly linked to existing (user-owned) repositories of previous texts. The general description of the current available TREVI prototype is shown in

In TREVI the specific emphasis on linguistic content rather than on simpler retrieval procedures results in the definition of a complex architecture for language processing based on the Object Oriented design method proposed in sections 5 and 7. The variety of textual information processed in Trevi has been modeled according to the OO paradigm, and design steps described in Section 7.1 have been followed. Figure 17 shows the functional decomposition of the core NLP engine available in TREVI.

The UML class diagram that represents the object model for textual information is shown in Figure 18. A set of classes and their relationship are defined in order to explicitly represent the linguistic information extracted during the document analysis. It represents an example of the contribution that the entire NLP chain provides to the target application.

The `ParsedArticle` class is defined to represent articles and the information resulting from the entire NLP processing of their content. All articles are made of at least one `ParsedText` object. A `ParsedText` object contains all the linguistic

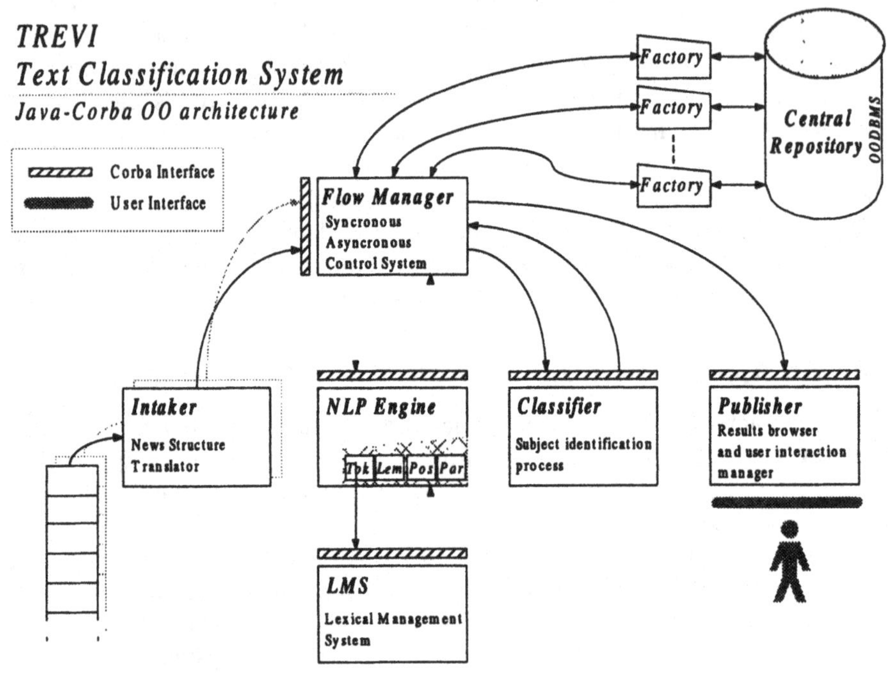

Fig. 16. A general description of TREVI prototype

information related to a text field of a structured article (e.g. the *title* or the *abstract* parts). A set of specialized `ParsedArticle` are introduced to represent different article types. A specific `ParsedArticleType`, (`PT1`), in fact, may include `ParsedText` objects that can be absent from another article type (`PT2`).

Figure 18 shows a collection of different textual objects used to store the textual information resulting from text analysis. The different classes are the following:

- `Token` : each `Token` object is related to a token of the raw text.
- `Lemma` : a `Lemma` object is used to store the information extracted by the `Lemmatizer` module. A lemma is related to a single token or a sequence of tokens (for compound terms like *New York* resulting from lemmatization)
- `ProperNoun` : a specialization of `Lemma` object that is able to take into account specific information related to proper nouns (e.g. proper name conceptual categories like *Company* or *City*).
- `Event` : a `Event` object is used to represent an event detected by the `Event Recogniser` module. Among the relevant properties of these objects are `Event Types` as well as a set of `Participants`.
- `Participant` : This is an abstract class for the `Event Participants`, each characterized by a semantic role. For example in *management succession*

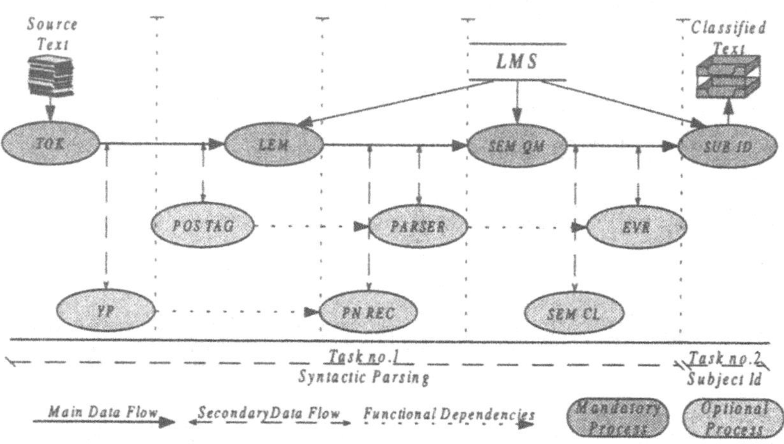

Fig. 17. Functional architecture of the NLP engine in TREVI

type of events, the *leaving manager* is a typical participant as well as the *source/destination company*.

- `SimplePart` : a simple participant refers to a `Lemma`.
- `ComplexPart` : a complex participant refers recursively to another `Event`.

The textual information extracted by the NLP component are then used by the next modules in the TREVI processing chain. The main advantage of the adopted linguistically motivated object-oriented specification has been a flexible modeling of the document categorization task. The transparent access to the contributions of the NLP engine (in terms of the structured `ParsedText` object) has preserved the TREVI designer to take care of any kind of data-level specification, thus supporting:

- flexible development environment, where different modules (possibly in different programming languages) have been transparently developed and integrated
- distributed and concurrent engineering of the different modules
- modular development and testing of the different components
- rapid integration and prototyping

8 Conclusions

The satisfactory design of a NLP system must consider conflicting needs expressed by the involved entities: academic and industrial research and development communities. It is a largely shared opinion that computational frameworks,

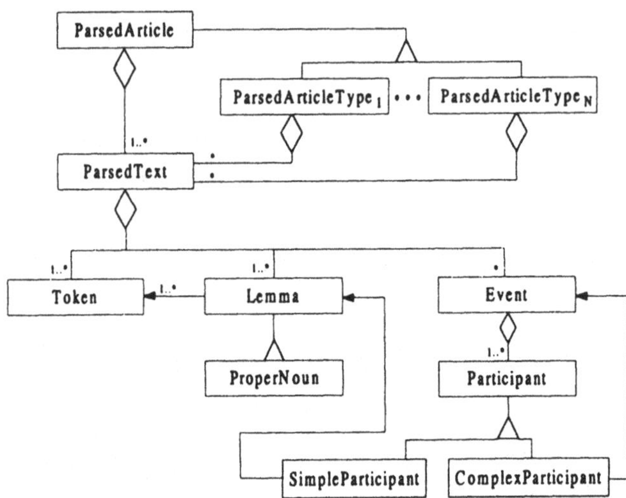

Fig. 18. Class Diagram for Parser contribution in TREVI

or software infrastructures, to support the design process are needed. The availability of software infrastructures is crucial for sharing the linguistic knowledge among language models and tools and for the engineering and scalability of the target NLP application.

In this paper a computational representation to express the linguistic information at a conceptual level able to optimize the design phase has been presented. An OO model has been proposed providing a systematic description (i.e. classification) of linguistic information and processes in order to satisfy *real* requirements of NLP applications. As result a general repository of linguistic objects, reflecting such classification, has been derived. The resulting data and processes are application independent and constitute a set of computational objects portable throughout different linguistic theories and application environments. This is one of the first attempts to provide a strictly computational and theory-neutral system for linguistic description.

An extensive use of the modeling method has been carried out in the development of lexical acquisition systems as well as applications. In the design of *Termex*, a system for the acquisition of a domain specific terminological database from an extensive corpus, the adoption of the defined representational framework has allowed the straightforward reuse of the resulting knowledge (i.e. terminology). The terminological entries resulting from the induction are directly served to several core NL processing phases (e.g. lemmatization and noun phrase recognition) that usually operate within different application architectures.

Further operational evidences about the benefit of the proposed approach have been observed during the development of a distributed text categorization system (TREVI). The adopted modeling method produced a set of general purpose and reusable linguistic processors (e.g. from the tokenizer to the robust parser). The adopted representation is linguistically adequate as the tested integration with existing LKBs (in particular Wordnet) demonstrates. The design of the TREVI system has been crucially facilitated by the adopted framework, where a Java/CORBA platform supports intercommunication among the different computational modules (linguistic and application servers). The results of TREVI in terms of categorization accuracy as well as the processing speed are very good and open to further extensions. Most of this benefits are due to the careful design allowed under the proposed framework.

It is worth saying that further research is needed to evaluate the expressiveness of the proposed set of linguistic definitions with respect to a larger set of linguistic theories and representation systems (e.g. unification-based formalisms). The lack of mechanisms (e.g. unification) so widely used within many methods and algorithms for language processing requires a careful analysis and extension of the proposed framework. It also plays a relevant role, given our first results, the work to be still done in testing the current framework. This will proceed by validating the OO descriptions and measuring their "coverage" with respect to different operational scenarios, where deeper linguistic capabilities are needed (e.g. text understanding in machine translation).

References

1. Tipster text program phases i & ii. In *Proceedings of Workshops sponsored by the ARPA TIPSTER Program for Advances in Text Processing.* Morgan-Kaufmann Publishers, 1996.
2. R. Basili, De Rossi G., and Pazienza M.T. Inducing terminology for lexical acquisition. In *Preoceedings of the Second Conference on Empirical Methods in Natural Language Processing, Providence, USA*, 1997.
3. R. Basili, Bonelli A. and Pazienza M.T. Estrazione e Rappresentazione di Informazioni terminologiche eterogenee In *Proceedings of the Workshop "Strumenti di Organizzazione ed Accesso Intelligent per Informazioni Eterogenee" of the AI*IA '98 Conference*, Padova, September 1998.
4. R. Basili, Di Nanni M., Mazzucchelli L., Marabello M.V., and Pazienza M.T. Nlp for text classification: the trevi experience. In *Proceedings of the Second International Conference on Natural Language Processing and Industrial Applications, Universite' de Moncton, New Brunswick (Canada)*, August 1998.
5. R. Basili, Catizone R., Pazienza M.T., Stevenson M., Velardi P., Vindigni M., and Wilks Y. An empirical approach to lexical tuning. In *Proceedings of the Workshop "Adapting Lexical and Corpus Resources to Sublanguages and Applications", LREC First International Conference on Language Resources and Evaluation, Granada, Spain*, 26 May 1998.
6. R. Basili, Pazienza M. T., and Velardi P. n empirical symbolic approach to natural language processing. *Artificial Intelligence*, (85):59–99, 1996.
7. R. Beckwith, Fellbaum C., Gross D., and Miller G. Wordnet: a lexical database organized on a psycholinguistic principles. In U. Zernik, editor, *Lexical Acquisition: Exploiting On-Line Resources to Build a Lexicon.* Lawrence-Erlbaum Ass, 1991.

8. E. Brill and P. Resnik. A rule based approach to prepositional phrase attachment disambiguation. In *Proc. of COLING-94, Kyoto, Japan*, 1994.
9. H. Cunningham, Humphreys K., Gaizauskas R., and Wilks Y. Software infrastructure for natural language processing. In *Proceedings of Fifth Conference on Applied Natural Language Processing, Washington, DC, USA*. Morgan-Kaufmann Publishers, March-April, 1997.
10. R. Gaizauskas, Humphreys K., Cunningham H., and Wilks Y. Description of LaSIE system as used for MUC-6. In G. Booch, editor, *Proceedings of the 6th Message Understanding Conference, MUC-6*. Morgan Kaufmann, 1995.
11. E. Gamma, Helm R., Johnson R., Vlissides J., and Booch G. Design patterns : Elements of reusable object-oriented software. Addison-Wesley Professional Computing, October 1994.
12. R. Grishman and Sterling J. Generalizing automatically generated selectional patterns. In *Proc. of COLING-94, Kyoto, Japan*, 1994.
13. D. Hindle and M. Rooths. Structural ambiguity and lexical relation. *Computational Linguistics*, 19(1), 1993.
14. L. Mazzucchelli and Marabello M.V. Specification of the overall toolkit architecture. In *EP 23311 TREVI Project Deliverable 7D1*, 1997.
15. D. McKelvie, Brew C., and Thompson H. Using SGML as a basis for data-intensive NLP. In *Proceedings of Fifth Conference on Applied Natural Language Processing*. ACL, Washington, DC, USA, March-April, 1997.
16. MUC-6. Proceedings of the sixth message understanding conference (muc-6). In *Columbia, MD*. Morgan Kaufmann, 1995.
17. OMG. *Common Object Request Broker Archictecture*. July, 1995.
18. M.T. Pazienza, editor. *Information Extraction - A Multidisciplinary Approach to an Emerging Information Technology*. Springer Verlag, Berlin, 1997.
19. N.K. Simkins. An open architecture for language engineering. In *Proceedings of Language Engineering Convention / Journees du Genie Linguistique,*. Addison-Wesley Object Technology Series, Paris 6-7th July 1994.
20. F. Smadja. *Macrocoding the Lexicon with co-occurrence knowldege*. Zernik, U.,ed. "Lexical Acquisition" Lawrence Erlbaum, 1991.
21. R.H. Zakon. actually on site: `http://www.isoc.org/guest/zakon/Internet/History/HIT.html`.
22. R. Zajac, Carper M., and Sharples N. An open distributed architecture for reuse and integration of heterogeneous nlp component. In G. Booch, editor, *Proceedings of Fifth Conference on Applied Natural Language Processing*. Addison-Wesley Object Technology Series, Washington, DC, USA, March-April, 1997.
23. U. Zernik. *Lexical Acquisition: Exploiting On-Line Resources to Build a Lexicon*. Lawrence Erlbaum Associates, Hillsdale, NJ, 1991.

Author Index

Lecture Notes in Artificial Intelligence (LNAI)

Vol. 1571: P. Noriega, C. Sierra (Eds.), Agent Mediated Electronic Commerce. Proceedings, 1998. IX, 207 pages. 1999.

Vol. 1572: P. Fischer, H.U. Simon (Eds.), Computational Learning Theory. Proceedings, 1999. X, 301 pages. 1999.

Vol. 1574: N. Zhong, L. Zhou (Eds.), Methodologies for Knowledge Discovery and Data Mining. Proceedings, 1999. XV, 533 pages. 1999.

Vol. 1582: A. Lecomte, F. Lamarche, G. Perrier (Eds.), Logical Aspects of Computational Linguistics. Proceedings, 1997. XI, 251 pages. 1999.

Vol. 1585: B. McKay, X. Yao, C.S. Newton, J.-H. Kim, T. Furuhashi (Eds.), Simulated Evolution and Learning. Proceedings, 1998. XIII, 472 pages. 1999.

Vol. 1599: T. Ishida (Ed.), Multiagent Platforms. Proceedings, 1998. VIII, 187 pages. 1999.

Vol. 1600: M. J. Wooldridge, M. Veloso (Eds.), Artificial Intelligence Today. VIII, 489 pages. 1999.

Vol. 1604: M. Asada, H. Kitano (Eds.), RoboCup-98: Robot Soccer World Cup II. XI, 509 pages. 1999.

Vol. 1609: Z. W. Ras, A. Skowron (Eds.), Foundations of Intelligent Systems. Proceedings, 1999. XII, 676 pages. 1999.

Vol. 1611: I. Imam, Y. Kodratoff, A. El-Dessouki, M. Ali (Eds.), Multiple Approaches to Intelligent Systems. Proceedings, 1999. XIX, 899 pages. 1999.

Vol. 1612: R. Bergmann, S. Breen, M. Göker, M. Manago, S. Wess, Developing Industrial Case-Based Reasoning Applications. XX, 188 pages. 1999.

Vol. 1617: N.V. Murray (Ed.), Automated Reasoning with Analytic Tableaux and Related Methods. Proceedings, 1999. X, 325 pages. 1999.

Vol. 1620: W. Horn, Y. Shahar, G. Lindberg, S. Andreassen, J. Wyatt (Eds.), Artificial Intelligence in Medicine. Proceedings, 1999. XIII, 454 pages. 1999.

Vol. 1621: D. Fensel, R. Studer (Eds.), Knowledge Acquisition Modeling and Management. Proceedings, 1999. XI, 404 pages. 1999.

Vol. 1623: T. Reinartz, Focusing Solutions for Data Mining. XV, 309 pages. 1999.

Vol. 1632: H. Ganzinger (Ed.), Automated Deduction – CADE-16. Proceedings, 1999. XIV, 429 pages. 1999.

Vol. 1634: S. Džeroski, P. Flach (Eds.), Inductive Logic Programming. Proceedings, 1999. VIII, 303 pages. 1999.

Vol. 1637: J.P. Walser, Integer Optimization by Local Search. XIX, 137 pages. 1999.

Vol. 1638: A. Hunter, S. Parsons (Eds.), Symbolic and Quantitative Approaches to Reasoning and Uncertainty. Proceedings, 1999. IX, 397 pages. 1999.

Vol. 1640: W. Tepfenhart, W. Cyre (Eds.), Conceptual Structures: Standards and Practices. Proceedings, 1999. XII, 515 pages. 1999.

Vol. 1647: F.J. Garijo, M. Boman (Eds.), Multi-Agent System Engineering. Proceedings, 1999. X, 233 pages. 1999.

Vol. 1650: K.-D. Althoff, R. Bergmann, L.K. Branting (Eds.), Case-Based Reasoning Research and Development. Proceedings, 1999. XII, 598 pages. 1999.

Vol. 1652: M. Klusch, O.M. Shehory, G. Weiss (Eds.), Cooperative Information Agents III. Proceedings, 1999. XI, 404 pages. 1999.

Vol. 1669: X.-S. Gao, D. Wang, L. Yang (Eds.), Automated Deduction in Geometry. Proceedings, 1998. VII, 287 pages. 1999.

Vol. 1674: D. Floreano, J.-D. Nicoud, F. Mondada (Eds.), Advances in Artificial Life. Proceedings, 1999. XVI, 737 pages. 1999.

Vol. 1688: P. Bouquet, L. Serafini, P. Brézillon, M. Benerecetti, F. Castellani (Eds.), Modeling and Using Context. Proceedings, 1999. XII, 528 pages. 1999.

Vol. 1692: V. Matoušek, P. Mautner, J. Ocelíková, P. Sojka (Eds.), Text, Speech, and Dialogue. Proceedings, 1999. XI, 396 pages. 1999.

Vol. 1695: P. Barahona, J.J. Alferes (Eds.), Progress in Artificial Intelligence. Proceedings, 1999. XI, 385 pages. 1999.

Vol. 1699: S. Albayrak (Ed.), Intelligent Agents for Telecommunication Applications. Proceedings, 1999. IX, 191 pages. 1999.

Vol. 1701: W. Burgard, T. Christaller, A.B. Cremers (Eds.), KI-99: Advances in Artificial Intelligence. Proceedings, 1999. XI, 311 pages. 1999.

Vol. 1704: Jan M. Żytkow, J. Rauch (Eds.), Principles of Data Mining and Knowledge Discovery. Proceedings, 1999. XIV, 593 pages. 1999.

Vol. 1705: H. Ganzinger, D. McAllester, A. Voronkov (Eds.), Logic for Programming and Automated Reasoning. Proceedings, 1999. XII, 397 pages. 1999.

Vol. 1711: N. Zhong, A. Skowron, S. Ohsuga (Eds.), New Directions in Rough Sets, Data Mining, and Granular-Soft Computing. Proceedings, 1999. XIV, 558 pages. 1999.

Vol. 1712: H. Boley, A Tight, Practical Integration of Relations and Functions. XI, 169 pages. 1999.

Vol. 1714: M.T. Pazienza (Eds.), Information Extraction. IX, 165 pages. 1999.

Vol. 1715: P. Perner, M. Petrou (Eds.), Machine Learning and Data Mining in Pattern Recognition. Proceedings, 1999. VIII, 217 pages. 1999.

Lecture Notes in Computer Science

Vol. 1685: P. Amestoy, P. Berger, M. Daydé, I. Duff, V. Frayssé, L. Giraud, D. Ruiz (Eds.), Euro-Par'99. Parallel Processing. Proceedings, 1999. XXXII, 1503 pages. 1999.

Vol. 1687: O. Nierstrasz, M. Lemoine (Eds.), Software Engineering – ESEC/FSE '99. Proceedings, 1999. XII, 529 pages. 1999.

Vol. 1688: P. Bouquet, L. Serafini, P. Brézillon, M. Benerecetti, F. Castellani (Eds.), Modeling and Using Context. Proceedings, 1999. XII, 528 pages. 1999. (Subseries LNAI).

Vol. 1689: F. Solina, A. Leonardis (Eds.), Computer Analysis of Images and Patterns. Proceedings, 1999. XIV, 650 pages. 1999.

Vol. 1690: Y. Bertot, G. Dowek, A. Hirschowitz, C. Paulin, L. Théry (Eds.), Theorem Proving in Higher Order Logics. Proceedings, 1999. VIII, 359 pages. 1999.

Vol. 1691: J. Eder, I. Rozman, T. Welzer (Eds.), Advances in Databases and Information Systems. Proceedings, 1999. XIII, 383 pages. 1999.

Vol. 1692: V. Matoušek, P. Mautner, J. Ocelíková, P. Sojka (Eds.), Text, Speech and Dialogue. Proceedings, 1999. XI, 396 pages. 1999. (Subseries LNAI).

Vol. 1693: P. Jayanti (Ed.), Distributed Computing. Proceedings, 1999. X, 357 pages. 1999.

Vol. 1694: A. Cortesi, G. Filé (Eds.), Static Analysis. Proceedings, 1999. VIII, 357 pages. 1999.

Vol. 1695: P. Barahona, J.J. Alferes (Eds.), Progress in Artificial Intelligence. Proceedings, 1999. XI, 385 pages. 1999. (Subseries LNAI).

Vol. 1696: S. Abiteboul, A.-M. Vercoustre (Eds.), Research and Advanced Technology for Digital Libraries. Proceedings, 1999. XII, 497 pages. 1999.

Vol. 1697: J. Dongarra, E. Luque, T. Margalef (Eds.), Recent Advances in Parallel Virtual Machine and Message Passing Interface. Proceedings, 1999. XVII, 551 pages. 1999.

Vol. 1698: M. Felici, K. Kanoun, A. Pasquini (Eds.), Computer Safety, Reliability and Security. Proceedings, 1999. XVIII, 482 pages. 1999.

Vol. 1699: S. Albayrak (Ed.), Intelligent Agents for Telecommunication Applications. Proceedings, 1999. IX, 191 pages. 1999. (Subseries LNAI).

Vol. 1700: R. Stadler, B. Stiller (Eds.), Active Technologies for Network and Service Management. Proceedings, 1999. XII, 299 pages. 1999.

Vol. 1701: W. Burgard, T. Christaller, A.B. Cremers (Eds.), KI-99: Advances in Artificial Intelligence. Proceedings, 1999. XI, 311 pages. 1999. (Subseries LNAI).

Vol. 1702: G. Nadathur (Ed.), Principles and Practice of Declarative Programming. Proceedings, 1999. X, 434 pages. 1999.

Vol. 1703: L. Pierre, T. Kropf (Eds.), Correct Hardware Design and Verification Methods. Proceedings, 1999. XI, 366 pages. 1999.

Vol. 1704: Jan M. Żytkow, J. Rauch (Eds.), Principles of Data Mining and Knowledge Discovery. Proceedings, 1999. XIV, 593 pages. 1999. (Subseries LNAI).

Vol. 1705: H. Ganzinger, D. McAllester, A. Voronkov (Eds.), Logic for Programming and Automated Reasoning. Proceedings, 1999. XII, 397 pages. 1999. (Subseries LNAI).

Vol. 1707: H.-W. Gellersen (Ed.), Handheld and Ubiquitous Computing. Proceedings, 1999. XII, 390 pages. 1999.

Vol. 1708: J.M. Wing, J. Woodcock, J. Davies (Eds.), FM'99 – Formal Methods. Proceedings Vol. I, 1999. XVIII, 937 pages. 1999.

Vol. 1709: J.M. Wing, J. Woodcock, J. Davies (Eds.), FM'99 – Formal Methods. Proceedings Vol. II, 1999. XVIII, 937 pages. 1999.

Vol. 1710: E.-R. Olderog, B. Steffen (Eds.), Correct System Design. XIV, 417 pages. 1999.

Vol. 1711: N. Zhong, A. Skowron, S. Ohsuga (Eds.), New Directions in Rough Sets, Data Mining, and Granular-Soft Computing. Proceedings, 1999. XIV, 558 pages. 1999. (Subseries LNAI).

Vol. 1712: H. Boley, A Tight, Practical Integration of Relations and Functions. XI, 169 pages. 1999. (Subseries LNAI).

Vol. 1713: J. Jaffar (Ed.), Principles and Practice of Constraint Programming – CP'99. Proceedings, 1999. XII, 493 pages. 1999.

Vol. 1714: M.T. Pazienza (Eds.), Information Extraction. IX, 165 pages. 1999. (Subseries LNAI).

Vol. 1715: P. Perner, M. Petrou (Eds.), Machine Learning and Data Mining in Pattern Recognition. Proceedings, 1999. VIII, 217 pages. 1999. (Subseries LNAI).

Vol. 1716: K.Y. Lam, E. Okamoto, C. Xing (Eds.), Advances in Cryptology – ASIACRYPT'99. Proceedings, 1999. XI, 414 pages. 1999.

Vol. 1717: Ç. K. Koç, C. Paar (Eds.), Cryptographic Hardware and Embedded Systems. Proceedings, 1999. XI, 353 pages. 1999.

Vol. 1718: M. Diaz, P. Owezarski, P. Sénac (Eds.), Interactive Distributed Multimedia Systems and Telecommunication Services. Proceedings, 1999. XI, 386 pages. 1999.

Vol. 1727: P.P. Chen, D.W. Embley, J. Kouloumdjian, S.W. Liddle, J.F. Roddick (Eds.), Advances in Conceptual Modeling. Proceedings, 1999. XI, 389 pages. 1999.

Vol. 1728: J. Akoka, M. Bouzeghoub, I. Comyn-Wattiau, E. Métais (Eds.), Conceptual Modeling – ER '99. Proceedings, 1999. XV, 539 pages. 1999.